THE
ANALEMMA
WALTZ

THE
ANALEMMA
WALTZ

A YEAR OF SOLAR AND PERSONAL REFLECTIONS

PAUL VINCENT

THE ANALEMMA WALTZ
A YEAR OF SOLAR AND PERSONAL REFLECTIONS

Scripture quotations marked KJV are from the Holy Bible, King James Version (Authorized Version). First published in 1611. Quoted from the KJV Classic Reference Bible, Copyright © 1983 by The Zondervan Corporation.

Scripture quotations marked NASB are taken from the New American Standard Bible®, Copyright © 1960, 1962, 1963, 1968, 1971, 1972, 1973, 1975, 1977, 1995 by The Lockman Foundation. Used by permission.

iUniverse books may be ordered through booksellers or by contacting:

iUniverse
1663 Liberty Drive
Bloomington, IN 47403
www.iuniverse.com
844-349-9409

ISBN: 978-1-6632-1168-2 (sc)
ISBN: 978-1-6632-1219-1 (e)

Print information available on the last page.

iUniverse rev. date: 11/18/2020

For Cathy

who has faithfully shared with me
the wonder of the
sacred space
that is our home.

CONTENTS

Preface and Acknowledgments..ix
Prologue: Moving Day 1

Chapter 1   December 17
             Merry Kenosis

Chapter 2   January 39
             Martin, Martin, Robert, and Harry

Chapter 3   February 60
             Clio, Farewell

Chapter 4   March...77
             Artisan!

Chapter 5   April 93
             The Big East

Chapter 6   May 131
             Eschewing the Asphalt Sea

Chapter 7   June 144
             The Meldung Paradox

Chapter 8   July 167
             A Death in the Morning

Chapter 9   August 180
             The Angel from the Tomb

Chapter 10 September...191
      One and a Half Cheers for an Elder Brother

Chapter 11 October 200
      The Fall of "Man"

Chapter 12 November..211
      The Joy of Sacred Doublethink

Afterword: The Great Appreciation 240
Bibliography..243

PREFACE AND ACKNOWLEDGMENTS

Anyone who reads the first sentence of the prologue of this book will instantly realize that it is not a work of scholarship. Rather, and as emphasized more than once in the pages that follow, the book is an attempt to treat issues of universal import as they impinge on one individual life—mine. For this reason, I have abjured the deployment of footnotes, believing that their use would convey a false impression of the kind and level of research I undertook and my purposes in writing in the first place. In sum, this is a book of essays, not treatises.

On the other hand, the "universal issues" I confront in the separate chapters have received scholarly treatment by others who are more or less experts in their respective fields and to whom I have applied for information and wisdom as the basis for distilling my own views. Hence I have appended a bibliography immediately following the afterword. But for this book, I felt a simple listing of sources was insufficient; accordingly, I adopted a tripartite methodology for source identification, my intention being to aid the reader who would like to verify an assertion or simply read further. Under one heading are works that are suitably brief and/or had a general—though not to be construed as unimportant—effect on my thinking. For these, I have included a simple bibliographic citation, which I hope will induce readers to peruse the book in question in its entirety, if their interest has been suitably aroused. In a second instance, I refer to a source perhaps two or three times as a support for my argumentation or as a manifestation of an alternative view. For these, I provided the appropriate page numbers in the book or article along with the publication information in the bibliography. Finally, in a number of cases, I refer multiple times to a number of specific sources because of my opinion regarding their singular importance—positive or negative—for the themes I am advancing in the essay. For this group, I list the publication information in the bibliography but the page citations within the text of the chapter in question. As perhaps was inevitable, there were more than a few close calls as to which category was appropriate for a given source, and I apologize in advance to any reader who finds my identification methodology inconvenient.

A glance at the bibliography will reveal that the author whose works I have most copiously quoted is C. S. Lewis. I make no apology for this. I regard Lewis as my spiritual godfather—a role he has filled for many, many others—and believe him to be a commonsense mystic, combining in his writing both a diamond-hard rationality and a countervailing spiritual richness that is elsewhere hard to find coming from the pen of a single author. Indeed, if a reader of this book finds it not to his or her taste but is nevertheless prompted to investigate Lewis further due to my references to him, I will regard this book project as having been a success based on that criterion alone.

As always, there are many persons to thank for the appearance of this volume, though responsibility for its contents is mine alone. I wish in the first place to thank my sister Barbara and her late husband, Norman, for many spiritually deepening conversations, the fruit of which I believe appears in a number of chapters. I am also indebted to my cousin Jan and her husband, Norman, for allowing me to be the witness to lives well lived and furthering my resolution to attempt the same. Indeed, I am humbled by the many members of my own extended family and that of my wife, Cathy, whose lives and virtues have provided me with seemingly endless occasions for meditation. I am grateful to all the persons, too numerous to mention by name, who read my previous book, *The Star at the End of the River*, and offered encouragement and helpful criticism. Once again, I offer my gratitude to the staff at iUniverse who aided me with the myriad details, of which I am largely ignorant, of bringing a book from an imperfect draft to publication. It will be clear only from a reading of this book itself why it is that I thank wholeheartedly those who constructed my house ca. 1880 and those involved with its remodeling one hundred years later—thus creating a beauteous interior pathway for the sun and the departure point for the contemplative journey herein described. Finally, in the matter of thanksgiving, I name my supportive, faithful, warmly encouraging wife, Cathy: anything I ever write will be dedicated to her.

Bristol, Rhode Island
January 2020

PROLOGUE

Moving Day

To be happy at home is the end of all human endeavor.
—Samuel Johnson

Is there anything more dispiriting than the sight of rooms in an empty, for-sale house, awaiting the longed-for buyer who will breathe life into them with furniture and the sound of human laughter? In my mind, one thing perhaps. That is the look of rooms piled high with boxes and the disassembled remnants of human inhabiting on moving-day morn—a time that is a curious mixture of melancholy and joyous expectation. I did not know which sentiment predominated, as my wife gave final instructions to the movers, just arrived, and I sat in a corner surveying the living room as if it were a foreign land, wondering if, even now, the interlocking gears of our property transfer—the closing, the termite inspection, even the moving men in my kitchen—could somehow be disengaged.

Ah, but that would put us athwart the iron laws of American home ownership, which, research indicates, dictate a change in residential venue about every nine years, or, if one cannot maintain that dizzying pace, certainly at least one move up from whence every homeowner must begin—the starter home. What an inelegant moniker, I mused, for the place in which Cathy and I had established so many happy memories over the past eight and one-half years (we slightly bettered the statistical average). But a starter home is undeniably what Cathy and I had bought. We had moved from an apartment in Cranston, Rhode Island, to a five-room ranch in Smithfield, an attractive

1

bedroom community northwest of Providence where we both worked. (One of Smithfield's claims to fame, which nevertheless had no role in our decision-making, is that it is the hometown of Sullivan Ballou, a Union officer who was killed at the Battle of Bull Run in the Civil War, but not before he penned a letter to his wife poignantly describing the inner conflict of a man pulled by duty to country from what was clearly a blissful marriage. The dramatic reading of Ballou's letter was one of the high points of the PBS series *The Civil War*.)

Months before moving day, when we were attempting to sell our house, we discovered that it had somewhat deficient functional utility, as the real estate professionals say, featuring only two bedrooms and one bath, when the typical buyer demands three and two, respectively. These deficits would not be counterbalanced in the minds of interested purchasers, we discovered, by a finished basement and an attractive yard, meaning that our net take from the transaction—if indeed it were ever to eventuate—was going to be a meager assist to our upward climb. As Cathy and I listened to the less than cheering news from our broker, we momentarily wavered in our resolve to sell but finally concluded that, for us, it was now or never.

After a relatively short interval, we found a qualified buyer, long before which happy outcome we were already searching for our next residence. As we began our foray, the question before the house (pardon the pun) was, Would we make a similar mistake with the next home we were about to buy? Namely, would we fail to keep in mind that it was to serve as an investment, a future negotiable asset, as well as a place to live? The French architect Le Corbusier has described a house as a "machine for living"; very well then, Cathy and I would look at all the working parts of the listings we investigated—room count, plumbing, electrical, neighborhood quality, curb appeal—to verify that they were well oiled and promised, within reason, to stay that way long enough to reward our investment at resale time. And we would look at all the prospects through the eyes of the typical buyer, whose needs and proclivities are, according to real estate manuals, the determinants of market value—thus guaranteeing a bevy of interested parties when it was time for us to move on again.

I couldn't do it. In the first place, once we made the purchase, I wanted my next move after that to be to the great assisted-living complex in the sky, so future selling prices were not at the top of my priority list. But, second, I wasn't able to bring myself to view a prospective home under such a mechanistic and functional modality. If pressed, I would deny that what I was holding out for could be reduced to such nonessential qualities as charm or quaintness; but, lacking any explanatory theory beyond personal taste, I was paralyzed in the face of the house as investment/ machine paradigm. In the end, and as reality often arranges it, we purchased the right house from my point of view, and I discovered the theory I was looking for later.

What saved the day, as usual, was Cathy's more balanced perspective. Fully cognizant of the importance of a house conceived of as a financial asset, she also yearned for that indefinable quiddity—the house as Emerald City—that already held my imagination captive. For me, what beckoned was a home of older vintage with the niches, alcoves, and other beguiling inefficiencies eliminated by modern construction techniques; but that meant searching for an older neighborhood in all the townships we surveyed. We began with our own town of Smithfield and searched along a geographic arc northwest of and including Providence. Cathy, in her more sensible way, made sure that we did not fail to consider newer housing stock available, on the off chance that a deal might be so favorable as to override our attachment to traditional architecture and neighborhoods. But,

3

on both counts, we found nothing to our taste and needs, even after widening the search parameters to include municipalities south and west of Providence and at greater distances from the city.

We were now faced with a grim reality if we wished to stay in Rhode Island (a necessity in my case, since I was a state employee): we would have to cross the bridge! The span in question was the Washington Bridge, linking the municipalities of Providence and East Providence, but more to the point, connecting the bulk of Rhode Island ("Providence Plantations") with a narrow swath of islands and peninsulas, between the bridge and Massachusetts, that reminded the explorer Verrazano of the island of Rhodes and bequeathed to the state its name. The bridge is dreaded by those who live on the east bay of Rhode Island and at the same time must commute to Providence for work, thereby being vulnerable to the almost daily backups on Interstate 195, inducing some to chomp on their steering wheels. But, unless something broke in Providence Plantations, it appeared that we were about to join this unhappy company.

This eastern sector of the state extends a good distance from the capital—in Rhode Island terms, that is; Californians and others from large states would find the local notion of *far away* laughable. On the east side of Narragansett Bay, at about thirty miles from Providence, is Newport, a principal tourist mecca in these parts and sort of an indoor/outdoor museum of the Gilded Age. And—would you believe it—you can still travel farther than this and be in Rhode Island. Newport and beyond were just too distant for Cathy and me. We confined our search to townships immediately across the bridge and, from there, in radiating circles outward: East Providence first, then Barrington, Warren … Bristol.

Bristol! A town resembling an angry lobster claw jutting into Narragansett Bay, the smaller portion of the claw—called Poppasquash—containing high-end homes and a gated community, within which resided for a number of years Bristol's most celebrated retiree—Anthony Quinn. Cathy and I of course would not, could not look for a house in this area. Much of the rest of the town was typically suburban, and Cathy and I were not boaters, an avocation of every second Bristollian. So why were we looking there?

Because Bristol had an old-town section with dozens of early federal period and some Greek revival homes. Because it had a main street resembling an Edward Hopper painting with a Civil War memorial and shops that still engaged in commerce in the shadow of big-box outlets not that many miles away. Because its grid of two or three north-to-south avenues and nine to ten right-angle intersecting streets was shaded by linden trees planted from a time beyond remembering. Because it had a town square with a concert gazebo surrounded by public and religious buildings that made it resemble a Shaker village. Because Andrew Jackson walked up Church Street from Bristol Harbor during a presidential visit in the 1830s. Because Bristol had the longest continuing Fourth of July parade in America and pretty much closed itself down during the surrounding days for oratory contests and band concerts. Because its people were an amalgam of old Yankee stock and Portuguese and Italian newcomers. Because Bristol was the closest thing to Grover's Corners in Rhode Island.

Actually, all these rationales occurred to me over time, after we had moved. The thing that initially brought us to Bristol was a house for sale just off the old section of town, which we had learned about in a FSBO magazine. If a real estate agent is Luke Skywalker, then a FSBO is Darth Vader—that is, *for sale by owner*, a program for promoting and marketing a home undertaken by the property owners themselves with no help from a real estate professional and therefore no surrendering of a 6 percent commission. The young gentleman owner's strategy was an open house that we attended. A single man who was moving to Nevada to start a new job, he had purchased the house from his aunt, who had owned it previously for years. And that was only part of the story: the house was 120 years old, just a bit young and one street away from being on the town's historic register, but its vintage and appearance were within the framework of what Cathy and I were seeking.

The house style was Dutch colonial; that is, the roof pitch was barnlike but dormered, thus portions of the upstairs walls were inclined inward as compared to the downstairs exterior walls. This was considered better than the undormered Cape-style house from the point of view of functional utility, not as good as a standard two-story colonial home. In this instance, the axis of the roof was perpendicular to the street line, accommodating—delightfully, from my point of view—a front porch. The front of the house faced a few degrees west of due north (I later verified that with the North Star), so entrance from the front was southward. Upon entering, one saw immediately to the left—eastward—several stairs up, which at the landing turned ninety degrees to provide the staircase—with historic vintage banister—to the second floor along the eastern wall of the house. As I glanced upward, I saw that the stairs turned right again, westward, with the equivalent number as the initial eastern-directed portion of the staircase. I thought for a moment about Jacob's vision in Genesis 28—a stairway to heaven. Would the second floor disappoint by this standard? I would have to wait to find out; our host was already beckoning us to continue the tour of the first floor.

To the right (west) of the front door on the first floor was the living room—conventional, except that a large portion of its interior south wall, where it would have joined the western exterior wall, was absent. Even before I reached this area, the young man was explaining to Cathy what he knew that a routine investigation by the house inspector we would surely engage would reveal, namely, that the house had suffered a fairly large fire in the recent past but before his ownership. In the reconstruction of the interior, the then owners had decided on an open floor plan. It was not surprising to me that Cathy, as she later told me, had already noted the singe marks on the staircase banister. At this point, the young man was talking very rapidly to Cathy, making the case that the fire was really a blessing in disguise—to wit, the structure still had antiquarian charm (exterior design, wide-plank flooring upstairs) but had also been redone with updated mechanicals on the inside. Not a totally irrational argument, I mused; but I was only half listening, since I was counting windows. The living room had two standard double-hung windows on the north wall and one on the west; but then, high on the west wall, where the dividing interior wall would have been, was a small octagonal glassed orifice—obviously a feature added after the fire. As I moved closely to inspect it, I now could see the entire north-south floor area, the southerly portion of which was clearly to function as dining area. But it was the windows again that drew my attention—two standard on the western wall; another large octagonal on the south wall at the southwestern extremity of the house; and then immediately to its left, occupying most of the southern exposure, a huge box bay window with enclosed landing. From here, the downstairs tour was quickly completed: to the left (east) of the bay window was the back door; then the first-floor bathroom; then the kitchen, with its exterior wall to the east, but its dividing wall with the dining room being now just a four-foot-high counter (another legacy of the fire), upon which were constructed Y-shaped ceiling supports; finally, a small, doorless

7

passageway on the northern wall of the kitchen leading to the entry area whence we had started—a full circle.

We proceeded upstairs. The landing at the top of the stairs (you were facing westward as you reached it) extended north to south under the roof axis and provided access to the upstairs rooms. But first it expanded at its northern extremity to something of a room without walls, jutting out like a hockey stick easterly into the stairwell. Surrounded by the banister on two sides, south and east, it was serviced by a window in the north wall and, breathtakingly, by a skylight—a four-footer—in the northeast portion of the roof. Here was sure to be a reading area if we bought the house. For the rest, it was a fairly conventional second floor: a bedroom at the northwest corner of the second floor, entered directly from the reading area (we were to use it as a den/TV room); another bathroom midway along the eastern wall down the corridor; and, at its end, two additional bedrooms. All of it was essentially nondescript, except for two features: each of the bedrooms had three-foot skylights on the lower roof, making a total of four for the upstairs; and the entire floor areas of the rooms had period wide-plank flooring, which the owner had painted a battleship gray but which we would later restore to its pristine wood-grain coloring. Walking barefoot on them was, I found, a delicious sensory experience.

Our tour ended with the musty, stone foundation cellar (it leaked); the backyard, a predictably conventional, grassed seven-thousand-square-foot rectangle with several large shade trees; and an extremely unattractive two-bay garage. These elements made for something of a downer after the upstairs, but as Cathy and I advanced to the street to take leave of our host, I peered down the array of houses. The view buoyed my spirit: here were charming 1920s/1930s vintage homes—mostly bungalows and cottages with front porches—which, along with the even older

8

trees that lined the thoroughfare, entirely captured my concept of a neighborhood. This in contrast to the more modern, treeless, suburban plats of nearly uniform ranches and Capes. Nevertheless, the many ambivalences that had emerged from our tour meant that Cathy and I had a hard decision to make.

In the end, the antique charm of the house, especially the flooring and the porch, trumped the leaky basement. We signed on the dotted line and, like other purchasers of older homes, inherited our share of problems. I had almost forgotten what initially drew me to the house until our return from an evening walk in the late fall after the closing. Cathy had left only a couple of lights on for security reasons, but as we approached our street, it seemed like the interior of our house was aglow with a half dozen chandeliers. I recognized with a start that such an effect could not be created by the paltry illumination that we had turned on before our departure but only by the surfeit of windows that seemed to magnify its power to bat-signal proportions. It occurred to me that, if artificial light could escape so readily at night from the house due to its multiplicity of windows, it should be lavishly vulnerable to incoming sunlight during the day. Why hadn't I realized this before? The truth was I had—on the initial tour of the house. I just hadn't associated my interest in the windows with my affinity for the ability of this, my future home, to capture sunlight at so many points in its interior.

From that day forward, I began to take more notice of the sun's invasion of my house; began to wait for the sun to hit interior portions of rooms and walls; began to know where sunlight fell at certain times of day at, say, the solstices and the equinoxes. The practice gradually evolved into a ritual not only of mind but of certain actions. Cathy and I had set up our dining room—the room that ends with the box bay window—with a dining room table north to south. Also, tangent to the window and its landing, we had placed a smaller circular antique breakfast table, since we ate breakfast separately on workdays due to commuting schedules. (As the table was simply flat against the window casement, we immediately dubbed the area the "breakfast unnook.") At these breakfasts, because of the early hour, the sun is not a factor. However, we had also developed a tradition of a bigger shared breakfast on Saturday midmornings, with long, lingering conversations over coffee. By this time of day, the sun is much more in evidence. From about Memorial Day (Old Style—May 30) to Independence Day, the sun's trajectory takes it above the roof of the bay window, rendering the smaller table usable. As late summer approaches, we have to move to the southern end of the dining room table, excluding cloudy days, of course, as the sun floods the breakfast table with its beauteous luminosity. From our new station, we observe the September and early October journey of the sunlight along the carpet between the two tables until, near Halloween, the sun forces us to move yet again—this time to the northern end of the table, where we eventually are confined to a sliver of space and saved from further relocation by the sun's retrograde motion after the winter solstice.

One may reasonably ask, Why not put up a large bamboo shade across the bay window and roll it up and down as needed? Answer: because our seasonal breakfast odyssey more nearly captures the true nature of the human situation than a technological fix for an inconvenience. No doubt, humanity was meant to solve such problems and has acquired the skills over centuries to do so; no one should berate this part of the human vocation, of which the entire race has been the beneficiary. In recent centuries, the Scientific, Industrial, and Cybernetic Revolutions have greatly advanced this enterprise, so much so, however, that human beings have increasingly become petulantly expectant of solutions to all dilemmas great and small. This is the downside of human progress: an addictiveness to instantaneity provided, for instance, by mobile devices that convince their owners that they are masters of all they survey.

In my judgment, the opposite is true. Humankind consists of a small group of sentient beings in a universe so large that it simply cannot be grasped by any available spatial analogy and can only be economically expressed in miles by mathematical notation featuring the generous use of exponents. Although humanity, through the agencies of engineering and medical science, has bent some earthly phenomena to its will, it is, in my view, powerless in the face of these awe-striking distances, which effectively place an absolute limit upon human striving. Manned space flight to Mars may be only a century or less away, but travel to the stars is out of the question and, I believe, forever will be, warp speed and hyperspace being available only in science fiction. The contrary view, that all is possible for the human race, follows upon what C. S. Lewis called the "fatal serialism" of the modern imagination. Thus Christopher Columbus, then Neil Armstrong, then voyages to the near reaches of the solar system, then ... What? A thousand- or ten-thousand-year journey to Proxima Centauri, our nearest stellar neighbor other than the sun, with likely no place to land a spacecraft and no way to return?

No, to these immensities we are no less vulnerable than our ancient and medieval ancestors—all of us feeling a bit terrified by the great spaces hinted at by the night sky, with some of us, then and now, nourishing a firm hope that, in the ultimate beyond, there abides a Presence that greatly cares for us. And so it is that Cathy and I continue our yearlong breakfast journey— to keep these truths in view and to cultivate that practice of *waiting upon*, so inimical to modern sensibilities but so necessary to the growth of the spirit—even as we balance our perspective by heating our English muffins in a toaster oven, delivered to us by the technological advancements attendant on the Scientific Revolution.

Of course, we would not be engaged in a traveling breakfast at all were it not for the tilt of the Earth's axis twenty-three and a half degrees from the perpendicular relative to its orbital plane—the Northern Hemisphere gradually inclined toward the sun, then away, over the course of the year—a phenomenon that also bequeaths to us the seasons in temperate latitudes. If one were to plot (or photograph compositely, as some have ingeniously done) the changing positions of the sun in the sky at the same time of day at uniform intervals throughout the year—at every Saturday breakfast at 9:00–10:00 a.m., say—the resultant assemblage of the sun's images or positions would resemble a narrow figure eight or infinity sign, albeit one loop of which, the southern, being much larger. The inequality in loop sizes is caused by the increased orbital velocity of the Earth during Southern Hemisphere summer, during which the Earth is slightly closer to the sun. The Earth moving faster means the sun appears to cover more ground (sky, that is) below the celestial equator, while we in the north are shoveling snow or celebrating Christmas.

This annual, figure eight path of the sun is known in astronomy as the analemma, and representations of it can often be found on old Earth globes in antique stores. It was heretofore very useful for timekeeping since the time of the sun's crossing of the meridian changes constantly throughout the year, varying from local noon in what is termed the equation of time. Absent the tilt of the Earth's axis and the analemma, Cathy and I would not have to alter progressively our Saturday breakfast regimen, and other portions of the house would not be bathed in light sequentially during the annual slow-motion solar dance.

Happily for me, the analemma, together with an abundance of windows, has made our entire home a solarium. Since I was already noticing these changes in solar positioning, I decided without much fanfare to keep a diary of the sun's movements within my house. Like Thoreau traveling widely in Concord, I would travel widely in my home. Or, to use a different figure, the interior of my house would become a perpetual Stonehenge; chairs, couches, walls, and floors transformed into stations of the sun's liturgical year. My decision surely generates another question: who cares? That is, since there are millions of houses in the world, why is the sun's path through *this* one worth memorializing?

I can only answer by citing three authors who inspired me to initiate such an activity. One is Gaston Bachelard, the twentieth-century phenomenologist philosopher, whose *The Poetics of Space* was one of the two or three greatest books I have read in my adult life. I discovered in this slim volume the theory and the name for feelings I was already experiencing: topophilia, the love of spaces. His essays were a summons to investigate the intimate geography of one's own domesticity. In Bachelard's words, a house has the energy of a human body, keeps man from being a despised being, and protects the dreamer. His writing is full of the joy of stairways, chests of drawers, corners, and interior lights. After reading *Poetics*, it is hard to resist the notion that he believed *every* house is a holy of holies and, as such, worth venerating.

The second author, not surprisingly, is Thoreau. Nothing in *Walden* delighted me as much as his somewhat detailed account of the rising and falling of Walden Pond from the 1820s to the 1840s. Mind you, this was not a monograph on the hydrology of the ponds of Eastern Massachusetts; it was a history of *this* specific pond in these designated years. It was as if these events were part of God's knowledge and happiness and that it was a sadness that they were not more widely known, and to remedy this, He had appointed a watchman of this particularity, Thoreau. The world,

I mused, was full of such particulars entrusted to each of us as stewards.

The details of the places of this world, so pointedly represented in the writing of Bachelard and Thoreau and so consistently ignored in our celebrity culture, bring me to the third literary inspiration for my journaling—Thornton Wilder's *Our Town*. In the opening scene of the play, the stage manager recites a catalog of specifics about small-town Grover's Corners, piling particularity upon banal particularity: latitude and longitude; location of churches, geological features, ethnic stock. It is clear from the length of the list that Wilder is up to something. What it is is not long in coming. Particulars are both precious in themselves and as linkages to the universal experience of being human—as the stage manager makes clear in his oration about the common folk of the ancient world—and to God, as is seen in the envelope address of a letter received by Rebecca's friend, Jane Crofut, which she excitedly describes to her brother George at the end of the first act (Jane's pastor had addressed the letter thusly: Jane Crofut, Crofut Farm, Grover's Corners, New Hampshire, USA, North America, Western Hemisphere, the Earth, the Solar System, the Universe, the Mind of God.).

The marriage of particular and universal—the metaphysical intricacies of which were a conundrum for ancient Greek philosophers—is for me a continual source of reflection and joy, so much so that my mind is constantly moving between these two poles of reality. That is one explanation for what follows in this book—a series of essays, which, morphologically speaking, attempt to mirror Jane Crofut's letter. Another is the pairing in my thoughts of nature and human history, emerging from childhood experiences of elementary school. At school, I could look out the window at the state of nature, governed, in part, by the Earth's present station in its orbital journey, and then inside where the walls of the classroom were apt to be decorated with whatever events we might be celebrating that month or season. Thus, wet ground covered by thawing snow is forever in my mind married to black construction paper silhouettes of Lincoln and Washington; falling leaves and a waning sun with Columbus sailing the ocean blue and New England Thanksgiving feasts; early spring green with the shot heard round the world. The year seemed so much longer then and so much more a ritual; losing those associated sensibilities is one of the things I most regret about growing up.

But this book would never have been undertaken had it not been for a third element, one that I hesitate to mention—that is the vocation of meditative thinking or reflecting. It has taken me nearly a lifetime to realize that thinking, in this sense, is the human enterprise with which I am most comfortable. I am fully cognizant of the breathtaking implications of such a conclusion: if I believe that my vocation is thinking, then I must regard myself as a thinker. The problem is that that term has already been appropriated and applied to persons of Olympian stature: Plato was a thinker, so too Marcus Aurelius and Pascal. It goes without saying that I am not in the minutest sense numbering myself in this luminous company. Moreover, I am a man of modest attainments and in no way a specialist in any of the heterogeneous subjects covered in the chapters that follow. Sometimes a nonspecialist's entry into a domain outside his bailiwick can be of interest precisely because he has already made his reputation in some other field: thus George Will, a political philosopher and commentator, wrote *Men at Work,* a study of the craft of baseball, a topic about which he is passionate but in which he has no direct expertise; and Roosevelt Grier, an All-Pro defensive tackle for the New York Giants, wrote about his avocation of needlepoint. One can readily see how the anomalous pairings of authors and topics in these two cases could create or enhance a market for their books based almost on curiosity alone. But I have no such bona fides as Will and Grier; hence, all in all, there is no conventional rationale for the publication of this book. I wrote it anyway.

The chapters of the book correspond to the months of the year and begin with the sun and its presence in my home and move on to an associated meditation, as suggested by contemporaneous seasonal and/or personal occurrences. As will be seen, some are longer than others, corresponding to the depth of my interest in the topic. The first chapter is December, not January, because that is the normal beginning of the year, liturgically speaking, in the Christian religion. Indeed, a prospective reader should know that in my earlier years, I studied for the Roman Catholic priesthood and that, as a consequence, matters theological predominate in this book. It will not take even a casual inquirer to discover that my thinking has a traditionalist bent and features some manifest dissatisfactions with the current state of affairs in our culture. If anyone finds these sentiments repellent or just distasteful, I bid him or her a fond farewell along with an offer of my gratitude for reading thus far.

But if these elements are not disqualifying to preliminarily interested parties, then I welcome them to a year of reflections on matters ultimate and penultimate together with twelve celebrations of the sun's way stations on its yearly journey across the sky and through my home.

CHAPTER 1

DECEMBER

Merry Kenosis

And the Word was God .... And the Word became
flesh and made his dwelling among us.
—The Gospel of John, chapter 1 (New American Bible)

He did not deem equality with God something to
be grasped at. Rather, he emptied himself.
—St. Paul's Letter to the Philippians, chapter 2 (NAB)

The sun at bay. That is the best shorthand description for what
I saw in the early afternoon of a December day as I looked out
the bay window of our house. Already well past the meridian and
careening toward the southwestern horizon, the sun, in this the
season of its Northern Hemispheric discontent, seemed to me
to be like a fox fleeing for the safety of a thicket, baying hounds
nipping at its tail. As I continued to gaze, historical metaphors
crowded into my imagination—Pompey retreating south after
the rout at Pharsalus or General Lee racing for the Potomac after
the Confederate debacle at Gettysburg, untroubled by a standpat
Union commander, General Meade, whose failure to follow up
on his victory by pursuing Lee's army prompted a long-suffering
Abraham Lincoln to explode with impatience.

Earlier that morning, just before noon, the sun projected a
narrow rectangle onto my bedroom dresser through the southwest
skylight. It is a function of how shallow is the sun's daylight

arc of travel in December that it is already shining through the southwestern skylight before midday. And it is in the southern extremities of the house alone that the sun holds its feeble sway during its subequatorial exile.

Actually, that is overstating it. Before it fell away onto my dresser, the sun had invaded as far north as the doorpost of the upstairs bathroom. And, recently, shortly before 2:00 p.m., the sun projected light from the downstairs, west-wall octagonal window onto the eastern end of our north-wall living room sofa. As it declined, and before disappearing completely, it traveled all the way to the north wall of the stairway—a locale that is flooded with incandescent morning sunlight in spring and summer but is now barely illuminated, as if by a candle about to be extinguished.

"About to be extinguished" is the mood for life at this time of year. Though most of December is technically in the season of autumn, there seems little autumnal about it—especially to New Englanders, who experience fall from its late September to early-November passage at a level of colorful brilliance not easily matched elsewhere. I am told that weather experts designate December 1 as the beginning of meteorological winter, and thus they have, in my view, more nearly captured the dreary truth about the last month of the year: to wit, that it is thirty-one days of barrenness and cold, made all the harder to bear since it presages two more months of the same and worse.

Yet December has escaped the disaffection that would seem naturally to attach to it and that is very commonly focused on its winter sister months of January and February by, for instance, the Florida snowbirds who live hereabouts but are long gone when the year is young. Why is December spared the opprobrium of the winter haters? The answer can be expressed in one word: Christmas. Because of the Feast of the Nativity, the whole month of December is counterintuitive, filled with frenetic hithering and

18

thithering—shopping, decorating, singing, celebrating—while our animal cousins have been forced into a more reasonable slow-motion subsistence or even extended sleep. Those who have charge of my religious tradition (Roman Catholic Christian) sometimes take strong exception to this December frenzy, regarding it as a regrettable jumping of the gun, since through most of December, we are in the quieter, expectant season of Advent and, liturgically speaking, not in Christmas until the end of the month. With due deference to the justice of the objections of these revered lords spiritual and recognizing the negative effects of the commercial vulgarization of the feast, I still am rather comforted that the culture has baptized the entire month for Christmas, because what Christians are celebrating—the birth of the Deliverer—can hardly be expected to be set within narrow temporal limits. That is what this time of year does to people during the longer nights; they are moved to joy uncontainable in light and its future promise. So it must have been, I muse, for our remoter ancestors who hailed *Sol Invictus*.

For Christians, the unconquered sun that arrives to warm the heart is in fact a son—the Son of God and the son of Mary. And though, for the reasons cited above, Christmastime is not necessarily convenient for the observance of theological niceties, the season is, within Christianity at least, a celebration of a very specific dogma—the Incarnation—which holds that the babe in the manger is a) fully God, b) fully human, excepting sin, and c) one in person. Formulaically, that is it. But it is plainly not enough; or, if for any member of the faithful it is, then the doctrine becomes sadly inconsequential beyond ritualistic assent Sunday after Sunday. In addition to the practice of mindless repetition, such an affectless placidity in the believer can be induced by the words that often accompany a dogma, terms like *binding* and *infallible* and *unchangeable*, conjuring up a spiritual landscape that appears forbidding and inhospitable.

It doesn't have to be this way. Yes, dogmas are authoritative statements, definitive and settled. But they are less like prisons than they are like mansions with rooms to explore, the title deeds for which have our names on them. By my lights, the doctrine of the Incarnation, in particular, can be thought of as an invitation to a lifetime journey, navigating between Christ's divine and human natures. And if it is true that we can never fully penetrate the mystery, we may at least end up by discovering our deepest selves. Of course, exploring the dogma of the Incarnation has been going on for centuries, undertaken by individuals many and various, not least among which are the professional theologians with an expertise in this specialty—Christology. To master or even to adequately understand the resultant reams of studies and books would require something on the order of a graduate-level education in theology with an additional grounding in ancient languages, not to mention an intimate acquaintance with Hellenistic culture.

My purpose in this essay is necessarily much more modest: to discuss the dogma of the Incarnation from the point of view of the literate layperson who *receives* it—homiletically and perhaps in the arena of spiritual direction—not from the perspective of the church teaching authority that *proposes* it, nor from that of the theologian who, with scholarly acumen, *interprets* it. My thesis is in two parts, namely: 1) that the insistence on Christ's divinity as well as His humanity is essential and is, in the end, the principal consolation of the human community, even for those who don't know of Jesus, don't care, or hold to another belief system or divine avatar; and 2) that, in my opinion, down through the years, there has been reluctance on the part of some critically situated individuals and even whole Christian denominations to embrace the full implications of Christ's human nature, to the detriment of the pilgrim believer who might otherwise have found a level of solidarity with the man, Jesus, that would have gladdened his heart and made the human journey that much more tolerable. This two-part discussion, in turn, corresponds to the two-word title of this chapter—*merry*, as related to Christ's divinity, and *kenosis*, a strange-sounding Greek word, as regards His humanity.

Merry

At this time of year, the word *merry* is paired off with *Christmas* in the conventional greeting that is offered reciprocally millions of times, especially when the mandarins of political correctness are not watching. But what has *merry* to do with the dogma of Christ's divinity? I suggest that we can begin to answer that question by a consideration of the words in translation of the "Cantique de Noel," known more familiarly as "O Holy Night." There, in the first stanza, we are told that, before the advent of Christ, the world lay "in sin and error, pining." That the world was and is in sin and error and in need of aid from some transcendent agency is a staple of all salvation religions, including Christianity. It is also empirically verifiable in the history of human cruelty and savagery and in each individual's failure, to a greater or lesser extent, to live according to the moral law, which, when we heed the better angels of our nature, we know binds us all.

Without in the least trying to detract from the salvation story that is essential to any orthodox Christianity and in no way attempting to minimize the seriousness of human sin and the situation of the individual who requires and longs for supernatural grace to be restored to spiritual health, I would like for the moment to put the emphasis on the composer's felicitously chosen word *pining*. This is because a consideration of salvation theology—whether, under the Protestant genius, involving a detailed analysis of the Pauline multiphased process of justification, adoption, and sanctification, or, under the Catholic genius, seeking to understand how the work of Christ is transmitted through the church's subdivided sacramental ministries—can at times fail to console. Frankly, it can be a grim business in which self-detestation appears to be a necessary ingredient. And the penitent could not be blamed for wondering if, considering the peril of his situation, eventual salvation was, as Disraeli said of life in Victorian Britain, "for the few and the very few." Indeed, for the soteriology of some Christian denominations, that is precisely the case. All in all, the whole arena of salvation is not one in which the word *merry* comes easily to mind; rather, the emotion of the saved person could more accurately be described as relief, as if emerging successfully but exhaustingly from a particularly daunting obstacle course aided, in whole or in part, according to different theories of grace, by Jesus.

I fear I am being irreverent. The truth is that the salvation journey I have described is just what thousands of people have experienced—people who have reached the end of their rope due to addictions, bad choices, or failure to honor commitments and who, in desperation, cried out for mercy and help to God. A singular case is that of John Newton, the eighteenth-century evangelical pastor who, recoiling from his past, including service on a slave ship, and turning his life around, bequeathed to us the beloved hymn "Amazing Grace," the first line of which is "Amazing grace, how sweet the sound, that saved a wretch like me." Far be it from me to denigrate this or any other salvation story; however, this is an empirical essay, and it is worth noting that in certain modern renditions of the hymn, the line was changed to something like "that saved and set me free." Why? The answer to this question is precisely the point I am driving at: some who are earnestly seeking God don't necessarily feel like wretches. For instance, me. I was brought up in the Presbyterian Church, and in my early adolescence, I attended an evangelical meeting at a sister congregation. At the conclusion of the service, as was the custom, anyone who desired was invited up to the front to give their heart to Jesus. I already loved Jesus, I thought, but being beset with the standard perplexities of my age group and wondering if there was something more I needed to do, I went forward. The minister conducting the service prayed over me and a few others and then, the service being concluded, directed me to a side pew where a counselor awaited. The counselor was armed with a huge Bible with multicolored tabs anchored to the pages. What happened next was a blur: the gentleman started citing scripture passages, furiously fingering the tabs and jumping from the Pentateuch to the Pauline epistles, back to Isaiah and forward to the prophet Amos—verse after verse of scripture testifying to the extremity of my situation. I had come into the service thinking that, despite my imperfections, I was on the road to God's kingdom; I found out that I was hanging onto a precipice by my fingernails. I thought I had done some reasonably good deeds in my life; I learned that my supposed righteousness was akin to filthy rags. I assumed that God the Father regarded me beneficently; I discovered that He couldn't even look at me without my appropriation of Christ's work on Calvary. There was nothing to do but give in and accept Jesus as my savior.

I cite this event without judgment; indeed, to differing extents, on different levels, using different nomenclature, I would not now disagree with anything I received that night. I include this anecdote for one reason and one reason only: the multicolored tabs. They bear witness to the fact that the degree of depravity that some Christians believe characterizes the individual person, the recognition of which is the necessary starting point to salvation, is not a universal human experience. Many have to be convinced of it or, as some have termed it, convicted by the Holy Spirit.

When the focus is on *pining*, rather than on *sin*, the situation, I submit, is different. The experience of a beautiful sunset, sublime music, agreeable friendships, the birth of children and grandchildren—all, while universally evoking joy and gladness, are pervaded with a sense of impoverishment. The human person, I aver, in all these situations aches or longs for something that these events hint at but cannot by themselves supply. Why? Because in addition to having fallen into sin (as many religions stipulate), humankind is also finite and limited but, it is also claimed by these self-same religions, with an appetite for and an openness to the infinite. According to this contention, human beings are composite, with a foot in two worlds—experiencing life sequentially, in eating, walking, sleeping, working, and timelessly, in love, aesthetic rapture, and moral sensibility.

No experience greater illuminates this fault line in human nature than death, especially the death of loved ones. Some Christian theologians, such as the Anglican John McQuarrie, contend that death is as much a function of human finitude as of sin. If so, pining is inevitable for those who experience human life in its hybrid nature. Only atheists are, or should be, immune. For them, death is technically a well-attested physical process, as inevitable as the sunrise. Yet it is clear they too undergo the acute pain of the loss of loved ones. One wonders if they at times regard the anguish of death as a very high price to pay for the advantage of consciousness, which is, by their lights, totally a function of sophisticated brain chemistry. For the rest of us, death is a dilemma that negates all that we have sensed about the largeness of human life. It is so out of joint that it leaves us convinced that the human journey is incomplete, even broken, awaiting a healing that, for some reason, many of us feel will be given to us.

From my perspective, however, a prophet bearing a message that appeared to assuage our longings in this matter would be insufficient; the Red Sea we are crossing is not a mere water barrier. That is why to cure the terror of annihilation that is the lot of humankind requires more than a firm hope or even an answer from on high. What is needed is someone who *is* an answer; a life lived among us of one who is life itself; someone we can touch and feel who answers our weariness and despair with the message that our burdens will be light because He is lifting them; and one who obliterates our greatest fear—death—by dying Himself and, having crossed over, appearing on the other side of the great divide in recognizable form.

I submit that this is news that makes the heart merry before any consideration of the details of salvation theology. Whether they know it or not, it is what animates holiday shoppers in their quests, families in their gatherings, and people watching *It's a Wonderful Life*. Unless it is true that God is with us in tangible form and that He invites us to share eternity, Christmas is nothing but a burnt-out crater. Moreover, *merriment* carries with it the idea of a sentiment widely shared, hence the greeting "merry Christmas" to anyone and everyone. But the development of a specific religious tradition—Christianity being no exception—often has the effect of channeling the truths and doctrines to adherents and believers only, to an *elect*—a term used throughout the scripture and in the life of the church but a word that, I now confess, in many moods I find distasteful.

There is irony here. The belief that Jesus is God can reasonably be said to be what distinguishes Christianity as a separate religion, and yet it is precisely this belief and its implications that shatter denominational boundaries. The event of Christ is too large to be confined to one faith community. For legitimate reasons of geography and heritage, it is clear that huge segments of the world's population historically did not and currently will not be converted to Christianity. Does that mean that they are outside the circle of those making merry due to the conquest of death that God has vouchsafed for us in Christ? God forbid. I am not a church officer or theologian and cannot speak with authority in these matters, but somehow it has to be explained that Christ, *especially* in regard to His divinity, is *for* everyone, even those whose allegiance is accorded to some other salvation drama.

Christmas then, for me, is the whole world's celebration, with no intent to offend my brothers and sisters of other faiths. In Christ, we discover God from God, Light from Light, True God from True God. Without this truth, we cannot in the end be merry; with it, all of us, Christians and non-Christians alike, truly are.

Kenosis

My Greek dictionary reveals that *kenosis* is a word meaning to "empty" or "drain out." It appears in conjugated form in the second chapter of the Letter to the Philippians, where St. Paul, perhaps transcribing an early Christian hymn, states that, in becoming a man, Christ emptied Himself of His equality with God— that is, His divinity. What constitutes that emptying process has been a subject of debate among scholars and theologians down through the centuries. Some have claimed that the divestment process was of almost everything associated with the deity— omniscience, omnipotence, sovereignty. Others have not been willing to go that far. The American biblical scholar and exegete Joseph Fitzmyer states that the passage in question advances the idea that Christ emptied Himself only of the glory of divinity to which He was entitled, not divinity itself. And yet the twentieth-century Catholic theologian Karl Rahner has stated that Jesus had everything that belongs to a man, including a finite subjectivity.

These ambivalences were already present in the early history of Christianity where churchmen affirmed that the joining of divine and human natures was effected in one historical individual and then sought to defend the proposition, not using mythological language but rather the Greek philosophical categories prevalent in the thought world to which it was proposed. The heresies about the Incarnation, which the fathers of the church combated successively in a series of councils in the first six hundred years of Christian history, can be conveniently described in a rather oversimplified shorthand as follows: Christ was not really God or equal to God. Okay, He was God, but He only appeared to be a man. All right, if it is to be claimed that He was both God *and* man, He is of necessity two separate persons; since that is not acceptable, if He is to be regarded as one person, then He only has one nature (divine), or His human nature counts for very little. To this last statement, the church also answered no, insisting on Christ's full humanity, soul and body.

Surveying the entire span of these controversies, it is not overstating it to say that they were primarily focused on Christ's human nature. Indeed, the affirmation of the divinity of Christ occurred fairly early in the process at the Council of Nicaea (AD 325); thereafter, the church was in a constant battle against those who were fighting a rearguard action against a fully human Jesus. Even as late as the middle of the sixth century, the church had to beat back an attempt to insist that Jesus had only one will (divine), resolving that He had a human will as well.

It is not hard to understand those who had objections to the orthodox view. Though human appearances of deities are a staple of religions worldwide, this Christian doctrine of the Incarnation—the proposition that the transcendent God was enfleshed in a particular human being, known to many, manifested in datable, historical time—was and is unprecedented and repugnant not only to the Judaism from which it emerged but to many of the philosophical currents then dominant. To me, it seems almost a miracle that the church over hundreds of years refused to entertain the smallest diminishment of Christ's humanity when it would have been so logical and natural to do so.

The Incarnation will always remain a mystery, but for the purposes of this essay, it is rather easy, based on the centuries-old witness of Christian orthodoxy, to encapsulate what it is *not*. The mistaken or heretical position is that when we view Christ, we are seeing a human body with a divine nature replacing what would have been a human consciousness and human faculties of knowing, willing, and feeling. God in a body. It is tempting to ask of Christian believers (myself included) whether this is more or less what they tend to think is the case, despite two thousand years of teaching to the contrary. Nevertheless, it is from the orthodox position—the full humanity of Christ—that has flowed all those sermons, all those books, all those comforting words in private when we were depressed or perplexed to the effect that Christ knows what it is like, that He really is one of us. Keeping all this mind, my meditative journey has been to reflect on the extent of the identification that Christ, being human but also divine, can have with the human race. How much kenosis (divine emptying) is needed, possible, and/or compatible with the content of the dogma of the Incarnation? In this regard, I have developed a personal evaluative tool for judging any given statement about Christ's human nature; I call it the *solidarity quotient.*

When we apply this standard to the theological reflection of the church in the fourteen hundred years since the finalization of the dogma, the results aren't all that encouraging. It is as if the church, having so courageously and resolutely insisted on the fullness of Christ's humanity in the original pronouncements, was now having a long and collective bout of second and third thoughts. An excellent short summary of this history is to be found in *Jesus: God and Man*, a book by another distinguished American biblical scholar, Raymond Brown. To cite just a few examples, Brown relates that it was customary down through the ages to attribute to Jesus full access to the divine essence and full knowledge of *created realities* (my emphasis). He refers to a theological tractatus that maintained that Jesus (by definition?) was potentially or, depending on the instance, actually the greatest philosopher, doctor, painter, and musician in the history of the world. This mode of reflection has lasted into modern times: Brown cites the encyclical *Mystici Corporis* of Pius XII (pope from 1939 to 1958), which stipulated that Christ enjoyed the beatific vision in the womb. And so on.

The Catholic Church has a hierarchy of dogmatic, doctrinal, theological, and legal statements as regards the level of assent to them required of the faithful. Not all those mentioned above are on the same level. But that is not my concern at present; let us assume for the moment that all the above is to be believed. How are they to be judged by the solidarity quotient? Is Jesus really one of us if He knows all created realities or has the beatific vision at all times?

Perhaps a look at the record of His life itself—the Gospels—will provide some help. The cautionary note here, as both biblical scholars and church authority would agree, is that these accounts are not conventional biographies or in their entirety historical narratives. They are faith statements and theological reflections on historical events. Nevertheless, there is enough of the latter that we see Jesus tired, disappointed, frustrated, afraid, and anxious. All helpful for human solidarity. On the other hand, these instances are perhaps outweighed by the general tenor of the writings, showing Jesus by and large in control of nature and events when He wants to be. This characteristic is especially marked in St. John's account, where Jesus's divine nature is underscored almost, but not quite, to the exclusion of the human.

Another tack to take is to come at this question from the other end: not to discuss what the church or the Gospels has or has not said about Jesus's humanity but instead to look at what musings an individual believer, armed only with the basic dogma (Jesus is both God and human), might have about it before he or she has been completely informed of the limit of speculation. I have not performed a survey or poll on this subject, so all I offer are my personal explorations, which take the form of a myriad of questions. Herewith, a few. Did Jesus have allergies or other health problems? Was He really handsome as the innumerable portraits of him indicate, or was He of average looks? What was His luck of the draw in regard to genes? Could He have had flat feet or bad skin? Would His hygiene standards put us off? Was He of, could He have had, an average or below-average IQ? Is any of this possible? And if it is not, how can we think of Him as identifying with all of us who are subject to such possibilities—the contingencies of being human?

If someone, perhaps in church authority, were to say that there are no answers to these questions, I could readily accept that. But if he were to say that such wonderings are silly or even blasphemous, I would not give my assent. The door to such ruminations was opened wide by the early councils of the church, which, when given more than one chance to do so, refused to retreat on the humanity of Christ. The legatees of this decision—lovers of Jesus and believers in His divinity—will rightly feel that they have a license to meditate on His human nature until the end of time. I, for one, have dozens of questions like the ones cited above; and doubtless, other believers would have theirs. While it would be fun to expand the list, I think it would be more helpful in trying to explore Jesus's solidarity with us to focus on two issues: 1) His sinlessness and 2) His knowledge.

It is understood that the church teaches that sin is not part of the essence of human nature but is a regrettable add-on, originating in primordial time; thus it is possible to be fully human without sinning. However, on a practical level—and this is the level on which the solidarity quotient principally operates—how can Jesus be like us or understand what it is like to be a human being if He never erred or sinned? There is no wiggle room in the content of the dogma on this question, but perhaps there is a way of understanding what it means to be without sin that does not altogether distance us from the incarnate Son of God.

Near the end of my service obligation in the Air Force, the chief of staff and the command structure launched a program designed to enhance mission capabilities. It was known as Zero Defects. The idea was to encourage competition among units to attain a pristine performance in everything from neatness of uniforms and cleanliness of barracks to 100 percent compliance with regulations across the gamut of military operations—aircraft maintenance, weather forecasting, flight training. Units that excelled were awarded certificates at well-publicized ceremonies. One hoped-for outcome was an augmentation of esprit de corps, and in some cases this was the result. But, as in any such campaign in a large organization, the program was greeted by some with more than a little cynicism.

When I reflect on the sinlessness of Jesus, it is the *zero defects* image that has in the past come to mind. I imagine Him at work in the carpenter shop in Nazareth, in the days prior to His public ministry, and accidently jamming his finger with a tool. (Or, was this impossible because, by definition, he was the perfect carpenter?) Was He able to utter the Aramaic equivalent of *dammit* or even *darn it?* Perhaps not. Perhaps the dogma doesn't allow for this all too human response; rather, it may require us, when we think of Jesus's conduct in His life, to use words like *immaculate, spotless,* and, yes, *without defect.* If so, so be it. But then the solidarity quotient is reduced to zero.

But just maybe there is a different way to process the concept. In his useful short book *Models of Jesus,* Catholic theologian John O'Grady, instead of simply citing Jesus's sinlessness, takes a stab at writing a character portrait of Him. In O'Grady's view, the human Jesus cultivated at all times an intimacy with God and put a premium on communion with Him; that is why He could reveal God as a dear father (Abba). Jesus sensed His own goodness and therefore eliminated the internal warfare of good and evil. As a result, He lived His life in an integral way, achieving a fusion of principle and practice.

What this brief sketch does, in my view, is enable believers to embrace Christ's sinlessness instead of simply affirming it in a mechanical way. The reason? We have all met people who have achieved these qualities at least partially; we can therefore imagine Christ's life as the highest exemplary level of something that beckons us all. At a stroke, O'Grady has been faithful to the dogma and made it a positive value for the solidarity quotient.

When it comes to Jesus's knowledge, I have harbored, like others, I believe, perhaps childish notions akin to those mentioned above in regard to His sinlessness. I imagined Jesus as He walked with His disciples doing calculus problems in His head or knowing the outcome of World War I. Again, these ideas can be called silly; on the other hand, what can reasonably be expected of people who are taught that Jesus had knowledge of all created realities? And how can He be like us armed with such knowledge? The answer of contemporary theology—cited or developed in the works of the aforementioned Rahner, McQuarrie, Brown, and others—appears to be that He cannot. They affirm, using various terminologies, that it is legitimate to speak of Jesus experiencing a developmental/progressive growth in His understanding and of having a human consciousness that shared the limited knowledge horizon of His historical milieu. If that is the case, then a true solidarity of the God-man with the human community is possible. For instance, it is conceivable to imagine Jesus, at one of the dinner parties He attended at the home of a Pharisee, meeting a rabbi recently returned from Rome and saying something like, "I've never been to Rome. What's it like?"

This issue came home to me personally when I began to study other world religions. I would come across something in the Upanishads or a Buddhist principle and sometimes think that it illumined aspects of the spiritual journey in a more incisive way than anything I had found in my own Christian patrimony of writings. I would immediately feel guilty and suspect that I was delusional since I had been told in any number of sermons, homilies, and books that Jesus was the greatest teacher who ever lived. But why? As anyone of us who has ever tried it can tell you, teaching is a human art/skill that takes application and effort to develop. Some are definitely better at it than others. That Jesus was a master teacher is clear from a reading of his pithy sayings, surprising and attention-getting illustrations, and memorable stories with several levels of meaning. How did He achieve this? Is it possible that it was through study and practice? When a homilist claims that Jesus is the greatest teacher in history, is he saying that an inspection of the dialogues of Plato reveals Socrates to be mediocre by comparison or that Jesus's parables are greatly to be preferred to, say, Aesop's fables? Or are we back to what appears to be a heresy, namely that Jesus is the greatest teacher because, as God's Son, He *has* to be? If so, then the solidarity quotient is in tatters because Jesus did not have to hone his craft like the rest of us did ours—by hard work. As for me, I can imagine the fully kenotic Jesus as not being afraid, at times, to take the focus off Himself, despite His divine nature and singularity in salvation history. Informed of a particularly well-wrought maxim of the Buddha or Confucius (if it were possible), He might well respond, "I wish I had said that." Or to His disciples, He might have said, "Remember my parables, but don't forget to tell stories of your own." Or is this, too, blasphemy?

Sometimes I have used the solidarity quotient to interpret, rightly or wrongly, scriptural incidents in the life of Jesus. Three especially come to mind. In the Gospels of Matthew, Mark, and Luke is recorded, with minor variations, the story of the rich young man. In brief, a young man (Luke calls him a "ruler") approaches Jesus to ask Him what is required to inherit eternal life. Jesus answers by saying that the man knows the commandments and then takes the trouble to recite a few, to which the man replies that he has kept all these. Jesus says that he lacks one thing: he must sell all his possessions and give them to the poor and then follow Him (Jesus). The young man turns away sorrowfully, for he was very rich. Jesus is then able to pronounce on the perils of riches as regards entrance into the kingdom of heaven. End of story? For the solidarity quotient, not quite.

Could it be that, on this occasion, Jesus was tired—perhaps it was the end of the day or, as only Mark records, He was setting out on a journey—since when Jesus says to the man, "You know the commandments," one can almost sense a slight irritation, as if to say, "Why are you bothering me with this?" But then, after the man stipulates his compliance with all these precepts, something happens: Marks gives us a detail, omitted in the other two accounts—the kind of biographical fragment that the Gospel writers, for their own reasons, are short on but one that has the flavor of an eyewitness remembrance and for which lovers of Jesus are forever grateful. Mark records that Jesus *looked* at the man—one of the few times in the Gospel narratives Jesus is said to have glanced at someone or something. (Another, recorded in Luke, is the unforgettable "And the Lord turned and looked at Peter" after Peter had denied three times that he knew Him). Moreover, Mark states that He looked at him *with love*! Is it conceivable that in this encounter we do not have the omniscient Son of God testing someone and knowing an outcome but the kenotic Son of God, the human Jesus, somewhat unfocused at the outset but then, realizing the depth of the man's sincerity, overcome with compassion? I wonder.

A similar incident, one that has challenged biblical scholars, is the story of the Canaanite woman, narrated in Matthew and Mark. In brief, a woman of non-Jewish parentage appeals to Jesus to heal her daughter who is possessed of a demon. At first, Jesus rather curtly dismisses her, emphasizing that His mission is to the children of Israel alone and adding that the children's bread should not be given to the dogs. But then the woman replies that even dogs get the crumbs that fall from their master's table. Jesus rewards her insight, persistence, and faith by healing (at a distance) her daughter.

What to make of this? Like the story of the rich young man, the incident appears to be a case of Jesus testing someone. Jesus's apparent coldness, says commentator John L. McKenzie, is more understandable in a Near Eastern context where a matching of wits was highly prized; indeed he believes that this is the most realistic aspect of the episode. But—think of it—here is a story where a daughter's health and well-being are at stake, and we see Jesus enjoying a bout of mental gamesmanship. Forgive me if I find this a bit hard to take and feel drawn to looking at it another way. Is it possible that the incident on which this story is based is one of a number of encounters in the Gospels where Jesus—a not fully omniscient Jesus—is prompted by someone to see things in a different light and, I am almost afraid to say it, to grow?

A final event in the earthly life of Jesus that has served as a lifelong meditation for me is the story of the raising of Lazarus. The incident is full of drama: the death of a friend, the anguish of his sisters, Mary and Martha, their disappointment that Jesus had not arrived in time to heal their brother before he expired, their sorrow transformed to joy as Jesus faces down death to revive Lazarus after four days in the tomb. The only problem is that this narrative is recorded by St. John, the Gospel with the thickest theological overlay. Thus, as commentator Bruce Vawter relates, the story is a kind of allegory where Lazarus is representative of all Christians, and the miracle is in reality a sign of the final resurrection and of the rising from sin to grace. Jesus appears in control at every point: knowing what He is going to do; delaying His coming, almost as if to ensure that Lazarus actually dies and is not just ailing; and using the death to display the glory of God. And, as Vawter states, the story makes no attempt to satisfy curiosity about incidental details. So much for the grief of the sisters and the actual additional suffering that Lazarus had to endure before dying.

Within this narrative, there is, for me, one arresting moment: John 11:35, the point when Jesus finally is brought to the tomb. As the translators of the King James Version rendered it, "Jesus wept." I remember as a boy in Sunday school being solemnly told that this was the shortest verse in the Bible. (Other translations have it "Jesus began to weep.") It is curious that in the otherwise superior miniseries *Jesus of Nazareth*, which Cathy and I view during Holy Week, the writers and the director simply overlook this dramatic juncture in the story. As for me, I imagine myself as one of the onlookers or, sometimes, as one in the whole world

community who, having dropped what they have been doing, step
into this scene and, awestruck, regard the Incarnate Son of God,
overcome with grief.

But what kind of tears did he shed? The thing about tears is
that they *happen* to people, that people crying are in almost all
cases manifestly not in control. But this does not fit the paradigm
of the Jesus of St. John, who at all times is the master of events.
I tremble to say it—but what other choice is there?—for the in-
command Jesus of this Gospel, only crocodile tears are possible.
Unless it is thinkable that, even for St. John, Jesus has His
moments. Is it conceivable that embedded in this story we have
one of those transition experiences in Jesus's life, that, at this point
in His ministry, having recognized His divine origin and power
and full intending to save Lazarus and all humankind from death,
He still was human enough Himself not to have fully gauged the
effect upon Him of the passing of a close friend?

In regard to all my musings about Jesus's humanity gleaned
from these stories in holy writ, I can sense in the background
the collective shaking of heads of scripture scholars and biblical
theologians. I have misunderstood the literature with which I
am dealing, they will say. The Gospels, as received, represent
wholesale modifications and reorganizations of the original orally
transmitted accounts of the life of Jesus in response to issues
and imperatives with which the early Christian community
was contending. Moreover, the final editors added their own
perspectives, perhaps with a view to the needs of the community
at a slightly later time. Accordingly, the historicity and the
immediacy of the events recounted in the Gospels being largely
lost, it is futile to probe these narratives looking for clues as to
workings of Jesus's psyche.

I am not qualified to dispute this assertion. I say only this:
the probing of Jesus's psyche continues apace in the homilies

of priests, books by bishops, and in counsel offered by spiritual directors. If they won't stop, neither will I.

In the Gospels, we see Jesus calming the sea, multiplying loaves and fishes, curing lepers. Could the One who is said to have done these things experience a growth in consciousness, change His mind, see things in a new way? At times, it seems to me unlikely and inappropriate to a dogma in which I have put my faith. At other times, I ache for it. And perhaps my longings are not misplaced. World literature is full of stories of kings and others in authority who traded places with, or disguised themselves as, low-born subjects to see what it was like or better understand those over whom they had to rule. A modern example is the film *Brubaker*, starring Robert Redford, in which a newly appointed prison warden goes undercover as an inmate to view firsthand the abuses that prompted his appointment. A kenosis of a kind, certainly, but, in the end, only a game of pretend. The self-emptying I have in mind, by contrast, is not to be too easily dismissed precisely because it is that of which only God Himself would be capable.

CHAPTER 2

JANUARY

Martin, Martin, Robert, and Harry

I am a man, nothing human is alien to me.
—Terence, second century BC

January has the feel of falling off a cliff. The holiday buoyancy that lifted our spirits, despite the cold, is gone, nay, has even become negatively charged, since we must now dismantle all the decorative reminders of Christmas and its attendant joys. For Cathy and me, this includes packing away her extensive collection of Father Christmas dolls—a bleak and melancholy task, which even Epiphany, fiercely maintaining a foothold at the beginning of the month, fails to allay. The sun is moving up, from the perspective of the Northern Hemisphere; but in January, winter is getting down. To business, that is. Except for skiers, the whole north temperate world, it seems, moves indoors to movies, card playing, and the football playoffs.

In January, as regards the sun's journey, I look for the incremental. On the seventh, after 3:00 p.m., I noticed the sun, through the west-wall octagonal window, hitting the banister posts of the northeast stairway, where only last month it was illuminating the more northerly stairs. On the fifteenth, at 3:40 p.m., I note that the sun has now moved sufficiently to the north in the upstairs bedroom to illumine the lamp on my bed stand more brilliantly than when it is actually on at night. January 22 at 4:00 p.m. finds the setting sun's more northerly declination allowing it

39

to escape the upstairs TV room, where it was previously confined, and to project light through its doorway onto the eastern wall of the house.

So much for the afternoon. What of the morning? The sun's more northerly and hence more generous trajectory has now reached the easterly kitchen window, where it projects light onto the north wall next to the refrigerator, a hopeful benchmark I noted on January 18 at 9:10 a.m. On the twenty-sixth at 7:16 a.m., I saw that, through the northeast skylight, the sun hit the north wall of the house for the first time this year. I will now have the pleasure of watching the sunlight move gradually along the wall westward, then southward across the bookcases on the west wall of the upstairs sitting area, to reach briefly the doorway to the TV room before beginning its lamentable recessional at the June solstice.

All these are but fleeting and meager portents of more fulsome illumination to come and, sad to say, the best that January can offer. That is why some have concluded that the most useful activity for a month of wan sunshine and forbidding temperatures—and of life confined indoors—is introspection. When I was studying to be a priest, a seminary to which our diocese sent candidates closed down its academic program during the entire month of January for a "desert experience" of spiritual exercises. And in his book *The Embers and the Stars*, the American philosopher Erazim Kohauk claims that it is the experience of oncoming darkness that has liberated the philosophical faculty in humankind, without the use of which human life would go brittle and shatter. So, reflection and introspection it is; there is a lot of oncoming darkness in January.

The subject matter that recommends itself to me for reflection during this month is tolerance—tolerance not so much as a concept but as a practicing virtue. There are two reasons for this. One is that tolerance has always been a difficult attitude for me to adopt, there being so much about which I feel strongly, even passionately. So, attending to it at all is, in my case, like experiencing Lent or the desert. The second is that January, by the coincidental aggregation of disparate events, ones that relate to the names that title this chapter, turns out to be the month for me to ponder and perhaps to celebrate tolerance.

But first it is important to clarify what is meant by a virtue. My ideas in this regard follow Aristotle's treatise *The Nichomachean Ethics*. For Aristotle, a virtue is not the opposite of a vice but "a disposition to achieve a mean between *contrary* vices," (emphasis added), a view that was echoed by St. Thomas Aquinas in the *Summa Theologica* ("Habits and Virtues," Question LXIV, Article One). This does not hold for every action or feeling. There is nothing virtuous about envy in moderation. But for many virtues, the analysis is valid. Thus bravery is not the opposite of cowardice but a mean between cowardice and rashness (foolhardiness); temperance, a mean between profligate indulgence and abstinence. Aristotle allows that for many virtues, the location is not exactly halfway between the vices but closer to excess or deficiency. In the two cases above, the virtue would be closer to the vice of excess: better Evel Knievel than a man dressed as a woman in a *Titanic* lifeboat; better a teetotaler than a drunkard. Still, better not to be like Evel Knievel at all and better to discover the joys of responsible delectation of wine or spirits.

How does this schema apply to the virtue of tolerance? Clearly, a deficiency of tolerance is, or leads to, intolerance. What would an excess look like? Can there be an excess of tolerance? To me, it seems possible, and I would characterize the excess of this virtue as indifference. When it was discovered that President Clinton had a dalliance with Monica Lewinsky, local news in this area interviewed people at random to get their opinions. One college coed averred, "If he's doing a good job, who cares who he's sleeping with?" Well, Mrs. Clinton, for one. It was apparent that conjugal fidelity was not high on this young lady's set of concerns ("who cares ..."). After hearing her sentiments, I speculated as to whether she had a boyfriend who also went to college, perhaps an honor student. Would she then say, "If he's getting good grades, who cares who he's sleeping with?" In any case, such thoughtless indifference hardly qualifies as tolerance, though it must be said that this cast of mind has on many occasions been so characterized.

Lack of clarity in the understanding of tolerance is further highlighted by the ubiquitous bumper sticker that reads "COEXIST." Ostensibly intended to promote amity among religious groups, it cleverly modifies the letters of the word, still recognizable as such, with the forms of religious symbols. So one sees the Star of David, the cross of Christianity (the T in *coexist*), the yin and yang, the crescent moon and star of Islam, among others.

It may be deemed mean-spirited to quibble with a bumper sticker that appears to be so generous and benign, but its message, if it can be called that, in part puzzles me. The problem is the grammar: *coexist* is obviously a verb, but what is its linguistic mood, or how is it to be conjugated? Is it, for example, a simple imperative ("Coexist!") or perhaps a hortatory subjunctive ("Let us coexist.")? And in these cases, who is doing the mandating or appealing? It makes a great deal of difference to me—and, for that matter, to the proper functioning of tolerance as a virtue—whether, on the one hand, it is the Dalai Lama saying, say, to the pope, "We must coexist!" or, on the other, a self-satisfied soi-disant intellectual who regards religion as an enterprise for the simpleminded urging the adherents of the different faiths with "Now, now, play nice, coexist!" or even a strident advocate of atheism (Richard Dawkins?) declaiming, "All religion is drivel and delusion anyway, so why can't you people just coexist?" For me, just as indifference often impersonates tolerance, so too, calls for tolerance that are heavily laced with condescension or hostility do not in any way deepen our understanding about its proper role.

Finally, there is an additional false positive of tolerance. Anthony Daniels, the British psychiatrist and writer, has noted that where heretofore tolerance was more or less identified with the inclination to leave people in peace to go about their lawful business despite disapproval of what they did (or perhaps thought?), now it has become a demand for total acceptance, approval, and even celebration. There is nothing wrong with acceptance or approval, if that is the point to which a person has arrived. It is just not the same as tolerance, at least as I see it.

A metaphor of common currency with a rural, outdoorsman flavor is represented in the saying, "I don't have a dog in that hunt." As is clear, it means that a person has no vested interest in an issue or aspect of life. Thus, if one keeps all his money under the mattress, he will have little concern about the Dow Jones average; if he has given up smoking, about the cost of a pack of cigarettes. But, returning for a moment to our bumper sticker, if he is a Christian of a certain stripe who believes it is critical that everyone acknowledge that Jesus Christ is the savior of the world, he will want to get the word out; he will have a dog in the religious hunt. In so doing, he is bound to meet adherents of the other faiths displayed on the bumper sticker. It is at that point, and only in such a case or those that are similar, that the intricate dance of tolerance can begin or, as so often, be stillborn.

The practice of the virtue of tolerance is given birth (or not) by the existence of doctrines/practices/ideas/convictions that separate, at least in part, the partners in what I have called a dance. I have found a particularly helpful book in this matter to be Stephen Carter's *Civility*. Carter, a professor of law at Yale, discusses civility in all its forms and manifestations, but one of his most piquant observations is that anything we feel so strongly about that we refuse to see the face of God in another is an abrogation of civility, civility being tolerance in action. I would add that this is especially the case when the other refuses to accede to the assertions we are advancing.

This then is at least a working understanding of tolerance in practice: a truth claim, a settled conviction, not shared by all, that makes its way in the world without fracturing the web of civility, without which the human community is brought to grief, and that recognizes, in a practical and not just theoretical way, the holiness of the other. And, to reiterate, without a truth claim or something akin to it—an attitude, a profound attachment—it is not tolerance that is at work in amiable human interaction but anything from indifference to acceptance to even veiled hostility.

I am now ready to lay my cards on the table as to what about January prompts a reflection on tolerance and what it further has to do with the names that head this chapter. It is first related to the Week of Prayer for Christian Unity, celebrated toward the end of January. Established in 1908 to promote amity and cooperation among the churches of Christ—and to effect a diminution of intolerance among the denominations—it was later known as the ecumenical movement. It began among Protestants, but, gaining momentum in the second half of the century, it added the participation of the Roman Catholic Church, fresh from a season of internal reforms minted by the Second Vatican Council.

It is important to understand the situation of the Christian religion before the advent of the ecumenical movement. Protestant Christianity broke away from Roman Catholicism in the sixteenth century over a variety of issues related to doctrine, church government, and worship practices. (For the moment, I leave aside the break between Western and Eastern churches, which, occurring earlier, gave rise to Eastern Orthodoxy; representatives of the Orthodox churches are also longstanding participants in the ecumenical movement.) Almost as soon as the split occurred, Protestants themselves began to separate and denominationalize over similar issues. Thus, not only is there not one Protestant church, there isn't even one Baptist, Congregational, or Methodist church. All of them are fractured by disagreements over biblical texts, over what constitutes fidelity to their founding tenets, or over what is legitimate in the way of adaptation to changing times.

Still, the differences among Protestants were, and to a certain extent still are, nothing as compared to those that separate Protestantism from Catholicism. My boyhood was in the pre-ecumenical days, and so these divergences were not just theological but had a personal, day-to-day impact. Living in a heavily Catholic state, I remember going to weddings at Catholic churches and feeling like a stranger in a strange land, replete with sights and sounds utterly different from my Protestant experience. I can still remember the chill of alienation I used to feel when opening a book by a Catholic author and seeing the words *nihil obstat, censor librorum,* and *imprimatur.* The Catholic Church seemed to me to be like a menacing and authoritarian empire ready to swallow us up, much like the denizens of the Land of Mordor tried to do to Gondor and the Shire in Tolkien's *The Lord of the Rings.*

Another boyhood memory, about 1955. The pastor of our church had secured a copy of the 1953 motion picture *Martin Luther,* starring Niall MacGinnis. I remember the minister, Mr. Simpson, standing in front of the retractable screen in the church basement, telling us solemnly that the movie was forbidden to be shown in Quebec. Then he started the 16 mm projector with its sound so sweet to school children of the era before DVDs and other such advances and signaling in school that, since the class was to be given over to audiovisuals, we would be liberated from diagramming sentences or learning the principal exports of Bulgaria. I remember little about the film except the strains of "A Mighty Fortress Is Our God" (we had sung it in church many times) and Luther's courageous appearance at the Diet of Worms where he uttered those time-honored words, "Here I stand."

In the study of history or the philosophy of history, there is the perennial question of what it is that actually determines the unfolding of the human story. Economic forces, geography, ideas, critically situated individuals—all these have been advanced as the predominant causative factors for the great events of the past. In the life and career of Martin Luther, I believe we have strong evidence that individuals of a certain genius *can* shape history into a form that simply would not have been possible without them. Yes, the Protestant Reformation would likely still have happened if Luther was not on the scene, but how different it might have been, how much more lacking in emotional power. In his struggles to find peace and reconciliation with God, Luther adumbrated the experience of thousands of others who could find no solace in the institutionally exhausted Roman Catholic Church of the early sixteenth century. For them, he paved the way into scripture and reliance on faith rather than works and, in so doing, gave relief to the weary and the overscrupulous, chief among them himself. He would be followed in short order by other reformers—Bucer, Knox, the cerebral Calvin—some of whom may have been greater theologians but none of whom nailed a list of incendiary theological issues to a church door before anyone else did so or appeared before the Holy Roman emperor and refused to recant beliefs that could easily have earned him an auto-da-fé. Luther, in short, was not just the first and, arguably, the greatest reformer, his life is the stuff of legend.

(There will likely be no film biographies or Broadway plays about John Calvin.) If Protestants practiced the veneration of the saints, surely Luther's name would head the list.

So, harking back to my childhood experience of the movie and in view of his manifest genius, it is of Martin Luther—the first Martin in my quartet of names—that I think when meditating on the dilemma of religious tolerance, especially within the Christian family of churches. And it is not because Luther exhibited such tolerance. That could not be reasonably expected considering the age of religious strife in which he lived. It is rather because I, to a certain extent, replicated his experience but in the inverse. In my young manhood, I found my Protestant background was no longer helpful to me. It seemed to me (underscoring how utterly subjective this is and intending no offense) that, at that time, the churches of the Reformation were divided between those that were breathlessly trying to render themselves relevant to the contemporary scene, whatever the cost to their heritage of belief, and those that nourished the smallest of orthodoxies almost to the point of denominational extinction. To me, Roman Catholicism seemed to provide an escape from this dilemma (though it must be added that it had more than its share of problems) and to be a haven where my innate attraction to the guardianship of tradition and the sacramentality of all existence was satisfied. I crossed over at the age of twenty-six, went on to study for the priesthood, left before taking orders, subsequently married Cathy, and then spent a good deal of time in lay ministry.

One of the duties I volunteered for in regard to the latter was attending ecumenical services, more or less as the representative of my parish, during the Week of Prayer for Christian Unity in January. To me, it was thrilling to view the clergy in their contrasting garb singing and praying together after centuries of angry words and spilt blood. In my enthusiasm and positive regard, was I, a relatively new Catholic, therefore exhibiting tolerance toward my former Protestant coreligionists? Hardly. I was and am a Christian before being either Catholic or Protestant. My introduction to Christianity—and, most importantly, to Jesus Himself—was under the tent of Protestantism. Even as a Catholic, I still feel strong positive emotions about meetinghouse architecture, hymns I used to sing, and Protestant ministers and laypersons who influenced me deeply. The best analogy I can offer to my situation comes from baseball. I am a diehard Red Sox fan, but I love Major League Baseball even more (Despite my Beantown attachments, my favorite figure in baseball history is Lou Gehrig, a Yankee) and do not miss the drama of the postseason even if, as has been often the case over a good deal of my lifetime, my beloved Sox are not in it. So, no, I am not tolerant of Protestantism; I love and accept it—a false positive of tolerance, as noted above.

The question of tolerance in religion is a special case that places extraordinary demands on the virtue. What is at stake here for toleration is not simply political differences or the disagreeable habits of a next-door neighbor but disparate visions of the fundamental realities that govern the universe. Moreover, my brief foray into thinking about this topic, as narrated above, has only scratched the surface. Contenting myself with the issue of Protestant and Catholic divisions and attempts at rapprochement, I have completely left out the far more complicated question of the divisions inherent in the world's major religions. What does tolerance demand here? Is it possible to be true to one's faith and still have cordial intercourse, even cooperation, with those whose belief system has completely different holy books, liturgies, and paths to redemption? The question is so large that, with the forbearance of the reader, I have thought it well to entertain it—to the extent my powers allow—in isolation in a later chapter (chapter 12). For the present, I only acknowledge that my own faith journey within Christianity, from Protestantism to Catholicism, and my attitudes thereafter, as noted, do not necessarily exhibit tolerance so much as a broad-based acceptance.

I move on to the next two names in my chapter heading—Martin (the second Martin) and Robert, as in Martin Luther King Jr. and Robert E. Lee. By a strange irony, these two historical figures, who engaged in different eras on opposite sides of perhaps the greatest ongoing struggle in American history, were both born in January, their birthdays being just four days apart (the fifteenth and the nineteenth respectively). Of course, Dr. King's birthday is now a national holiday; what is perhaps less well known is that Lee's birthday is (or was) a holiday in a number of southern states that formed the old Confederacy.

The battle for civil rights and equality for black Americans was joined on a number of fronts and by a variety of actors over the centuries of the history of the republic and has not ended even today. Several of the founders had misgivings about slavery's inclusion in the Constitution. During the pre–Civil War federal period, there were prominent figures, such as John Quincy Adams, who in his postpresidential congressional career battled slavery at every turn in the forums of government, and others, such as Frederick Douglass and Harriet Beecher Stowe, who fought against it in different venues or by different means. The Civil War, while it may have had several causative factors, in the end was really about slavery and its extension into the territories. And then there was the "long twilight struggle" against the Jim Crow regime in the South in the years following the end of Reconstruction in 1877 until the 1950s and '60s, when Supreme Court decisions and congressional legislation finally began once and for all the process of dismantling the structure of racial subjugation in our country.

I have unforgivably telescoped this whole history; I should have mentioned many other persons and incidents in this story. But historical narration is not my purpose. Rather, my intent is to say this: it is saying far too little to claim that Martin Luther King occupies a prominent place among others in the unfolding of these events. It wasn't just that he was a superb rhetorician, personally brave, and gifted with leadership skills; he was indispensable. He stands to the American civil rights movement as his namesake, Martin Luther, does to the Protestant Reformation: both events would have been far different in character without the presence of these two individuals. In his sermons, in speeches, and perhaps most importantly, in his responses to provocations, Dr. King's decision constantly to frame the civil rights struggle in biblical terms and by the invoking of the transcendent moral law proved efficacious; they were the swords by which he finally slew the dragon. Our present difficulties in securing racial equality and reconciliation—and I do not wish to minimize them—are essentially related to the sometimes not inconsiderable task of dealing with the dragon's death throes.

It is from the perspective of a believer in the truths forwarded by Martin Luther King Jr.; from the mindset of a resident of the North (in terms of the 1860s); and from the historical imagination of one who still cheers Joshua Lawrence Chamberlain's bayonet charge on Little Round Top, helping to prevent the collapse of the Union left flank on the second day of the Battle of Gettysburg, that I come to regard the man and the legend known as Robert E. Lee. Of the many debates that still rage over the man more than one hundred forty years after his death, one is surely resolved to the point where the following statement is unassailable: Lee was a great military leader. Taking charge of the Army of Northern Virginia in the spring of 1862, he saved the Confederate capital from falling to General McClellan and then went on to conduct three years of military operations, winning most engagements with a succession of Union commanders and, in the end, being defeated essentially by the horrendous attrition of Southern casualties.

When it comes to the generic qualities of the man, I am almost afraid to say that he bears some resemblance to Martin Luther King. Lee had enormous reserves of personal courage to the point of audacity. Like King, albeit in a different arena of human activity, he had the ability to inspire adherents to self-sacrifice in the pursuit of a larger vision. Then there was something courtly about the man, incarnating perhaps the best of the so-called southern gentleman. In this sense, he seems anachronistic—an ancient warrior or medieval knight thrust into command of armies in a time when all redolence of honor was quickly being drained from warfare.

Robert E. Lee is surely not a saint, as pointed out, for example, in Michael Fellman's critical study, *The Making of Robert E. Lee.* His record on slavery and black Americans, though significantly better than some of his Southern contemporaries, is decidedly mixed and does not survive the scrutiny of twenty-first-century eyes. However, sometimes a man can best be evaluated by his ability to rise above his less praiseworthy inclinations. There is the famous incident in St. Paul's Episcopal Church in Richmond in the late spring of 1865 after the South had surrendered. An African American parishioner, in defiance of all traditional protocol, advanced to receive communion as the first in line. As related in Jay Winik's *April 1865: The Month That Saved America*, the congregation, including the presiding clergy, froze, not knowing what to do—until, that is, a graying white man strode to the communion rail to receive the sacrament along with his fellow Christian, after which the remainder of the membership quietly followed suit. With such small gestures, the journey of peacemaking begins. The white communicant was Robert E. Lee.

This pairing of names and personalities—Martin Luther King Jr. and Robert E. Lee—would seem to provide for me a fertile ground for the practice of tolerance. On the one hand, there is a man who was martyred in a cause that was intrinsically noble and in service to the highest principles of divine and natural law. On the other, I see a man who in the previous century devoted all his considerable talents to sustain and protect a system bent on the perpetual subjugation of human beings of a certain race. Do I tolerate Lee then? I am afraid that, as with my sentiments about Luther and Protestantism, the answer is again no. The problem is that, despite the repugnance I feel for the cause he defended, I admire Lee for his courage and quiet dignity. I am in the position here of Winston Churchill, who in January 1942 and on the floor of the House of Commons saluted German General Erwin Rommel across the gulf of war for the latter's superb tactics in the North African campaign. It goes without saying that Churchill found the Nazis odious in the extreme, but he discovered more than a little ... to tolerate? ... no, to admire in Erwin Rommel. For both Churchill and me, the search for an arena of challenge for the virtue of tolerance must lie elsewhere.

Fortunately, I have one more January name to consider— Harry, as in Harry Blackmun, the Supreme Court justice who wrote the majority opinion in *Roe v. Wade*, handed down on January 22, 1973. Invalidating the abortion laws of the fifty states, *Roe v. Wade* essentially created a right to an abortion for any or no reason throughout most of the pregnancy term, with some pro forma restrictions for the last months. Worse still, its deployment of fetal viability—the gestational threshold for a preborn infant to have a good chance of survival outside the womb—to designate in practical terms the beginning of human life has had deleterious ripple effects upon American society, encouraging a coldly pragmatic and mechanistic understanding of the human person. Due to *Roe v. Wade*, the United States has one of the most liberal abortion regimes in the world.

At last, I believe I have found a venue for the practice of tolerance, if I am up to it, for I am unalterably opposed to the practice of abortion. To me, it seems a vast mistake of our civilization—a deliberate and highly imprudent refusal to see the balanced goods that are at stake in the human reproductive process but to see only the rights of one of the parties involved and to relegate the other to a kind of ontological oblivion.

This is not overstating it. Pro-choice advocates, who much prefer talking exclusively in terms of reproductive freedom, sometimes are forced against their instincts into the precincts of philosophy with disastrous results. A few years ago, Wesley Clark, running for the nomination of the Democratic Party for president, was asked by a reporter his view on when human life begins. "With the woman's decision" was his reply. I feel comfortable in affirming that such a proposition—the assertion that an individual, in this case a pregnant woman, can be a kind of metaphysical gatekeeper, that the humanity of a preborn baby is contingent on the weight given to such competing imperatives as career prospects, convenience, finances, or even health—is repugnant to large segments of the Western moral tradition. We have had brutal practices in the past: some ancient societies, much to their shame, allowed the exposing of infants, unwanted for a variety of reasons. However, *Roe v. Wade*, and the abortion mentality that is its legacy, has bequeathed to us something new: the exposure of infants elevated to the conceptual level. The effect is to provide a matrix of new or revised values whereby the conscience can be deadened to the preborn infant's humanity and deafened to his/her claim to life. Far be it from me to deny that many of the decisions for abortion are agonizing and attended by much remorse. Still, the *theory* that underlies the Supreme Court's decision encourages adopting a moral calculus in regard to the infant in the womb, especially in the early to middle stages of gestation, that is chillingly close to that of a terrorist contemplating the people on a bus he intends to blow up.

The conventional wisdom tends to connect antiabortion thinking in large part with the Roman Catholic Church. But it is possible to be against abortion without any such association. A noteworthy case is that of civil libertarian and free speech advocate Nat Hentoff. Hentoff, who regularly wrote for the *Atlantic,* the *New Republic,* and the *New Yorker,* could not easily be confused with a Catholic or a conservative, yet he has maintained that a consistent ethic of the protection of the dignity of human life must extend to the womb. Reflecting on the case of Hentoff and recalling episodes in the abortion debate over the years have convinced me that the pro-choice position is not only immoral but an assault on reason and common sense; that is, it is not only without Jesus (or Moses) but without Socrates as well.

The legal landscape post *Roe v. Wade* is full of anomalies. Fetuses can inherit property but technically speaking have no right to life. In some jurisdictions, a murderer of a pregnant woman can be charged with a double homicide, apparently even if the woman had scheduled a future appointment at an abortion clinic. Then there are the evasive euphemisms that the pro-choice position must brandish, such as referring to preborn infants as *fetal tissue.* None of this would survive a Socratic dialogue any more than hamburger does the grinder.

My wife, Cathy, who has had a successful career as an administrative assistant and business manager at several Catholic parishes, related to me a telling incident. The parish in which she was working at the time had a kindergarten to eighth grade school.

She was touring it with the pastor and a contractor who was to be retained for repairs, when a third grader with an ear-to-ear grin approached her. With no associated explanation, she asked, "Want to see a picture of the new baby?" Cathy assumed that the girl's mother had just given birth to a new brother or sister. What she was handed instead was a photocopy of a sonogram. Sonogram technology has changed nothing in the matter of abortion law, but it has made much more problematical the abortion regime's project of obliterating from people's imaginations the humanity of what, in many cases, is scheduled for termination. Expectant parents are routinely proud displayers of sonograms to anyone who crosses their path. The idea that what they are showing people is a picture of a choice and not a human being would likely strike them as strange and repulsive, but, under current law, that is surely what it is.

This double vision of a sonogram—confirmation of the existence of a new member of a family or evidence of the need for pregnancy termination, according to the wishes of the parent or parents—reminds me of the continuing crisis of the 1850s, leading to the Civil War in America. In accepting his party's nomination for the US Senate from Illinois in 1858, Abraham Lincoln delivered his House-divided speech, in which he claimed that the nation could not continue half-slave and half-free but would become "all one thing or all the other." He knew that it was untenable to perpetuate a system where persons of a certain race were regarded by some as human beings but by others as property. Just the year before, the Supreme Court had decided the case *Scott v. Sandford* (often called the Dred Scott Case), in which a slave (Scott) who had lived for long periods in free states sued for his freedom. One of the conclusions in the majority opinion of Chief Justice Taney was that Scott had no standing to sue because, being of an inferior race, he had no rights; he was, in effect, chattel property. Taney thought that would settle the issue in perpetuity, perhaps that America could now become "all one thing." However, the Civil War and the constitutional amendments that followed overturned this finding: America would be "all the other"; that is, the full equality of black Americans would now be officially recognized.

I often wonder if those who are pro-choice on abortion regard *Roe v. Wade* as being similar to the constitutional amendments abolishing slavery and providing African Americans with equality before the law, that the decision effected the liberation of women from a kind of servitude. In reality, *Roe* is the Dred Scott case of the twentieth century, denying to a certain class of individuals their humanity and relegating them to the status of property to be disposed as their "owners" choose. That is why *Roe*, like *Scott v. Sandford* and contrary to the earnest hopes of its defenders, has settled nothing. Opponents of abortion will continue to fight a rearguard action against it and its noxious concept of viability in state legislatures and the courts into the future as far as the eye can see, and, in my view, with growing success.

I confess, to my shame, that my antipathy to the abortion culture has extended in some cases to a number of its proponents. I once watched a debate on the issue between Helen Alvare and Kate Michelman. Alvare, a lawyer with an advanced degree in theology, used to be the American Catholic bishops' point person on life issues; Michelman, at the time, was president of NARAL-Pro-Choice America. The contrast between the two individuals couldn't have been sharper. (I am obviously prejudiced, but I invite readers to look at a recording of the program to confirm or take issue with my assertions; it was an episode of the old CNN debate program, *Crossfire*.) Alvare was intelligent and forceful while outlining the pro-life position and turned her head to look at Ms. Michelman and listened attentively and politely as the latter made points when it was her turn; Michelman, by contrast, wouldn't even do her opponent the courtesy of glancing at her and advanced her side of the issue as if the whole debate was a needless annoyance and Alvare beneath contempt. In my view, it was not the best of days for the pro-choice camp.

My aversion to my adversaries on this issue is compounded due to some of the more distasteful sloganeering of aggressive pro-choice activists. I find the saying "Get your rosaries off my ovaries" particularly off-putting. Its coiner, in a clever attempt at internal alliteration (rosaries/ovaries), reveals more than a modicum of disrespect for Roman Catholics and no regard at all for their feelings by deploying in such a way the name of an object that they believe to be sacred (very little tolerance there, as I see it). Moreover, the saying is witless, confusing as it does the purely cultic elements of a religion, which are denominationally specific and could never be imposed on nonmembers under American constitutional guarantees, and the moral elements, some of which transcend denominational boundaries and even the precincts of revealed religion itself. It is well known that the original Hippocratic oath, which doctors used to take upon entering their profession, forbade them from performing or assisting in abortions. And like Nat Hentoff, the father of medicine and others in the ancient world, who bequeathed it to us, were *not* Catholic.

I have gone on at some length in registering my opposition to the pro-choice view on abortion and its advocates to delineate the position in which I find myself. I am certainly not indifferent relative to the issue or accepting of the other side's arguments, nor am I, as was the case with Robert E. Lee, an admirer of many of those with whom I disagree. This then is a viable test case for the practice of tolerance; indeed, I am at the very bottom of Mount Tolerance, looking for a way to scale its heights. Put another way and in the form of a question, How shall I enter into the dance of civility with my opponents on this most intractable issue?

I will start with Woman. Not, for the moment, women but Woman—that is, the female side of human nature and its history. I have often been resistant to those who say that women down through history have been oppressed, responding that, up to very recent times, life was hard for everyone, men and women alike. Both suffered the common ills of premodern history—malnutrition, lack of sanitation, disease—and each had specific difficulties to bear: women forced to adorn themselves in discomforting ways or to unreasonable degrees, treated like property, and vulnerable to rape and physical abuse; men laid low by backbreaking agricultural labor or dying far from home in wars fought many times for reasons they did not understand.

All this is true, but, coming from a male, far too glib. Though each gender could point to its own vicissitudes, there is one utterly defining human experience that Woman is heir to and of which men know nothing: that of a fetus growing inside of one's body. Even when that new life is welcome, there is an element of terror associated with it, as the embryo invades the private space of another human being and taxes her physical well-being. The female body, engineered for the process of initial custodianship of the next generation of human life, is thereby much more psychophysically complex and prey to many and various pathologies that will never darken the lives of males. For these reasons, any pro-lifer who is quick to use the term *murderer* for women who choose to end their pregnancies has, in my view, not only offended against the precepts of the Sermon on the Mount but insufficiently pondered the distinction between abortion and more conventional homicide as regards moral responsibility.

In addition to the physiological facts on the ground, there are the numberless and shameful cases in history of Woman, burdened with these gender-specific responsibilities, abandoned by the coresponsible males. This is where one can begin to use the moral imagination, envisioning Woman-with-child in all her incarnations—perhaps young, penniless, ill from pregnancy, panic-stricken about how to care for her soon-to-arrive son or daughter, fearful of the very real dangers of the birth process, and, perhaps saddest of all, alone.

Is it any wonder that Woman, that is, women as self-advocates, has in recent history insisted on Her right not to be abused and treated shamefully and to be recognized as an equal partner with men in the life of the world? A necessary ingredient in this achievement for some has been the appropriation of total control by women of their own bodies, even to the extent of life and death decision-making with regard to preborn human life. Those who believe this have, in my view, not only misunderstood the position of the human person within the moral universe, they have taken a wrong turn that promises cataclysmic outcomes for our civilization. But, while my mind will not be changed by their arguments, my heart has been expanded by the brief thought journey into the life of Woman described above and many more that I hopefully will undertake. Tolerance of my adversaries in this controversy is what I believe—no, what I feel— lies at journey's end.

There is something more. As noted above, one way to practice tolerance is to find the image of God in those with whom you disagree. I begin to see how this is possible for the issue of abortion. When I look into the faces of pro-choice advocates, I see also the face of Woman—that is, women who have been despitefully used, women who have been ignored and abandoned, women who have … suffered. It is not hard for me to see God in their faces. It is the God of my own religion, the One who came among us as a human being and also suffered.

CHAPTER 3

FEBRUARY

Clio, Farewell

The historian cannot state the facts and sit
aloof, impartial between good and ill.
—Henry Osborn Taylor in *The Mediaeval Mind*

The Earth has moved more than a month along in its orbit from
the winter solstice, and it is beginning to pay February dividends.
The southeast upstairs skylight now has an emboldened morning
sun projecting light into the northwest corner of the computer
room. On the afternoon of February 16 at 4:30 p.m.—4:30!—I
noted that the sun was still up and projecting light *south* of the
lamp on my night table. The afternoon is not yet lingering—that
would be too strong a word for February—but the sense that it is
longer is now palpable.

Indeed, on February 18 at 4:50 p.m., I saw the setting sun
filtered beautifully through the lilac bush in my driveway, much
as it does to my joy in October. This surprised me but shouldn't
have, since February is roughly October's correlative as regards
solar declination. Think of it in terms of the equinoxes, which, for
the sake of convenience, can be designated as March 20 (spring
equinox) and September 20+/- (autumnal equinox). On or about
both of these dates, the sun sits in the sky directly over the Earth's
equator but poised to head in opposite directions. Thus, in terms
of the solar itinerary, the early part of March corresponds to
the latter part of September; the late portion of March to early

September; the early days of February to late October; the late days of February to early October, and so on. The months of June and December, hosting the two solstices—that is, the limiting points the sun can travel in either direction—are their own correlatives in the two halves of the respective months. So ... the low-hanging sun shining through my lilac bush as viewed from the front porch on the eighteenth had a delightful Columbus Day look but a decidedly non–Columbus Day feel.

February is not all sweetness and strengthening light. My mother used to say we could always expect the worst snowstorm of the year around Valentine's Day. In 1978, she was just about right (though off by a few days) when southern New England experienced a paralyzing blizzard that strangled the region for more than a week. Just a couple of years ago, a February snowstorm knocked out power to our town. It was fun ... for a day. The ingenious Cathy rigged up blankets to enclose our kitchen, which is without walls due to the downstairs open floor plan, and boiled water in huge pans on the stove for heat (we still had gas), while we slept on air mattresses on the floor and did our bedtime reading by flashlight. It gave me the idea that, over the course of a year, we should sleep on the mattresses in every room of the house to get the different feel of the rooms from near floor level (I called it "sleeping around at home"). It is still in the conceptual phase. And finally, of course, on the debit side of the February ledger is the fact that Cathy and I are still eating our Saturday breakfasts at the north end of the dining room table, awaiting the sun's descent to the floor off the south end sometime in April.

Despite these negatives, I have an enduring affection for February. I have elsewhere called February "low spring," referring thereby to the sense one has from the weather, the light, and the emergent sounds, that new life is ready to burst all its winter restraints. The fact that in my religious tradition Ash Wednesday occurs fairly often in February only underscores the thematic that nature has given me; for the ashes, among other things, signal a journey from death to life. Then there is the Valentine's Day lift of our spirits with all the craziness and profundity that a celebration of love and falling in love include.

But the event above all others that confirms my February devotion is Abraham Lincoln's birthday on the twelfth. I am one of the legions who have fallen in love with Abe (I call him sometimes by his abbreviated first name because I feel like I know him), and the affair began in my childhood. I read a boy's biography of our sixteenth president and was immediately blown away by the seeming romance of his life. Stories of his courage, homely wisdom, honesty, and sincerity—some of which may be partially or wholly apocryphal—impressed me no end. I was particularly in awe of the fact that he was largely an autodidact and yet achieved so much with the English language. As I journeyed through life, I would sometimes cross paths with people whom I would never have guessed had an affinity for Lincoln. A secretary in one of the high schools in which I taught had her personal area covered with Lincoln photos and sayings. When I asked her about it, she without hesitation responded, "I simply love the man!" The former chief justice of the Supreme Court of the state of Rhode Island, Frank Williams, who has spent a good deal of his nonjudicial life in scholarly pursuit of the president, has written a book of essays about him (*Judging Lincoln*) and is a key member of the Lincoln Forum, an organization that keeps the conversation about the president going in perpetuity. (Can you imagine a Millard Fillmore Forum? No disrespect intended.) That is what Lincoln does to people: though in his grave for more than 150 years, he gathers them to himself as if he were still alive.

In my adult years, I read a number of biographies and critical studies of Lincoln, and the ideal was stripped away a bit. I tardily realized that he had a family and had to make a living, collecting fees from the not always estimable railroads and other well-heeled clients. I discovered that he actually *wanted* to be president—the office wasn't thrust upon him—and that his ambition, in the words of his law partner, William Herndon, was "a little engine that knew no rest." (Horrors!) I was slightly scandalized by the fact that he was a wily politician and engineered his own nomination from a distance, outmaneuvering other seemingly more seasoned hands at the political game, as well as more eminent statesmen and office holders. It gave me pause to think that Lincoln might have more than a passing interest in and attraction to the tactics of political operatives who run contemporary campaigns for aspirants to high office. Finally, I came reluctantly to understand that Lincoln, once president, superintended armies in a war that, at its outset, was still executed in set-piece battles under codes of honor but later changed into a war of attrition with an appalling loss of life and the ravaging of the lives and property of noncombatants, and that he was not an unwilling participant in this metamorphosis in order to further his war aims.

So is the bloom off the rose? By no means. The story of Lincoln is just as inspiring with the warts as without. First, there is the evidence of the regard of individuals who were brought into the ambit of his personality—former competitors for the presidency like Secretary of State William Seward and former skeptics and deriders like Secretary of War Edwin Stanton—who, after prolonged exposure to Lincoln, became what can only be described as adoring collaborators. Clearly, if there is such a thing as the mythological Lincoln, it was not created out of whole cloth but was based on the very real qualities of the man.

But even more compelling was the transformation of the man himself. By Lincoln's middle years, when he was an up-and-coming lawyer in Illinois, his political philosophy, keeping in mind his humble beginnings, was a sort of chamber of commerce, cheerleading type Whig/Republicanism—championing the impulses of those who were ambitious to succeed in life and prosper materially. On its face, there is nothing wrong with this, and, indeed, these ideas never left him. However, Lincoln's political ascendancy coincided with the culmination of a series of events leading to the greatest national crisis in American history. At stake were issues of greater moment than personal economic opportunity, namely the ability of representative government to endure and the prospect of the growth and extension of race-based slavery.

Entering this maelstrom as the chief magistrate of the nation changed Lincoln or, better, brought to the surface the deeper currents of his personality. In addition to being an able war administrator, he began to be a brooder on the arc of human history, a traveler into the mysterious borderland where the divine and human touched, and an eloquent transcriber into prose of the hopes and dreams of his suffering countrymen. In my judgment, the Lincoln story is as impressive as any in world history; it is indeed the stuff of myth, not in the sense that the story is counterfactual but in the sense that it gives us access to truths that transcend the events themselves.

Still, skepticism about Lincoln and the lingering suspicion that there has been a deliberately crafted Lincoln legend will not be quenched and was in evidence in my boyhood in a newspaper listing for a movie to be shown on TV. Back in the days when there was no cable TV or movie-subscription services, old movies were shown on the regular broadcast channels on Saturdays or Sundays or after the weeknight late local news. Indeed, for a number of years, they were competitors with *The Tonight Show* for late-night viewership. The movie in this instance was a February showing of *Young Mr. Lincoln* starring Henry Fonda, and the newspaper reviewer saw fit to comment, much to my annoyance, "History takes it on the chin again."

First—full disclosure—I love the movie. It is an essential part of my yearly February 12 Lincoln Festival, along with a renewed hearing of Aaron Copland's *Lincoln Portrait.* (I have three versions of this concert piece, with three different eminent actors in the role of Speaker; in my judgment, Gregory Peck's performance is the best.) And I am not the only one who views the film positively; a number of critics believe the movie is a classic. Henry Fonda, with his measured speaking style, thin frame, ambling gait, and, at times, melancholy mien, is perfectly cast as the young Abe and delivers an Oscar-worthy performance. Of course, the mythological Lincoln is very much in evidence: his decision to become a lawyer occurs in a melodramatic scene at Ann Rutledge's grave; Lincoln offers to be defense attorney for two young men accused of murder, when no reasonable fee could be expected; and there is the final scene when a triumphant Abe, after his victory in court, walks up a hill to the strains of the "Battle Hymn of the Republic." On the other hand, there is the opening scene of the movie, where Lincoln, a candidate for the state legislature, delivers a short speech outlining his political views. The mythological Lincoln might have said something about the moral unacceptability of slavery; the Lincoln of the movie instead recites a humdrum, and historically accurate, list of bullet points regarding the standard Whig platform of tariffs and internal improvements.

But perhaps the greatest criticism of the movie with reference to historical accuracy relates to the famous almanac murder trial, which is the centerpiece of the movie's plot. The movie places the trial in the late 1830s when Lincoln was a fledgling barrister trying to make his way in the profession. The historical trial (Yes, Lincoln skeptics, there was such a trial!) occurred in 1858 when he was already well established and indeed a figure of at least regional renown. And I would submit that the details and circumstances of the actual trial exceed the drama of that of the movie. Here was Lincoln with the presidency beckoning and a Senate race against Stephen Douglas for which to prepare—the campaign that gave us the Lincoln-Douglas debates—being asked to defend an accused murderer, who was not a stranger, as in the movie, but the son of a lifelong friend. In my opinion, the conflicts inherent in the facts of the trial—facts that in some respects forced an agonized Lincoln to weigh against each other the twin imperatives of advocating for a friend while still being faithful to the truth—as well as the interesting astronomical details regarding the moon's position and phase on the night of the murder are at least as dramatic as Hollywood's rendering. In regard to the latter, Lincoln had asserted that the moon was too low for witnesses to clearly see his client perform the murderous act as they had asserted, producing an almanac that specified an early moonset. But many people remembered seeing the moon out earlier that fateful night, and some accused Abe of using a false almanac. However, recent research, as reported in *Sky and Telescope* magazine (August 1990; March 2009) has resolved the case in Lincoln's favor. On the night of the murder, the moon was at the lowest southerly declination possible in an 18.6 year cycle, dramatically contracting the time span between meridian transit and moonset. For more on this remarkable story—no, history—I invite readers to inspect John Evangelist Walsh's book *Moonlight: Abraham Lincoln and the Almanac Trial.*

The whole phenomenon of Lincoln—myth and fact—has prompted me in recent years to think about the study of history. Inclining me to this exercise is also the fact that I was once at the apprentice level in this trade—that is, I majored in history in college. I remember sitting in my senior class called Introduction to Research in History, a requirement for majors, listening to the professor discuss the sublime—Is their meaning in history?—and the mundane—how to set up four-by-six note cards and use a bibliography of bibliographies. We all had to write a senior research paper, not on topics of our own choosing but on ones selected from the professor's list of only those for which our library had ample primary sources. Mine was on the machinations of Otto von Bismarck, the Prussian chancellor, furthering the chances of getting a member of the Hohenzollern royal family chosen for the vacant Spanish throne after 1868. I remember poring through pages and pages of cables and messages from Bismarck to his diplomatic personnel and secret agents in Spain, trying to discover whether he was deliberately attempting to embroil Napoleon III of France in a war, which indeed occurred over this issue in 1870, or just trying to push the envelope as far as possible in the cause of Prussian aggrandizement. (In the end, I couldn't decide.) But the biggest memory I have of this class (the year 1966) is this: there were more than thirty of us, more than thirty majors in history in the senior class alone!

It prompts this question: Does anyone major in history anymore? Almost all the young people of my acquaintance who are college bound are concentrating in fields such as software design or communications, few in the so-called liberal arts majors that were heavily subscribed in my youthful day. Colleges themselves are fast becoming—and marketing themselves as— career-preparation academies, and the concept of college-level education is quickly being transformed for most into a kind of high-level vocational training.

I have no wish to denigrate those who pursue this type of education, still less to imply that it is not important to keep postgraduation employment possibilities in view when contemplating or enrolling in a collegiate program. Indeed, universities have for years maintained within their borders whole colleges, such as pharmacy, nursing, and engineering, devoted to just this purpose. But alongside these there were always the indispensable liberal arts and the concept of a humanistic education where one learned how to think critically, became acquainted with the patrimony of Western civilization, and engaged in the Great Conversation (the actual name of a course at a liberal arts college!) about the "permanent things." The end in view here for an individual was not so much what he or she was going to do but what kind of a person they were to become. There was also the sense that devotion to knowledge for its own sake and cultivation of the faculty of informed appreciation was necessary for a full humanized life and should be pursued prior to, or at least concurrent with, targeted career preparation. In my view, it is not overstating it to say that, as of this writing, this paradigm of education is disappearing with an unseemly velocity, to be replaced by what almost might be described as a worship of the technical and the functional.

The study of history is one vocation that is a casualty of the above-noted development, but history, as a field of inquiry, has additional issues specific to its domain. It is worth noting that among the muses of Greek mythology, most of whom were devoted to art and literature, there was one for history, Clio. Under her patronage, it seems, the human story was to be regarded as a kind of moral drama, and its study a branch of inquiry under the heading of what we would now term the humanities. Today, history is classified as one of the social sciences, along with economics, psychology, and sociology. How it migrated to its new home is an interesting story.

The term *science*, from the Latin *scire* (to know or know how), could refer to any ordered form of inquiry. Thus, etymologically speaking, theology is a science (indeed, the "queen of the sciences," as our medieval ancestors had it); however, in the contemporary world, few outside of specialists in the field would ever refer to theology as a science. *Science* today, perhaps to the chagrin of social scientists, means natural science—that is, physics, chemistry, biology, and allied disciplines.

Science or natural science was born or, depending on one's take on the intellectual history of the last three thousand years, reborn during the Scientific Revolution of the sixteenth and seventeenth centuries. During this era, a new kind of thinking emerged—quantitative, empirical, methodical, nonpresumptive. Thus the new astronomy, beginning with Copernicus, asserted that the Earth revolved around the sun, not because a competing authority to Ptolemy so stipulated but because over time and through patient observation and testing, it could be shown to be true. Technological innovations based on the new science, which were quick to arrive, provided continual vindication for the new way of looking at the world.

In an arresting metaphor, C. S. Lewis has compared the science of the Scientific Revolution to a lion cub whose gambols delighted its master in private. He meant that the full implications that science posed for the study of the human person—including the study of the human past—were not apparent for some time. Indeed, many early pioneers of science, including Kepler and Newton, were theologically inclined and even religious mystics. The lion cub had not grown up and "tasted man's blood," to continue Lewis's metaphor.

When did this occur? I am not a specialist in this field and can only hazard a guess, but in the Enlightenment of the eighteenth century, we perhaps see the beginning of a theory of the human person as being totally analyzable using the tools of scientific analysis. If history had heretofore been regarded as an arena for the viewing of virtuous versus malevolent conduct and the learning of lessons, Enlightenment thinkers and their progeny would now put humans where they thought they belonged—under a microscope. The eighteenth-century French philosophe Denis Diderot is a classic example. A materialist and quasi-determinist, he was the compiler of the famed *Encyclopedia*, which aimed to disseminate all human knowledge on the emerging scientific basis. But he was also haunted by the implications of Enlightenment thinking and its disenchantment of the universe. In one of the saddest lines in all historical writing, Carl Becker in *The Heavenly City of the Eighteenth-Century Philosophers* describes Diderot thusly: "to the end of his days his soul was filled with discord; his mind unable to find any sufficient reason for virtuous conduct, his heart unable to renounce the conviction that there is nothing better in this world than to be a good man."

But the die was cast. Over the next century, the Darwinian revolution would cement in the minds of many a totally materialistic and organic understanding of humankind; while, at century's end, the value-free paradigm for studying human behavior, most notably associated with German sociologist Max Weber, would complete the transformation of historical studies into a social science, more pointedly, the sociology of the past. And it is not saying too much to state that, for many social scientists, the day cannot arrive too quickly when their domain will be considered a science, pure and simple (I have noted the predictions of some biologists that, due to ever more refined brain mapping, the discipline of psychology will be transferred from the social to the natural sciences sometime in the twenty-first century).

With regard to historical writing, the change did not occur all at once and perhaps is still in process. Edward Gibbon, writing his chronicle of the decline of the Roman Empire during the years of the Enlightenment, deployed value-laden terminology at every turn, describing the barbarian invaders of Rome and their Hun tormentors using terms like *vulgar* and *savage*. In the next century, Carlyle's history of the French Revolution delivered similar praise and blame without hesitation.

Moving into the twentieth century, we can begin to notice historians conscious of themselves as observers in some sense apart from the historical flux they are recounting, almost as if they were population biologists recording the activities of quasi-social animals like prairie dogs or chimpanzees. One sees this a bit in macro-historian Arnold Toynbee's *A Study of History,* a prodigious attempt to treat civilizations worldwide as if they were organisms with classifiably similar stages in life processes of growth and decay. Despite the format of his study, it would not be fair to designate Toynbee's effort as conventional social science; the scope of his history is far too ambitious for that. Besides there is still too much of Toynbee's humanistic education that gets through, and he is still operating under a moral canopy, inimical to true science, as for instance when he describes the forces that eradicated the Roman peasantry as "social evils." A contemporary historian / social scientist would surely use the term "social factors." Nevertheless, the approach of Professor Toynbee study has a bit of the flavor of natural science, especially in his effort to demonstrate taxonomical parallels.

On a somewhat more modest scale in the writing of twentieth-century historians is that of Harvard professor Crane Brinton. I must confess that I have a soft spot for Brinton. He used to deliver lectures, which I faithfully watched, on PBS back when it was called the "educational channel" and more or less lived up to that designation. Today, a PBS station is far more of a mixed bag, awash in nostalgia rock concerts, where, back in the day when Brinton was on (the 1950s and '60s), the only music I remember being broadcast in my locality was that of the Boston Symphony Orchestra in concerts hosted by the aristocratic William Pierce.

In any case, the subject of Professor Brinton's lectures was his classic work *The Anatomy of Revolution*. In the very title of the book, one can already see the allure of natural science, as if what we were about to do was dissect specimens. Brinton performs a study of four revolutions in modern times—the English of the 1640s, the American, the French, and the Russian—discovering commonalities in the major characters and stages of the revolutionary process and, in regard to the latter, coining such terms as "thermidor" (after the French Revolutionary name for August) to describe the reaction against radical rule and reigns of terror. In the opening pages of the book, Brinton lays his cards unabashedly on the table, stating that in studying revolutions, he is carrying on his work in the manner of the natural scientist.

There is much of value in Brinton's book, and from my perspective, there is nothing in principle wrong with the comparative study of civilizations or revolutions. My objection relates to what was only nascent at the time Brinton and Toynbee were writing but is more much more manifest now—the behavioral/scientific model of the study of the human past, which is much more comfortable with repeatable phenomena and tends to play down the singularity of persons. It is a sure bet that if *Anatomy* were to be written today, it would be heavy with graphs and statistical analysis that attempt to put the science in social science.

If I were to choose a metaphor for history as social science / the sociology of the past, it would be Toto in the film *The Wizard of Oz*, who pulled away the curtain to reveal that what we thought was an awe-striking personage was in reality a pathetic and somewhat confused little man. The social science mantra is that people—in the case of history, the people of the past—are uniformly less than what we might have thought them to be, that they are most definitely nothing more than the sum of their parts, their parts requiring further study according to the scientific method. The job of the historian is to probe the not so admirable underbelly of the human story and to put the spotlight on the clay feet of our idols, which is why young people can be forgiven if they confuse the study of history with investigative journalism and expect a course in history to provide them with endless permutations of the discovery that J. Edgar Hoover was a cross-dresser.

In this model of the past, what is to be resisted above all else is the notion that, while social science can reveal some truths about humanity, there is something about mankind that is not amenable to the analysis proper to animals, plants, and inanimate reality; that the human community partially operates in an arena of good and evil; and that human beings also exist in a spiritual universe that means their history matters in ways and to extents that they cannot fully grasp here below.

Curiously, a short poem that sums up the issue at stake here is Walt Whitman's "When I Heard the Learn'd Astronomer." In the poem's nine lines, Whitman tells of his attendance at an astronomy lecture, in which the presenter's seemingly interminable disquisition, replete with charts and graphs, eventually drove him outside where he "look'd up in perfect silence at the stars." Whitman's distaste for the details and the numbers notwithstanding, we need both—charts and graphs *and* contemplation of that which reduces us to silence. And this point is made with regard to a natural science, astronomy; how much more critical for the study of the human story?

Where is to be found this "both and" historical writing— namely, ordered systematic study of the past coupled with the humility that comes from knowing that human life counts for something beyond our ken? There are still many examples, though certainly diminishing in number and perhaps lacking in esteem from academic historians. One can be seen in the life's work of the British historian of the last century Christopher Dawson—a scholar whose reputation is beyond gainsaying (he once occupied an endowed chair at Harvard) and for whose body of work the term *impressive* falls far short of adequate. Yet in his book *Progress and Religion*, in part a study of the relationship of religion and culture, he had the temerity to declare that a return to the Christian tradition in Europe is absolutely necessary to provide the spiritual foundation for the maintenance of human freedom. I shudder to think how a paper with such an avowal would be received today at, say, the annual meeting of the American Historical Association. Another example is *The Civil War*, a military history by Shelby Foote. No one can claim that Mr. Foote has not got down into the details of analytical history in more than 2,800 pages of text. Yet the book is also a narrative—indeed that is the book's subtitle ("A Narrative")—which the author clearly *loves*. Somehow we are invited in, asked to become a part of the story; thus Mr. Foote's achievement is that we are not only informed but edified, which may be precisely the problem from the point of view of the social scientist.

Then there is the case of John Lukacs. Lukacs was a well-known and prolific historian of the twentieth century with an emphasis on Europe and the Second World War. His short book *Five Days in London: May 1940* is typical of his work. Professor Lukacs has a thesis—namely, that in the late spring of 1940, Britain was in no position to win a war with a revivified Germany on the march and overwhelming Western Europe with superior armaments and military skill. On the other hand, the English didn't have to lose either: barring a successful invasion of their shores, they could carry on in a beleaguered fashion, awaiting a misstep of Hitler, which would bring others with greater resources in on the Allied side at a later date.

Such were Churchill's thoughts at the time, but it was a close-run thing; there were others who believed that as the armies of the Wehrmacht approached the channel ports, the only course was to make an armistice with Hitler or face an invasion (which didn't happen) or, at least, aerial bombardment of the homeland coupled with aggression against outposts of the British Empire (which did). To me, the story is full of drama, but Lukacs goes about his business calmly using the conventional tools of historical research: minutes of cabinet meetings; diplomatic dispatches; diary entries of the principal policy makers; even newspaper articles and polls to report the mood and disposition of the populace during the crucial days covered.

Yes, Lukacs's book is a standard history, except, that is, until near the end of the narrative. There, summing up his findings, he relates that, due to some strong sentiment within the British cabinet that ultimately did not prevail, Hitler did not know how close he came to winning the European war in May–June 1940. Says Lukacs, Hitler did not know "by the grace of God." With the deployment of this one phrase, the author of *Five Days in London* offended against all social science orthodoxy and, no doubt, precipitated a bout of condescending sneers in faculty lounges worldwide. But somewhere Clio was smiling.

It puts me in mind of a vignette related to me by a priest-professor during my seminary years. When he was a boy, he told me, his family spent part of the summer in a small, rented house on Casco Bay north of Portland, Maine. One afternoon in August 1941, he and his father were scanning the eastern horizon with binoculars and saw Franklin Roosevelt at the stern of the presidential yacht, *Potomac*, taking the sun. They did not know it then, but the president had only just returned from secretly meeting Churchill aboard the USS *Augusta* to draft a charter that in essence defined the values against which the aggressor powers of the world were currently making war.

On returning to my room, I realized that I had been deeply moved by the story. Imagine espying the president of the United State fresh from participating in a pivotal moment in world history! I further realized that it was just such emotions that had drawn me to the study of history in my formative years. Today, I fear, those who have charge of the discipline in academia would advise me that to pursue historical studies requires that such sentimentality—I would call it a kind of reverence—be rudely put aside in favor of the exclusive and unsmiling application of social science methodology.

And that is why to such historians I must bid a not so fond adieu (oops!)—farewell, that is. I would bid a fond and somewhat sad farewell to Clio too, but I'm not sure it is needed. I suspect that she left her post some time ago.

CHAPTER 4

MARCH

Artisan!

For everyone who exalts himself shall be humbled
and he who humbles himself shall be exalted.
—Luke 14:11 (NAB)

Things are getting serious with regard to sunshine now that we have crossed into the month of the vernal equinox. By serious, I refer in part to my Sunday newspaper reading, which I have habitually undertaken in the upstairs reading area in the northeast corner of the house. But as March progresses, I have noted in the morning a glancing blow of sunlight on my reading chair, meaning that during late spring and summer, the northeast skylight will capture the sun's morning rays and make for uncomfortable sitting. For Sundays with the newspaper, I will temporarily relocate—except, as always, on cloudy days—to the couch in the computer room. On the morning of March 6 at 8:30 a.m., I noted that the rising sun cast light onto the kitchen floor for the first time, where in February, its shallower path only made it to the north wall.

In March, during the sun's afternoon westerly descent, it projects light flat onto the china cabinet from the west-wall octagonal window, lighting up magically Cathy's mineral collection. All during the winter previously, the afternoon sun shone feebly through the octagonal window into the northern interior of the house. But now it reaches to the border of the living room and the more southerly dining room, which will henceforth be the sun's afternoon haven, at least for a season. Best of all, the setting sun, lower in its afternoon trajectory, has finally reached the downstairs northwest window, flooding the parlor with equinoctial light—a light deprived to me at the autumnal equinox due to the interference of a large air conditioner.

March is nettlesome to me because it is then that we switch to daylight saving time. (When I was a boy, the change occurred on the last Sunday of April.) The change in time, which Cathy detests, wrecks havoc with my record of solar jottings. It of course affects nothing of the incrementalism of the sun's slow-motion dance, but it changes everything in regard to the *perception* of the sun's journey, because our human activities are married to clock times, the artificiality of which are twice underscored in the course of a year.

On the plus side, the sun crosses the celestial equator on March 20 and fills dwellers in the Northern Hemisphere with hope for warmth and more clement weather, despite the occasional early-spring snowstorm. For a number of years, I celebrated the equinox by balancing eggs on end, a difficult process even then. The theory, as I understood it, was that as the contents of the uncooked egg slowly settled to the bottom (the egg was standing on its wider end), and with the sun poised above the celestial equator, a certain cooperation of forces obtained, as at no other time of year except the autumnal equinox, allowing the egg to stand precariously erect. The whole process appealed to that portion of my mentality that finds pleasure in harmony of the spheres type thinking and emphasizes the importance to humanity of the cultivation of the habit in certain circumstances of waiting upon events.

I still believe that there is value in such sentiments, but equinoctial egg balancing does not validate them. As astronomer Dr. Philip Plait makes clear in his indispensable book *Bad Astronomy*, there is nothing about solar positioning that aids an egg in staying erect, as can simply be proved by attempting the maneuver on any other day of the year (the book contains a photograph of erect eggs on one such random date). Dr. Plait's crisp prose is a pleasure to read, even if the effect in this case is the equivalent of finding egg on my face. In fact, to my mind, Plait makes only one false move: he ventures into the nonscientific territory of attempting to assess the motivations of egg balancers, deeming their enterprise "strange," as strange, says he, as dancing at Stonehenge to celebrate the vernal equinox.

To which my response is that there is nothing more natural than to want to dance in celebration of the sun's crossing of the equator, even if you understand all the niceties of celestial mechanics and the physics of moving bodies (i.e., the Earth) that govern the process. The dance impulse and the egg-balancing attraction do not just proceed from ignorance but from a sense of awe and wonder—attitudes to which, I fear, Dr. Plait may be tone-deaf. His opinions also signal, at least to me, a disturbing addition to some scientists' mental furniture in their incontestably valuable role of disabusing the rest of us of fallacies and superstitions about the way the known universe operates. That is a certain gratuitous hubris, a kind of arrogance that implies that, because we understand the properties of physical reality that eluded the grasp of our gullible ancestors, we now in a sense own them or have tamed them or, at least, completely demystified them. As has already been stated in this book, in my judgment, nothing could be further from the truth—a contention that will be discussed further in the chapter that immediately follows.

Back to March. One final point that confirms my affection for the month is that it contains my birthday, the eighteenth—a birth date I share with Grover Cleveland, he of the split presidential terms and of the lovely wife less than half his age. I am very blessed to have married into a large family: Cathy has twelve siblings, most of whom are married, and more than thirty nieces and nephews. I always get a birthday celebration with the other March honorees. On my side of the family, marking my birthday usually takes the form of dining out with my sister Barbara and her husband, Norman. Sometimes there are variations: on my fortieth birthday, Barbara signed us up for an all-day learning experience in astronomy, a delightful departure from the dinner custom (we of course had dinner as well). And a few years ago, I came up with my own idea: an excursion to a museum I had never visited.

The museum in question will remain nameless; I will only describe its location as being in our regional vicinity. It attracted me because I learned that it had recently changed its mission to the exclusive display of so-called decorative arts and crafts. I don't know exactly when or where this type of art captured my fancy. Perhaps it started in my extreme youth when looking at my grandmother's blue willow dishes, a similar collection of which Cathy and I started and expanded after we were married. When Barbara, Norm, Cathy, and I travel to northern New England for our annual October weekend excursion, I enjoy exploring antique and craft stores looking for lovingly created flatware and vases, and at the Boston Museum of Fine Arts, I have always gravitated to the colonial furniture gallery

My birthday visitation, however, was a bust. The museum in question did have some attractive table settings, but its largest gallery was devoted to art with commentary on (then) current social and political issues such as the Columbine massacre, the Terry Schiavo case, and endangered species. There were porcelain hand grenades, sculptures of children holding automatic weapons, and landscapes with oil spills. Our local metropolitan newspaper had its art critic do a review—one which I had, alas, failed to read—cleverly titled "Crafted to Provoke." My birthday enjoyment was significantly diminished and only partially alleviated by the dinner we shared later.

The question is why. The short answer is that I resent artists using their creations to baldly comment upon complex issues that require the nuance and distinction making that only prose discourse can afford. Strictly speaking, an artist, unless he or she has additional credentials in political theory, history, philosophy, or social or natural sciences, has no special authority to enter into these spheres. Viewing these kinds of exhibits is like being forced to enter into a debate where only one side gets to express, or heavily imply, its view, while the other must remain silent, or, as in my case, do a selective slow burn. Art is a precious endowment of the human community, but it is a terribly blunt instrument to probe issues where people of goodwill can be found on both sides. My negative experience with commentary art has convinced me that art museums should be polemic-free zones.

That is the (relatively) short answer. The long answer has to do with the purpose of art itself, the role of the artist in society, the relation between so-called fine art and decorative or functional art, and the difference, if any, between the artist and what is sometimes termed an *artisan*.

The first author I discovered who addressed these issues was cultural historian Jacques Barzun in his comprehensive tome *From Dawn to Decadence: 1500 to the Present; 500 Years of Western Cultural Life*. Barzun traces the distinction between types of artists (artist versus artisan) and arts (fine versus decorative) to the Renaissance of the fifteenth and sixteenth centuries. Beginning in that period, if one worked in fine art, one rose in status. Also, says Barzun, the artist began to be concerned about making a name for himself, where heretofore he had been relatively anonymous—a contention supported by Richard Tarnas in his richly detailed historical narrative, *The Passion of the Western Mind*, where he notes that the poet Dante, only a century and a half before, regarded himself as being akin to those unknown artists who built the medieval cathedrals. Finally, we see in the Renaissance era the beginning of the artist's self-assessment as an extraordinary person and, as a consequence, exempt from convention and the law.

Going forward, these trends only hardened. In the Romantic movement of the nineteenth century, and perhaps before, there is the dawn of the notion that the prototypical artist requires a so-called bohemian lifestyle and that the rest of us—the common run of humanity—must accept such peccadilloes as marital infidelity, the overindulgence of drugs or alcohol, and the exploitation of patrons' generosity as the price that must be paid for artistic masterworks. As Arthur Herman relates in his study of the intellectual history of the West, *The Cave and the Light,* artists at this time also began using the word *avant-garde* to suggest their status as pioneers and path breakers for the human race. Putting it in slightly different terms, historian H. Stuart Hughes has stated that in the Romantic movement, we see the emergence of the artist as a rebel and alienated from society. At the beginning of the twentieth century, originating in France but spreading rapidly, was the concept of *epater le bourgeois* (shock the middle class), where, for some in the artistic community, the badge of artistic merit was earned by the degree to which their creations assaulted the cherished beliefs and habits of living of museumgoers and patrons. Such exhibits as "Sensation" and artworks such as *Piss Christ* are just two of the more egregious examples of this regrettable development, which has, in the contemporary world, reached what might be termed an *apex of reciprocity*—that is, many artists regard it as the highest aesthetic to pour contempt on their viewers, while the latter are more than eager consumers of such art, not even allowing themselves a nervous smile or raised eyebrow, lest they be branded philistines.

In my judgment, the key to understanding how art in some respects has gone off the rails lies in probing the aforementioned distinctions between fine and decorative art, artist and artisan. Though a case can be made for such categorizations, they are not as neat as, at first glance, might be imagined. It is true, nevertheless, that artifacts and crafts are typically functional, a factor that places limitations on the artisan's freedom: plates, cups, and rugs, after all, have to be useful for the intended purpose. On the other hand, so-called fine art is classically understood to be art for art's sake and can, in principle, be fully expressive of the artist's imagination.

The distinction breaks down a bit when one considers a Grecian urn, to which the poet John Keats wrote an ode, praising it as the epitome of beauty. Privileged as I was to be stationed in Europe during military service, I viewed what may be the finest collection of them in the National Archaeological Museum in Athens. It would be hard for anyone inspecting these treasures, I would argue, to classify them as artifacts even though they are, in a sense, domestic tools. By contrast, a sculpture for a cathedral, such as the *Pieta*, would certainly be considered fine art, yet an artistic creation in this circumstance has to be subordinated to an extrinsic purpose—namely, creedal orthodoxy and the facilitation of worship. Or eighteenth-century portraiture, usually displayed in the fine arts section of a museum, could be deemed to be compromised—as far as the working definition of fine art is concerned—by unknown instructions to the artist of the person represented.

The great explorer of these anomalies is Helmut Ruhemann in his brief study *Artist and Craftsman: Contrast, Similarity, Influence.* Ruhemann admits that there is a distinction between fine and decorative/functional art—he calls them *free* and *applied* art, respectively—but underscores as the most salient truth in this area of inquiry that they fundamentally belong to the same field of human activity. (Translation: Picasso, were he so inclined, has no business looking down his nose at a glassblower.) Most of the world's art is applied art, Ruhemann continues; art created for its own sake is a fairly recent development. Like Barzun, Ruhemann believes that the idea of the artist as self-exhibitor in his or her own medium (Ruhemann calls this the concept of the "artistic genius") is a development of the Renaissance, with its focus on the glory of the human person. Another element that muddies the distinction is the fact that many artists who we would classify under the rubric of fine art were also involved in applied art: Matisse, for example, worked in textiles; and Barzun notes that the Spanish Baroque painter Velazquez was entered on the payroll of Philip IV as an upholsterer. Still, according to Ruhemann, there was a final divergence between the two, beginning in the nineteenth century, that is, from that point artists and artisans were no longer necessarily thought of as belonging to the same field of human endeavor—this, despite such notable exceptions as the arts and crafts movement in England, associated with William Morris, and the Roycroft community of craftsmen in the United States.

Since that time, the so-called crafts have continued much as before, the artisan's freedom continuing to be restricted by the functional imperative inherent in his or her creations, and the craftsmen themselves, while not necessarily anonymous, most typically having only a local or regional reputation. During the same period, artists in the so-called fine arts have more and more engaged in a spree of narcissism. As art critic Roger Kimball has noted in several essays in his book *The Fortunes of Permanence*, currently the skill often associated with the production of great art has been downplayed in favor of the choice of appropriate subject matter, that is, subject matter that is regarded by the nonartistic majority as *inappropriate*. Kimball notes that this kind of art, which appears to have as its purpose to shock and scandalize, has ironically become yawningly conventional—what he terms the "domestication of deviance." He adds that art that ennobles and gratifies viewers is the most conspicuous casualty of this lamentable development.

My sentiments in this matter parallel those of Mr. Kimball, but that does not necessarily mean that my taste in art is confined to Norman Rockwell–type illustrations. Actually, I am drawn to painting and sculpture that might be classified under the genus abstract expressionism. When I began to notice the subtle gravitational pull of some of these creations during museum visits, I was perplexed; but upon further reflection, I realized that what attracted me was not so much the expressionism as the abstract element. What draws me to this kind of art is the same as what captivates me about more conventionally representational art or any art where *it* is present. The *it* can be identified in one word: form.

I first heard this term in my high school art-appreciation course, where the instructor quite understandably struggled to describe it, while at the same time maintaining that it was an essential ingredient in any artistic creation and challenging us to look for it in our museum visits. *Form* is like the term *spirituality*: extremely hard to define, but you know it when you see it. It is the arrangement of shape and color in a way that communicates the artist's attempt to transform instants of time into timelessness. Hardly an adequate definition, but it does contain one key word: *communicates*. True art, in my judgment, requires the artist to have viewers in mind, to respect them, even appeal to them. The proper artistic temperament is not focused on the artist's self-assessment as genius, above the world and disdainful of its inhabitants, but is rather heavily seasoned with humility and the hope that the receiver can see together with him. That is why British philosopher Roger Scruton, who has written extensively on aesthetics, has said that the creation of beauty is less an act of self-expression than an act of self-denial, by which the artist invites the receiver to construct with him a mutually consoling world. As I see it, the failure of the artistic community to distinguish between art so conceived and that which passes for art but is little more than bullying and incivility is one of the regrettable outcomes of the overweening relativism that afflicts all aspects of life in the contemporary human community.

So much for art, but what about the personal profile of the artist? It is clear that I (and perhaps others) prefer artists who are humble, diligent, seeking to please, and even pious to an extent—all behaviors associated with middle-class striving, which many artists in the modern age detest. But, to my chagrin, the evidence from Caravaggio to Pollack is all against me; that is, it would seem that unconventional, immoral, even, at times, boorish behavior is a necessary ingredient in artistic genius. It is the conventional wisdom, but is it true?

A startling comment by a teacher who was once my carpool partner may shed some light on the issue. He turned to me on one occasion when I was driving and said that he had come to the conclusion that there was no such thing as adolescence. Puberty, he said, is a biological fact; adolescence, a social construction. As the discussion prompted by this conversational bombshell continued, it was clear that he wasn't talking about all characteristics classified by behavioral scientists or mental health professionals as *adolescent*—awkwardness, anxiety, sexual identity issues—all related to hormonal and physical appearance changes. Rather, he was speaking of what adolescence *connotes* in recent and contemporary American society: disrespect for adults and all that is outside the current youth value system, premature sexually suggestive behavior, peer/identity preoccupations such as gothic accouterments, endless time on the telephone or mobile device, loud music, drug experimentation—the whole panoply of attitudes and behaviors that sometimes goes by the oxymoron *teen culture* and is taken for granted in TV sitcoms and video advertising as unavoidable in dealing with young people over twelve and under twenty. My friend speculated, with neither a positive nor a negative judgment, that all this was the fallout of a permissive society and/or a modern mass media civilization. It was perhaps an inevitability, but that was not his point. These behaviors are not organic in a teenager. Was there this kind of connotative adolescence among the medieval French peasantry? In ancient Egypt? My teacher friend thought not. I suspect he was right.

I believe something like this analysis to be helpful in evaluating the contention that artistic ability and unconventional, even immoral, behavior are *organically* connected. My view is that they are not; the connection is circumstantial, having to do with historical developments cited above that affected both the artist's self-understanding and growing notoriety. However, what is needed to make my case more persuasive are examples of the inverse, that is, artists of recognized accomplishment but whose lifestyle was as commonplace and banal as your next-door neighbor mowing his lawn.

If pressed, I reckon that I could come up with a few who showed the argument to be valid, but I need only one, especially if that one, as in this case, provides by himself evidence so unassailable that he might as well have QED entered after his name, who is indeed the exception to the artist-must-be-unconventional idea that in the end *disproves* the rule! The person in question did not practice his craft in the visual arts but in music and, as it happens, is, like Grover Cleveland (and me), another March birthday honoree (March 31). His name—which, in my view, should only be uttered with the circumspection appropriate to that of a saint or benefactor of civilization—is Johann Sebastian Bach.

I had only a record jacket (later CD jacket liner notes) education about JSB until coming upon Christoph Wolff's weighty biography, *Johann Sebastian Bach: The Learned Musician.* By my lights, the book is a remarkable achievement, but it can be slow going for the musicologically challenged. Herr Wolff's level of detail is amazing; sometimes the book reads—no disrespect intended—like an extended résumé of a candidate for employment, because that is what Bach often was, changing jobs periodically—Arnstadt, Weimar, Cothen, Leipzig—as more attractive opportunities presented themselves. Wolff even includes tables detailing Bach's salary and benefit packages (pp. 175, 406, 539–541)! After reading an account of his life, whatever one's opinion of JSB, I think there would be unanimous assent to the following proposition: there will never be an *Amadeus*-type play or movie about Bach. There was no wife stealing from a friend and supporter (Wagner); no curse of the gods type tragedy coupled with explosive behavior (Beethoven); no passionate love letters to stage actresses (Berlioz); and no frustrated love for the wife of a mentor (Brahms with Clara Schumann; and, if Brahms biographer Jan Swafford is right, Brahms with Clara's daughter, Julie!). Instead, Bach went to work each day without much fanfare and with, it appears, the goal of pleasing his employers—various civic/religious entities who hired him as music director/organist/Kapellmeister. It seems evident that he loved his wives (his first wife, Maria Barbara, died suddenly at the age of thirty six), was solicitous for the progress and education of his children, and was genuinely and deeply spiritual.

Further gleanings from various parts of Wolff's biography, reassembled, give (at least to me) a very attractive picture of the man who was Johann Sebastian Bach. Sprung from an extended family of musicians, Bach thought of music as his trade and said of himself, "I was obliged to be industrious; whoever is equally industrious will succeed equally well" (p. 50). Unless one ascribes to JSB a kind of false modesty bordering on disingenuousness, which seems totally out of character for him, then we have here one strand of evidence of Bach's humility and self-regard as something other than the artistic genius. There were others. Bach tried to meet Handel, whom he greatly esteemed, on more than one occasion, traveling to the latter's locale only to find that Handel had departed. It is at least arguable that the respect was not so nearly mutual (pp. 208–209). But Bach admired many other musician/composers: Wolff cites the incident in Bach's youth where he mostly walked a distance of 250 miles to hear Buxtehude play the organ (p. 96) and refers to JSB's large musical library, assembled over a lifetime, of *other* composers' works (p. 332–333).

In fact, an *admirer*—of things and people—is perhaps Bach's most noteworthy persona (as contrasted with *artistic geniuses*, large amounts of whose admiration is often saved for themselves). As a young man, he did not follow the typical musical apprenticeship, which would have been more convenient, but, in addition to his musical training, studied classics, theology, history, geography, and physics—the standard curriculum for university entrance (p. 53, 55–58). Though never matriculating himself, he had to pass rigorous examinations in Latin and theology to qualify as Kapellmeister in Leipzig (p. 240). It is safe to say that Bach held the fruits of learning in high regard to the end of his days. Indeed, in one case, he took a post that was not as appealing precisely because it was at a celebrated preparatory school (St. Thomas) where his children could get the benefit of a first-class education (p. 306). In due course, three of his sons so educated were able to go on to universities, a privilege that had eluded their father. In my lifetime, I have known and esteemed many parents who made similar sacrifices; but, I fear, some in the artistic community, on hearing this vignette about Bach, might respond, "How bourgeois!"

On taking a post as organist at Arnstadt, he was summarily informed that his duties would include the upkeep and maintenance of the organ (p. 79). It is as if an airline pilot were suddenly told that he would be required to take on the additional role of aircraft mechanic. Bach didn't cavil; instead, he used the mandate to develop expertise as an assessor of organ design and performance, a useful and sometimes profitable sideline for the rest of his life (p. 415). It appears that JSB, to the sneering contempt of some, was a prototype of the power of positive thinking and of making lemonade out of lemons. Wolff also mentions that Bach kept students throughout his life (p. 331)—probably because he needed the income for a large and growing family but also, the evidence suggests, because he enjoyed the interactions, this in marked contrast to Handel and Telemann (and, one might add, to the Mozart of *Amadeus*, who, in a response typical of the artistic genius, tells his father that he doesn't want students because he needs time for composition).

"Time for composition." This is where the story of Johann Sebastian Bach approaches sublimity. The demands of his employment and the myriad concerns related to a large family, Wolff says, made his compositional productivity border on the sheer incredible (p. 278). Composing in those relatively few free hours or moments left to him, Wolff further comments, required of Bach extraordinary concentration and discipline (p. 254). But we are speaking here only of impressive quantity; what of quality? Suffice it to say that JSB shows up regularly on musicologists' lists of the greatest composers (a list that, I suspect, Bach would believe was a bad idea) in the number one slot. Bach was a pioneer in many compositional forms; Wolff says some of his works had no precedent or parallel (p. 379). But—and here is the key point as far as I am concerned—he did his path breaking while still trying to bring his listeners along and always with the intention of giving glory to God.

Every Bach devotee has a dilemma like the following. I believe the *Passacaglia and Fugue in C Minor* for organ to be the most transcendent thirteen-plus minutes in music. But then what about the three minutes and five seconds (Glenn Gould tempo) of the *Prelude and Fugue in G Sharp Minor* from *The Well-Tempered Clavier*? Oh, but I am forgetting the *Aria variata alla maniera Italiana*. And, come to think of it, I left off the *Kyrie* from the Mass in B Minor. And on and on. Each Bach lover has different starting points, but each tries, and fails, to designate his or her favorite piece, such is the vast array of JSB's output that approached musical perfection. In my judgment, no other composer has ever or will ever match this nexus of quality and quantity.

In his self-regard, Bach was an artisan, a tradesman, a craftsman. He died not knowing that he would be deemed the greatest composer of the West and a great man of history. But I do not believe that he, to his everlasting credit, would have cared. Rather, he was content with the smaller public—family, friends, students, employers—that loved and esteemed him. It is certainly true that others of his contemporaries thought of themselves as craftsmen, a point underscored by James R. Gaines in his interesting book on Bach and Frederick the Great, *Evening in the Palace of Reason*. The artist-as-hero idea, cited above as having begun in the Renaissance, took time to develop and spread. On the other hand, it is hard to resist the notion that JSB exceeded all creative artists, in his or any age, in the matter of modesty and self-effacement. In any case, it still remains that the elements of his character (or that of the Bach's time and place, if one were to insist)—diligence, piety, respect, fidelity, and humility—are ones that the artistic community of today, in my opinion, desperately needs to recover.

As for Bach himself, his life can be summed up in a slight paraphrase of Eric Hoffer's bon mot—the "Triumph of a Square,"; but, perhaps more pointedly, and for the edification of everyone, including "artistic geniuses," it is better to say that Johann Sebastian Bach is the greatest exemplar in human history of the perennial truth: "He who humbles himself shall be exalted."

CHAPTER 5
APRIL

The Big East

Religion … should not attempt to dispute what
science has actually proved; and science should not
claim to know what it does not know, it should not
confuse theory and knowledge, and it should disavow
any claim on what is empirically unknowable.
—Wendell Berry

At the beginning of April, Cathy and I celebrated our first Saturday breakfast at the south end of the dining room table. In looking back over my log, I realize that the unscientific nature of my solar journaling and the variations in dates when a Saturday occurs at this point in the sun's journey mean that I cannot pinpoint an exact date when sunlight falls off the south end of the table. Sometime in March to early April is the best I can do, and since comfort at eating breakfast is the criterion, we sometimes make the move when there is still a sliver of sunlight left at table's end or on one of the chairs.

I note some other major changes now that the sun has more appreciably advanced into the north celestial hemisphere. On April 5 at 6:00 p.m. (really 5:00 p.m. under standard time), I saw that the setting sun now illuminated my bedroom night table from the more northerly west window of our bedroom and not the skylight. On April 11 at 6:40 a.m., the rising sun through the northeast skylight shone almost completely on the southernmost of the two bookcases at the west wall of the upstairs sitting area, the light slowly descending in a narrow angle to graze the northern bookcase's bottom shelves. Five days later, it did not touch the northern bookcase at all, and by the twentieth, the sun was casting light into the upstairs TV room through the permanently open doorway. In March, I had delighted in the sun's lighting up of Cathy's mineral collection downstairs as it descended and cast light through the west octagonal window onto the china cabinet. Now on April 22 in the afternoon, the sunlight through the same window clears the china cabinet southerly and, since there is no wall here, shoots straight through to the kitchen, illuminating the salt and pepper shakers in their customary place of repose east of the stove.

April has been described by the poet as the cruelest month and sometimes lives up to the designation in these parts by afflicting us with a freak snowstorm. Farther north in New England, April snowstorms are much more common and facilitate the delightful activity known as spring skiing. But in southern New England, April snow, though usually of small accumulations, is almost universally detested and psychologically harder to bear than midwinter storms, since the sun's crossing of the celestial equator was supposed to spare us from such adversities.

On the other hand, April features such welcome events as Easter (most years), the beginning of the Major League Baseball season, preliminary planning for Cathy's vegetable garden, and, for me, the first serious nighttime observing with my mounted binoculars (as I have gotten older, I am more of a winter-observing no-show). Then there is the April phenomenon for which I wait all year: the emergent early-spring green of the leaves of the maple tree owned by the town and directly north of our house. An exquisite shade of light green, it lasts only a short time as the leaves grow larger and darker.

Cathy and I have another April tradition—a weekend excursion to Cape Cod. We've been doing it for about twenty years and have developed a routine of activities, which, though repeated every year, has yet to become tiresome or boring. We chose April—usually the end of April—because clement weather most times has arrived, but it is still too early for the crowds of tourists and beachgoers who flood the Cape all summer long, beginning in late spring. Of course, the Cape has changed much over the years—even from the time of Patti Page's 1950s song "Old Cape Cod"—and has its share of suburban sprawl, including unattractive strip malls. But Cathy and I typically seek out the other Cape, the Cape of legend, and we have probably hiked every trail from Sandwich to Provincetown, especially that place endowed with such grandeur on the eastward face of the outer arm—the Cape Cod National Seashore.

When pausing at that shore and gazing eastward, my mind often turns to two illustrious predecessors who similarly looked out from places not that far from where I have stopped. One is Henry David Thoreau, a wry assessor of people and a keen observer of detail, including shifts in sand and ocean at various places. Thoreau visited the Cape several times beginning in 1849 and left us a diary of sorts of his findings, titled simply *Cape Cod*. What impresses me about this record is the fact that Thoreau walked with a companion a twenty-eight mile journey on the outer Cape, a commonplace distance for a foot journey, it seems, in those days. In his writing, he constantly quotes from ancient texts in Latin and Greek and, at the same time, identifies elements of the flora by their scientific names. It saddens me to think of what we have lost in our educational practice, realizing that heretofore there were individuals who were equally comfortable in such disparate areas of learning. Some of his observations rise to the level of poetry, as his thoughts when he retires at night in the lighthouse in Truro, meditating on how many seaborne eyes are directed his way for guidance into safe harbor.

But what entrances Thoreau the most, what he returns to most often in awe is the beach—the eastern length of the outer Cape— speculating on what is directly across the Atlantic latitudinally and noting that there is nothing between him and Europe but the ocean, which he terms "savage." In this almost worshipful sentiment about the beach and the ocean, he resembles the second Cape diarist that often comes to my mind: Henry Beston. Beston was a New England nature writer who off and on, beginning in 1925, spent a two-year minimalist residency in a shack he had constructed on the beach near the Coast Guard lighthouse. The result was a chronicle of the shore and its flora and fauna over a year's time—the classic *The Outermost House*. Beston's writing is a delight to me, since he felt strongly about things for which I have a similar enthusiasm. For instance, he emphasizes the importance of the night for the human person and wonders whether moderns are in fear of it; he also calls on humankind to observe and share in the natural drama of the sun's yearly journey, an activity that inspired me to begin my own solar journaling; and he demonstrates in regard to nature both gratitude and reverence.

Like Thoreau, Beston loved to gaze eastward at the ocean immensity and speculate, albeit with more specificity than Thoreau, about what lay eastward roughly along the same parallel of latitude, identifying the Spanish province of Galacia, the town of Pontevedra, and St. James Compestela. He calls attention to perhaps a little-known fact that the peninsula of the Cape— speaking of its outer arm where his cabin was located—stands farther out to sea than any other portion of the Atlantic coast of the United States. What this yields for visitors to the Coast Guard lighthouse area is an ocean panorama that is marked by what can only be called a shoreline convexity; that is, there seems to be no encroaching shoreline perimeter north or south as there is in so many ocean vistas in New England and elsewhere. It is all ocean and all east, periphery to periphery. I have called this vision, this Cape-induced phenomenon, "The Big East."

Who notices such things? Thoreau and Beston, for two, and a far, far distant third, me. I think it is fair to describe such noticing as Thoreau and Beston were doing to be in the province of the naturalist, a term that, like humanist, is hard to define and has many resonances and overtones. The work of the naturalist is best understood when it is contrasted with that of a specialist who appears to have an interest in the same entities: the scientist. It is of course true that the scientist and the naturalist can sometimes be and have been the same person. But the endeavors are distinct. For the scientist, nature is a riddle to be solved, eliciting, primarily, from the practitioner the sentiment of curiosity. How do things work? Is the appearance of a natural event in some way deceiving? Does the behavior of any natural existent—a star, a mushroom—confirm or fly in the face of previous knowledge of it or its class of objects? The naturalist, by contrast, is bent more toward appreciation. He notes things simply because they are there and he has seen them; he is in every observation searching for what John Burroughs, another famous American naturalist, called the "wordless spirit of nature."

For instance, Beston was a close observer of everything surrounding his cabin, from beach grass to butterflies, but is especially good in describing the sound of the surf—its relentless seething, hissing, and grinding, to cite just three near onomatopoeic words he deploys to convey to his readers the experience. Was any of this narrative a contribution to the store of knowledge related to the physics of wave action? No, it was more like a love letter, a thank-you note, even a prayer.

The mention of prayer brings up the dread topic of religion, toward which, I must confess, this essay is remorselessly tending. But, before entering its precincts, a kind of autobiographical full disclosure in the matter of science is in order.

My early teen years were in the late 1950s—a half decade marked by the Soviet launching of the *Sputnik* satellite, coupled with some early US rocket failures, that prompted a round of hand wringing by elites, much like today, that America was falling behind the world in science. At the time, I was known to be a pretty good student and, coincidently, had, at the behest of a school mate, entered upon the hobby of astronomy. For an entire year, I spent as many clear evenings as possible at the end of my street, watching and identifying constellations in their seasonal succession. When it was evident that I was serious enough about this avocation, my father bought me a small telescope. It was a great sacrifice for him on his wages—one for which I am forever grateful. He would be dead in less than two years.

The combination of societal anxiety that we were falling behind the Russians, taken together with my interest in the night sky, naturally drew me in the direction of science. At the age of fourteen, I decided that I wanted to be an astronomer. But there was a problem: as any of my guidance counselors could have told you, my talents—such as they were—lay in the direction of the verbal rather than the mathematical side of human knowledge. Moreover, even my interest in astronomy consisted largely in a kind of awe at the night sky, rather than the insatiable curiosity about what makes it tick that characterizes the budding scientist. Still, I held onto my dream of an astronomical career long after it was not feasible, joining an astronomy club and the Science Club at school. For a while, I was that most pitiable of creatures: a science nerd who was not as good in science as many who would not be caught dead sporting a pocket protector. By the time I entered college, history and philosophy would be my majors.

But a funny thing happened on my journey away from science as a vocation: I had invested enough time and effort in astronomy that I brought it along with me, adopting it permanently as an avocation. Normally, what it is that I do would fall under the heading of *amateur astronomy*, a term that refers to a vibrant American and global subculture with its own associations, magazines, and observing networks of thousands of enthusiasts. However, I prefer a self-designation of *night sky observer* to amateur astronomer. Amateur astronomy is quintessentially a science hobby. Typically, hobbyists are persons with high mechanical and/ or science aptitudes; many have large instruments, observatory class equipment or make their own telescopes; some do quasi-professional work that can be entered into databases useful to full-time astronomers. An example of the latter is the American Association of Variable Star Observers (AAVSO), whose members keep track of the magnitude fluctuations of assigned stars and forward their reports for use by professionals who do not have the time for the periodic canvassing of the thousands of stars under this category.

I, on the other hand, am out under the sky more for personal/ aesthetic/spiritual fulfillment. But that does not mean I care nothing for the science that interfaces with these concerns. I have observed for years with telescopes and mounted binoculars using star maps and handbooks that require a grasp of celestial mechanics. I have become practiced in the rough determination of stellar apparent magnitudes. I am minimally conversant in the classifications and distributions of star clusters, nebulae, and galaxies. I am somewhat adept at the estimation of angular separations of double stars. And I have kept a thirty-year log of my observations, including drawings of astral configurations. I like to think that I am in a small way a naturalist, taking note of celestial phenomena and following in the footsteps of Thoreau, Beston, and others whose gaze was more terrestrially inclined. In sum, my avocation of night sky observing is in the main an act of appreciation of the nocturnal canopy above, but it has been greatly enhanced, if not made possible at all, by the science that gave me the optical tools that I use and the understanding of stellar apparitions that I am viewing—that is, my appreciation extends to the scientists who enabled me to pursue this endeavor for nonscientific ends.

And now to the point of this essay. I have spent a considerable portion of my adult life pursuing activities within the domain of organized religion. As noted previously, I studied for the Roman Catholic priesthood for several years; later, I taught theology in several Catholic high schools; and later still, I was active in adult education and other forms of lay ministry in my parish. And during all that time, I, from the house of religion, looked across the street, as it were, to the house of science with respect and gratitude. Increasingly, however, especially in the last twenty years or so, the favor is not being returned. There has emerged on the scene a new kind of muscular atheism, forwarded and promoted largely, though not exclusively, by certain men of science who regard the house of religion and its inhabitants with condescension, disdain, and even acrimony.

These individuals include the so-called Four Horsemen of modern militant atheism: Richard Dawkins, Daniel Dennett, Sam Harris, and Christopher Hitchens. Dawkins, an evolutionary biologist and professor at Oxford, has written, among other books, *The God Delusion* (hereinafter *God*); Dennett, a philosopher and cognitive scientist at Tufts University, has written *Breaking the Spell: Religion as a Natural Phenomenon* (hereinafter *Breaking*); philosopher and scientist Sam Harris is well known for his short book *Letter to a Christian Nation*; and journalist, historian, and controversialist, the late Christopher Hitchens, is justly famous or notorious, depending on one's point of view, for his take-no-prisoners book, *God Is Not Great: How Religion Poisons Everything.*

One way to analyze the modern atheistic assault on belief in God—certainly not the only way—is that it is two-pronged: one line of attack is concentrated on the idea of God and supernatural reality without regard to religious institutions per se, and the other is concerned with these institutions, that is, religious denominations and their practices, traditions, and their alleged record of historical infamies. All four of the above cited authors deal with both aspects of the issue, but I think it is fair to say that Hitchens and Harris (at least the Harris of *Letter to a Christian Nation*) concentrate on the latter. For instance, Hitchens has a humorous excursus called "A Short Digression on the Pig; or, Why Heaven Hates Ham" (it was read by Salman Rushdie at Hitchens's memorial service), in which his acid wit is used to some effect in attempting to skewer the dietary rules of two religions. The book contains a lot more of this. And Sam Harris waxes nearly apoplectic in relating a contemporaneous gathering of theologians in Rome, in what he terms an example of "misspent human energy," to discuss the doctrine of Limbo.

Religion being a human institution, whatever else it is, any denominational entity that has been around more than a millennium and has had sufficient numbers of adherents throughout its history has a record of thought and behavior that includes its share of tragedies, fatal contradictions, and just plain foolishness. This is the main grist for the mills of Hitchens et al. To defend, say, Christianity from all their charges would require many more pages than I am willing to dedicate to the process and much more specific knowledge than I possess. I am much more taken with the other prong of atheistic criticism—the principal focus of Dawkins and Dennett—namely the attack on belief in a supernatural dimension to the universe, pure and simple. It is not that I am qualified in this matter either; it's just that I believe the issues here are clearer, making a discussion of them from the point of view of an interested layperson at least minimally fruitful.

There are several general observations to make about the muscular atheistic attack on belief under this heading. First, there is the aforementioned condescension. Dennett uses the term "brights" (as in "us brights") to describe atheists and those who insist on a naturalistic explanation of all phenomena in the universe. He maintains (*Breaking*, p. 21), not very convincingly, that there is no implication here about the mental capacities of believers. As for Dawkins, it is more a matter of tone: his impatience with and contempt for believers just jumps out at one from any random page of *The God Delusion*.

A second point concerns what is perhaps the most crucial plank in the platform of modern militant atheism, namely a disrespect for NOMA. NOMA—an acronym for Non-Overlapping Magisteria—is a term coined by the late paleontologist Stephen J. Gould in his book *Rocks of Ages: Science and Religion in the Fullness of Life*. For Gould, the business of science is ascertaining the factual character of the world; religion is, by contrast, concerned with purposes, meanings, and values. In Gould's opinion, the two entities should stay within their separate spheres. To which Professor Dawkins essentially says, "Rubbish!" Science should get into the area of religion, explaining it empirically as it would any other occurrence in nature (hence the subtitle of Dennett's book, "Religion as a Natural Phenomenon"). Indeed, Dawkins cannot believe that Gould was serious about his concept and was rather being overly diplomatic (*God*, p. 81).

This brings us to the third general observation, namely the modern atheist's attempt to explain the human experience beyond the basic bodily functions that science can describe quantitatively. The answer is the theory of memes. Both Dawkins and Dennett provide full treatments of it in their separate books. Dawkins calls memes "units of cultural inheritance" (*God*, p. 222); Dennett describes them as "replicators," "elements of culture that may be considered to be passed on by non-genetic means" (*Breaking*, p. 345), and "cultural recipes" (*Breaking*, p. 350). They amount to an attempt to explain human history in those matters that make it so markedly different from the natural history of, say, other primates or, for that matter, any living thing. Though the transmission of memes is by other than the genetic process, in Dawkins's mind at least, they sort of act like genes. Hence he uses quasi-scientific terms like "memeplexes" and "memepool" (*God*, p. 230).

There are, in my opinion, two important caveats to keep in mind when reflecting on the theory of memes. First—and this point is applicable to the modern atheistic assault on belief more generally—if one is discussing the existence of God, then technically, for the sake of argument, it is deemed to be an open question. Hence one looks at a given phenomenon and evaluates whether a naturalistic inference or a positing of divine intervention provides the best explanation. For the past four hundred years, science has been winning most all these engagements. But this is not the case with memes. That is, memes do not prove the nonexistence of God; they are rather what one is left with if the existence of God has been ruled out in the first place. That is because—and this is the second caveat—the theory of memes is not science or the result of a scientific investigation. They cannot be demonstrated by repeated laboratory experiments or inferred with absolute confidence from exhaustive data sets like the fossil record. They represent, rather, a brilliant conjecture on the part of those who have already decided the issue of God's existence negatively before the debate begins.

A final observation concerns an arresting metaphor that Professor Dawkins provides his readers: "crane" versus "skyhook" (*God,* p. 188 and elsewhere; this metaphor is also attributed to Dennett). The crane—in Dawkins's description, an "upward ratcheting, self-bootstrapping crane"—is Darwinian evolution, which shows how living creatures evolved by slow, gradual degrees from simple (emphasis on "simple") beginnings. The "skyhook"— and the pejorative overtones are certainly intended—represents the explanation favored by believers that the story of the universe and of life and of humankind is attributable to an outside designer (i.e., God). In my opinion, Professor Dawkins has provided participants in the debate a brilliant shorthand for organizing the issues, one which will be used below.

To explore more fully the arena of controversy occasioned by the onset of contemporary muscular atheism, I have chosen for a closer look neither Dawkins nor Dennett but a third participant: the emeritus physics professor Chet Raymo. The rationale for this choice equates to the *Our Town* paradigm of this book, which seeks somehow to integrate the personal and the local with the universal and transcendent. Thus, Professor Raymo taught at Stonehill College in South Easton, Massachusetts, which, except in the Rhode Island concept of distance, would be deemed to be just a hop, skip, and a jump from my home in Bristol. More to the point, I actually met Professor Raymo when he gave a lecture titled "The Soul of the Night," based on his book of the same name that was being contemporaneously published. The book in question is actually quite characteristic of his published output, containing as it does the signature Raymonian mélange of solid astronomical information, cutting-edge research, and philosophical musings. Chet Raymo is most definitely a naturalist; there is a high level of appreciation in his writing. He is also spiritual person of a sort. He penned a meditative work called *Natural Prayers*—a title that

I am sure would give Richard Dawkins dyspepsia—and most of his books are peppered with allusions to mystics like Meister Eckhardt and concepts such as panentheism.

What Chet Raymo is definitely *not* is an adherent to any conventional theistic theology, and though he may be the kinder, gentler face of atheism (and I believe he would deny that he *is* an atheist), he is most assuredly and happily, it seems, in collaboration with the Dawkins and Dennetts of this world in the mission of relegating traditional Western religion to the dustbin of history, as can be seen from two of his later publications—*Skeptics and True Believers* and *Walking Zero*.

Skeptics and True Believers (hereinafter *Skeptics*) is an extended essay narrating the divergence between science and religion on the great questions of the nature of the universe and the meaning of human life. In the book, "true believers" is a catchall category that includes everyone from devotees of astrology and UFO enthusiasts to, it appears, advocates of standard monotheism. In the cleverly titled *Walking Zero* (hereinafter *Walking*), Raymo makes a foot journey along the prime meridian in England in close proximity to which were the domiciles, laboratories, and observatories of a number of luminaries of modern science, the triumphs of whom Raymo details in the several chapters of the book. It is safe to say that emerging, ever more confident, science, elbowing out conventional religious modalities of thinking, is the hero of both volumes.

I think the salient features of both books can be conveniently treated under several headings. First, the closest the professor comes to the more unpleasant aspects of the writing of Dennett and Dawkins is in his treatment of the intellectual value of theism, specifically Christian theism, the derision and condescension being just a bit more muted. Speaking of the separate appeals of science and religion, Professor Raymo describes them as a choice between a "hard truth and an easy high" (*Skeptics,* p. 119); it is essential, he says, that the church undermine science (*Skeptics,* p. 67); believers, he avers, are opting for "the thumb, the security blanket, the parent's embrace" (*Skeptics,* p. 126); and speaking of the faith of religious believers, he uses terms like "warm and fuzzy" and "teddy bears" (*Skeptics,* p. 144).

In regard to the above, I am left wondering if Raymo has any idea what has been going on in Catholic and the wider Christian theology in the last century. Referring to his earlier days as a student at Notre Dame, he mentions a textbook by Frank Sheed (a nonprofessional theologian) used in his class, which attempted to prove the validity of the Catholic faith (*Skeptics,* p. 18). It is not clear to me that the professor is aware of the difference between dogmatic or apologetical theology, on the one hand, and philosophical/foundational theology on the other. The latter is not concerned with explicating or proving the truth of church doctrines but exploring the relevance of theological language and belief in God in a postscientific and post-Enlightenment era—and no teddy bears allowed. No serious theologian, to my knowledge, goes about his/her work without first confronting the challenges to belief of modernity, but you would never know it by reading the works of Professor Raymo.

Finally, in the matter of condescension, Professor Raymo deploys (twice) the time-honored metaphor that he believes holds in thrall true believers—the gray-bearded God (*Skeptics,* p. 28 and 30). Since anthropomorphism is the trump card by which Raymo and other critics of theism believe they have disarmed Western religious belief, it is worth pausing to consider what is or has been intended by the image of the bearded God.

The key here is to distinguish between the order of being and the order of knowing. When it comes to (well-attested or alleged) realities that cannot be perceived by the senses, the investigator proceeds from what is known empirically, then analogically or metaphorically, to describe the nonsensible entity. It really cannot be otherwise, as describing electricity as "juice," computer information storage as "files," the entire electorate as the "body politic," outlying banking locations as "branches," a generous person as having a kind "heart," and thousands of other examples clearly show. But in regard to the entity that transcends the senses that is at issue here—namely, God—the salient point is that that which is in the order of being comes first, is more real, if you will. Thus, it is *not* the case that God is like an elderly man with a beard but that an elderly man with a beard is something like God, as are mountains, California redwoods, seahorses, and science writers who attempt to disparage belief in Him. The elderly man metaphor was deployed because of such features as consciousness and the wisdom attributable to old age, but it was never seen to be as exhaustive of God's being—which Professor Raymo at least appears to think—as any number of biblical references demonstrate.

Professor Raymo, I would surmise, believes that the old man metaphor limps terribly, even fatally. One can certainly make that case, but it pays to remember that other kinds of metaphors limp too. In his book *Miracles*, C. S. Lewis tells an amusing story of a woman of his acquaintance who was brought up by "high-minded" parents to believe that God was a "perfect substance." Though Chet Raymo might not endorse the figure, I am sure he would regard it as far superior to the old man metaphor. The trouble was that, when the girl grew up, she realized that she thought of God as a vast tapioca pudding. And even Professor Raymo might have his own problems with metaphor making. Speaking of the big bang, he relates that the billions of galaxies that astronomers have discovered originated in a cataclysmic explosion from a "seed of infinite energy" (*Skeptics*, p. 134). Who knew that energy had seeds? The fact is it doesn't. The good professor is using a botanical metaphor, one that visibly limps: seeds come from already existing plants, a biological necessity that cannot be accommodated in this analogy.

The bottom line is that Raymo is gratuitously ungenerous to theistically inclined believers, about the depth of whose spirituality in individual cases he knows absolutely nothing, and seems further to be ignorant of the fact that faith in a personal God can be as profound as that of belief in a God without attributes—indeed, for some ascetic traditions, believers hold to both conceptualizations in a kind of creative tension—or a God who is deemed to be a "perfect substance."

For my money, Professor Raymo is even worse when it comes to his narrations of the history of religion and the history of science. In regard to the former, unless I seriously misunderstand him, Raymo makes some fairly substantial category errors. Speaking of the Renaissance, he states that, with that cultural upheaval, Europe turned its back on the myth of the eternal return and cyclical history (*Walking*, p. 154). The implication here is that previously, Christianity, holding sway over European culture, was immersed in such a mindset. But this simply isn't true. The Christian liturgical year is of course cyclical—fasts, feasts, and seasons rotating year after year. But what might be termed the Christian philosophy of history, in a sharp break with much of ancient pagan thought, is about as rectilinear as it can get—creation, redemption, eschaton. Similarly, Professor Raymo says that since the time of Meister Eckhart (early fourteenth century), the dominant Judeo-Christian tradition has understood the material world to be "intrinsically evil" (*Skeptics*, p. 132). Again, false. Whatever the Judeo-Christian view of the consequences of sin, it never held to the intrinsic evil of created reality. Christianity, in particular, was, in its early days, resistant to competing Gnosticisms with their contempt for the physical. And this was from the *very* beginning. The resurrected Jesus— appearing to the disciples, whom they thought was a ghost— asks them if they have anything to eat (Luke 24:41). There is a straight, uninterrupted vector from this incident, where Jesus ends up partaking of a piece of boiled fish, to the Catholic love for the holiness of things—water, oil, wine, bread, beads, candles, art—to the dogma of the resurrection of the body. Finally, Raymo notes the complicity of Christians in the slave trade, comparing them unfavorably with Darwin and Thomas Huxley, who were on the side of "progressive social and political change" (*Walking*, p. 111). Raymo has heard of Bishop Samuel Wilberforce, whom he gleefully describes as being bested by Huxley in a debate over human origins (*Walking*, p. 110); what isn't clear to me is if he has ever heard of Samuel's father, *William* Wilberforce, whose Christian faith was *the* primary motivating factor in his leadership of a successful campaign to abolish the slave trade in the British Empire.

But this is how it goes with Chet Raymo: it is history as the saga of heroes (scientists) and villains (the conventionally religious), and no inconvenient distinction making is welcome. Typical is his statement that "with the Renaissance, Europe embraced progress, individual creativity, and empirical learning, and turned its back on tradition, religious conformity, and the authority of the past" (*Walking*, p. 154). Never mind that part of the Renaissance humanist project was precisely the recovery of the ancient past and ancient Latin and Greek authorities and that its almost worshipful regard and celebration of the dignity of man does not fit comfortably with the Raymonian view that human beings are as incidental to the cosmos as mayflies are to Earth (*Skeptics*, p. 222). In this matter, Professor Raymo seems to me to be seriously conflating, if not completely identifying, the

Renaissance and the Scientific Revolution—two movements that were related perhaps but also quite different in character. Indeed, as discussed below, it may have been the view of humankind of the Middle Ages that is less incompatible with science than that of the Renaissance. No serious historian would write like the professor. This is history as the talking points of an ideological mindset; if it were a film, it would be directed by Oliver Stone.

This cartoon version of the history of science to which Raymo and the muscular atheists subscribe runs something like the following: In the Graeco-Roman world, there were serious attempts at the proto-scientific—as opposed to the purely philosophical—analysis of reality, undertaken by such pioneering figures as Eratosthenes, Aristarchus of Samos, and Archimedes, to name just a few. Then, with the political collapse of the Roman Empire, the Western world entered a protracted dark age, in which the Christian religion enslaved human minds (although, as Arthur Koestler demonstrates in his history of astronomical discovery, *The Sleepwalkers*, the turn away from proto-scientific speculation in the Hellenic intellectual world occurred centuries before the founding of Christianity). With the Scientific Revolution of the sixteenth and seventeenth centuries, Western man threw off this prison of ignorance and brought the human community into a bright and progressive new era. From what has already been related, Chet Raymo would likely associate himself with a reasonable facsimile of this assessment. All doubt is put to flight when he asserts that, with the establishment of the Royal Society in England in the seventeenth century, modern science was taking up where the Alexandrians left off two thousand years previously (*Walking*, p. 129).

This story of the centuries-old war between science and religion, and the superiority of the former over the latter, has been eagerly forwarded by antireligious intellectuals at least since the

Enlightenment and, by now, has hardened into a cultural trope. An example of how it has lodged in the popular imagination can be seen in the play *Inherit the Wind*—a rendering of the Scopes Monkey trial of 1925, in which a Tennessee high school teacher was arrested and tried for teaching evolution in high school in contravention of state law. Made into a motion picture in 1960, the film, in my view, is a priceless cinematic treasure, primarily because of the cast: Spencer Tracy as Henry Drummond (the character based on the famous American defense attorney Clarence Darrow), Frederic March as Matthew Harrison Brady (the character based on three-time presidential candidate and Fundamentalist Christian William Jennings Bryan), and, in a surprisingly strong, against-type performance, Gene Kelly as acid-tongued reporter E. K. Hornbeck (loosely based on the American journalist and essayist H. L. Mencken). Leaving aside the fact that the play differs from the historical events in some important details (the name changes, it appears, gave the playwrights a license to diverge from history), it is clear that the writers and the director have stacked the deck against religious belief and are forwarding their own political/cultural agenda. The Brady/ Bryan character, for the prosecution, is portrayed as a pompous, strutting buffoon constantly outwitted by Drummond, defending the teacher, as he, Bryan/Brady, falls into the former's rhetorical traps and gets tangled in the contradictions of sacred history. Drummond/Darrow? He is cool, informed, urbane, in control, and gently humorous at every turn. He wins by a KO. You can almost hear the playwrights and director applauding.

Is this picture accurate? Not really. Evidence for this contention comes from an unlikely source: Stephen J. Gould in the aforementioned *Rocks of Ages*. While seriously disagreeing with Bryan's biblical theology and views on science, Gould shows how Bryan's motivations and concerns were multifaceted and worthy of consideration. He was not as one-dimensional and not nearly as bad as represented in *Inherit the Wind*. And perhaps Clarence Darrow was not as good. Six years after the Scopes trial, Darrow appears to have met his match and more in a lengthy exchange with English Catholic writer G.K. Chesterton on an American speaking tour. Debating the future of religion in a packed auditorium, Darrow was, according to firsthand accounts, impatient, testy, illogical, and somewhat ill-informed as he crossed swords with his opponent who, representing the validity of religion, was good-humored and dazzled his listeners with insightful paradoxes and incandescent metaphors. It was *Inherit the Wind* in the inverse. A poll of the audience taken at the conclusion as to who won the debate gave the nod to Chesterton by better than two to one.

This *Inherit the Wind* version of the battle between science and religion and what I believe to be its, at least, partial unmasking serves as a cautionary note when one is presented with the easy categorizations of some histories of science, like those of Chet Raymo. In the opening chapter of C. S. Lewis's *English Literature in the Sixteenth Century*, a tour de force of intellectual history titled "New Learning and New Ignorance," the author patiently shows how magic and astrology, superstitions that Raymo would likely believe are of a piece and that were left behind with the advent of the Renaissance, were in reality completely opposed to each other and that, what may be termed, high magic was popular with intellectuals and early scientists inconveniently far past the Middle Ages. On the other hand, as theologian David Bentley Hart has shown, some of the foundations for modern science were laid in the medieval European universities and by such figures as Albertus Magnus and Robert Grosseteste in the twelfth and thirteen centuries. Historian Christopher Dawson is even stronger on this point, averring that it is difficult to see how the Scientific

Revolution of the sixteenth and seventeenth centuries would have even been possible without the medieval (yes, medieval!) passion for disputation and belief in the rationality of the universe and the power of the mind to investigate the order of nature. Such nuances are lost on Chet Raymo, who, it appears, regards historical eras as watertight compartments.

This tendency can be further illustrated by a consideration of Professor Raymo's assessment of the cultural consequences of the Copernican heliocentric theory. Raymo says flatly that the Copernican revolution removed humankind from the center of the universe (*Walking*, p. 154). But did Western man believe he was at the center of things previous to this? It is not at all clear that he did. As Lewis shows in the abovementioned work, for ages, men had known that the Earth was infinitesimally small in relation to the universe and was at the distant reaches of the cosmos farthest from the light. Positional centrality, which was really more in the nature of being at the bottom of the universe, had not necessarily implied preeminence, so much so that the German humanist Cusanus (1401–1464) thought that the new theory of the Earth's movement actually raised it in dignity (a fact also noted by Koestler in *The Sleepwalkers*). On the other hand, does noncentrality prove that humankind is of small significance in the universe, as Chet Raymo clearly believes (We are "dust motes," *Skeptics*, p. 166)? Again, not necessarily, on the principle that it is dangerous to draw metaphysical conclusions from scientific premises. Such, it appears, is the view of Harvard astronomer *and* Christian believer Owen Gingerich (How would Chet Raymo classify *him*?), who sharply distinguishes between the heliocentric theory, which is not so much a theory as a scientific fact, and the Copernican principle that humankind is of no account in the vastness of the cosmos, which he treats as an ideology. In other words, the size of the universe and the motion or nonmotion of the Earth imply precisely nothing about the importance of humanity, and making such value-laden inferences is sheer conjecture whether undertaken by churchmen or scientists.

With Chet Raymo then, we have unwarranted condescension toward theistic religion and, arguably, a misleading and tendentious history of science and religion. A third problem with his thought centers around his use of Ockham's razor in the analysis of the human phenomenon. William of Ockham, a fourteenth-century Franciscan friar and scholar, was the originator of the philosophical school of nominalism, which took to task the idea that there were universal essences that inhered in things and could be captured by the mind in concepts. His hardheaded rejection of such entities, entities that could not be verified empirically, is seen by some as a foreshadowing of the scientific mentality of two centuries later. As was his famous razor, an epistemological principle that stipulated that the simplest explanation for a given phenomenon is almost certainly the best. Stated in a slightly more nuanced form: that explanation for a given occurrence is best which explains satisfactorily most of its aspects and features while, at the same time, requiring the fewest assumptions. Of Ockham's razor, Chet Raymo says that it is the skeptic's (and by *skeptic*, I take him by now to mean any rational, enlightened person) "guiding principle" (*Skeptics*, p. 72).

The razor, I think most everyone can agree, has been a valuable tool in delivering scientific truth by concentrating the human mind on the investigation of secondary causes and rejecting unverifiable primary causes such as a pantheon of gods and goddesses. Thus in the Disney film *Fantasia*—another cinematic treasure—a petulant Zeus, above the clouds, hurls lightning bolts at hapless individuals to the tune of Beethoven's Sixth Symphony. But lightning bolts are better explained *and* verified by the physics of cloud formation and electrical energy. In like manner, it is more sensible to attribute the details of initial sexual attraction to the biochemistry of hormones than to a chubby, winged imp shooting arrows. As noted above, science has been consistently winning these contests of explanation over recent centuries; thus has it disenchanted the world but, at the same time, vouchsafed for the human race accurate knowledge, not to mention cures for diseases and triumphs of technology.

An interesting aspect of Ockham's razor is that, after repeated successful applications, at some point it seamlessly morphs into the scientific principle known as the uniformity of nature (sometimes called uniformitarianism), to wit, the universe (or multiverse) is a closed system of matter and energy events in space/time that are uniform and hence uniformly knowable and predictable, in past, present, and future. It can be easily seen that the postulation of a God outside the system who can interrupt its uniform flow by random interventions is inimical to this scientific axiom. However, in regard to the scientists already cited and others, it is not clear to me that, when they talk of the impossibility of a theistic God, they are invoking uniformity or the razor. If it is uniformity, God has already been ruled out, *but by an assumption*; if it is the razor, He still has a fighting chance.

Why do I say that? Because there is one aspect of nature, to which, if scientists apply the razor fairly and honestly, the results are *not* as definitive as in the instances of lightning bolts and sexual attraction. I am speaking of the case of the human person, specifically human consciousness. The stakes are extremely high in this issue. Witness the proliferation of institutes, seminars, and international conferences on the mind/body relationship. One gets the sense from reading scientists' proceedings in this area of inquiry that, if they could crack this nut, if they could locate human consciousness without reservations on the crane, if they could at last explain the totality of human behavior and knowledge in terms of brain biochemistry (plus perhaps memes), then they would have achieved the biological equivalent of a theory of everything and won the last battle against belief in God.

How goes the war? If you are Chet Raymo, science is already victorious and alone in the field. Says he: matter/spirit dualism is bankrupt (*Skeptics*, p. 127); contemporary science says there is no soul (*Skeptics*, p. 135); the mind is the brain (*Skeptics*, p. 193); memory is electrochemical (*Skeptics*, p. 185). And there is much more from him in this vein. Professor Raymo, like his muscular atheist collaborators, understands human consciousness as an outcome of the drive to greater complexity inherent in the self-bootstrapping evolutionary crane. Human consciousness then is comparable to the previously noted wizard of Oz behind the curtain—that is, a furious concatenation of biochemical processing that produces an epiphenomenon known as *you* and *me*.

So, why are they still having mind/brain conferences? Why not call it brain/brain and be done with it, save for continued research in the area of brain mapping? Because, despite Professor Raymo's confident—one might say cocky—declarations, there are still issues and problems with regard to a crane-based theory of human consciousness. Consider the case of a woman who comes home from work to find her husband in the parlor with an ear-to-ear grin. "Honey," he says, "good news from the oncologist: the tumor in my brain is shrinking!" Back to what antecedent does the possessive adjective *my* refer? On Raymo's premises, there is no possessing entity of the brain: your brain *is* you, or the closest thing to it. But this example, and thousands like it, show that conceptually based language assumes that humankind can transcend its neurochemical brain processing as if it had a metaphysical place to stand separately from it. If the muscular atheists are right then, much of human life *as experienced* is utterly illusory. It is the same with the case of human knowledge. A thinker like Karl Marx might aver that a person's views on anything are a function of his economic class. Except of course the statement that this is true; for that, Marx has escaped the deterministic matrix in which humankind is enmeshed. All knowing implies this ability to transcend the flux of reality events and make statements about it. Put another way, the theory of memes, which purports to explain the entirety of human culture, cannot itself be a meme. This is not to claim that the brain and electrochemical processing are not necessary for human cognition. No one is forgetting that to be human is to have a body, including a brain. The question is, Is it sufficient? If cognitive scientists believe that it is, then human consciousness is in the end a chemical formula, the intelligibility of the universe is at risk, and the act of knowing reduced essentially to a dog chasing its tail.

The muscular atheists would of course laugh this off as the scattershot criticisms of a rank amateur. But I suspect that it would be a nervous laugh. The distinguished professor of psychology at Harvard, Jerome Kagan, notes that many scientists—he calls them reductionists—wish to replace psychological terms with language referring to molecules, receptors, and activated neural circuits but insists that the meaning networks for words that name psychological events are distinct from those that name brain activity. Even Daniel Dennett has admitted that brain structures cannot be isolated as a substrate for a particular meme (*Breaking*, p. 349), though one gets the impression that he earnestly wishes that they could. And in a rare moment of epistemological humility, Chet Raymo owns to the fact that consciousness has so far resisted scientific understanding and is the last recalcitrant mystery (*Skeptics*, p. 186).

The difficulty is that the theory of evolution, so successful in explaining the development of species, so spot-on in chronicling descent with modification, tells a story the primary characteristic of which is its markedly gradational velocity. It is the tortoise of the tortoise and the hare: slow, gradual changes over millions of years. I remember seeing a chart in my ninth-grade biology class showing life forms of different and increasingly complex biological classes in slowly rising steps until there were crouching apelike figures who got further and further from all fours, with an erect man standing at the end. Accurate? In some respects, yes; in others, completely misleading. Nothing is clearer than that human beings are close cousins of primates; body morphology and, now, genome analysis attest to that. Indeed, it is said that the genome of a chimpanzee and that of a human being are very nearly identical. What do chimps have? Rudimentary social groupings with alpha males and/or females; cooperative hunting; even the use of primitive tools. What do human beings have? The Toccata and Fugue in D Minor, the Sistine Chapel ceiling, and *Hamlet*. So much for comparisons in space. What about in regard to time? Suddenly, in the past, a primate begins to draw pictures of animals besides hunting them. I say *suddenly* because, whether this occurrence is numbered in the thousands, tens of thousands, or even hundreds of thousands of years ago (the Lascaux cave paintings are estimated at seventeen thousand years old), it is a drop in the bucket relative to the time line of evolution. There is simply no precedent for a development like this on the crane. Neither is there one for human language, despite the complexity that studies have shown to be constitutive of the signal systems of higher mammals. As Walker Percy has argued in the funniest book ever written, which is also deadly serious—*Lost in the Cosmos*—human language is a unique system of intersubjective meanings based upon a rule-governed syntax. Thus, higher animals have highly sophisticated signals for mating and fleeing danger; human beings write novels. The bottom line is that humankind can be considered as similar to other life forms in regard to evolutionary history but also as qualitatively different. Phrasing it alternatively, from one point of view, a chimp can claim a sort of extended family membership with the human race; from another, a chimp is closer to a paramecium than to a man.

Thus we return to Ockham's razor to evaluate two competing explanations for the origins of the human story: a) God endowed a candidate primate with consciousness, including an aesthetic sense, therefore he began to draw pictures on cave walls; or b) a primate gradually stood erect and developed opposable thumbs, therefore he began to draw pictures on cave walls. As noted above, if the principle of the uniformity of nature is brought to bear on this choice of explanations, one *has* to opt for b, at least as a starting point, even if it is wildly inaccurate and requires wholesale revision. But if it is the razor alone that is deployed, the choice is not as clear as to what is the simpler explanation. Option b wins the day, of course, if we are talking merely about simpler; the dilemma is that b, though simpler, is in no sense an explanation. It appears that, as far as resolving the riddle of human consciousness is concerned, the victory run of science using Ockham's razor is finally over, as is clear from the evasive language that scientists are forced to use whenever attending to the matter. For instance, when Chet Raymo, in discussing hominid ancestors of humankind, speaks of their "dawning self-awareness" (*Walking*, p. 122), to what exactly is he referring? In what did that "dawn" consist? And what precisely is the "self," since human beings, by his lights, have no soul? Such phrases as "dawning self-awareness," it is manifest, are contentless placeholders for the truth that scientists dare not avow, namely that scientific analysis has not even come close to an explanation of the phenomenon of man.

An individual who would like to take a stab at such an explanation is New York University professor Thomas Nagel in his book *Mind and Cosmos*, the brazen subtitle of which—"Why the Materialist Neo-Darwinian Conception of Nature Is Almost Certainly False"—is nothing less than a shot across the bow of the heretofore unsinkable muscular atheist battleship. The most important thing to know about Professor Nagel is that he is not a Bible thumper; indeed, he is averse to divine explanations of consciousness (p. 12), and it is not even clear that he believes in God at all. What *is* clear, as he says, is that psychophysical reductionism, of the kind practiced by Dawkins et al., flies in the face of common sense (p. 4, 5). Professor Nagel is not shy about his opinions; his unblushing assertions are precisely what is needed to restore balance to the debate between militant atheists and those who take exception to the more outrageous of their statements but fear the opprobrium of the scientific community if they respond. Herewith a sampling, in slight paraphrase, of the more pointed Nagelisms: People have been browbeaten into accepting psychophysical reductionism (p. 7; it is long past time when this needed to be said!); advocates of intelligent design do not deserve scorn since they are raising legitimate questions (p. 10); the belief in the intelligibility of the natural order, which science assumes, antedates the Scientific Revolution (p. 16, again, as noted previously by C. Dawson and D. B. Hart); the causation of consciousness by brain activity does not make it intelligible (p. 47); evolutionary self-understanding undermines moral realism (p. 28); a biological origin of language is unlikely (pp. 76–77); thought moves us beyond appearance to something we cannot regard merely as a biologically based disposition (p. 81).

But *Mind and Cosmos* is about more than laying down markers. Nagel presents and elaborates upon a thesis, namely that an understanding of the universe requires that *mind* be accounted a fundamental constituent of nature (p. 16) as much, one might say, as the elements in the periodic chart of the atom and not as a, perhaps accidental, derivative of them. The fleshing out of this hypothesis occupies the latter half of the book and will not be rehearsed here. I include his book only to underscore the point that it is possible to counter the arguments of the muscular atheists and on their own territory. With taking leave of Professor Nagel, I cannot resist, however, referencing his opinion that a theistic account of human consciousness, which he rejects, has the advantage over reductive naturalism in that it "admits the reality of more of what is so evidently the case" (p. 25).

The final point in Chet Raymo's assault on believers relates to the intersubjective, pan-millennial intuition that human beings are immortal and that there is something beyond the empirically perceived matter/energy matrix of reality. Says he, things will be so much better if we can surrender the dream of immortality (*Skeptics*, p. 246). Taking his presentation as a whole, including his attraction to such terms as "thumb sucking," "teddy bears," and "security blankets," to describe some religious believers, it is not too much to infer that, when he writes "dream," he is implying that those who hold to a belief in "something more" are children or childish and that it is through science that we "wake up" and "grow up." Very well, if Raymo believes that conventional believers are mental/spiritual children, let a child respond to him. In this case ... me.

My response takes the form of a story, the story of what I deem to be my second mystical experience (my first is related elsewhere). It occurred during the summer after my eighth birthday and began when I was playing with friends in my backyard on a Wednesday afternoon. My mother appeared at a screened window of our third-floor flat and said, "Paulie, come in now and get cleaned up for supper." Usually such a command would lead to a rather unpleasant conversation between us, if I were not disposed to comply, but in this case, she disappeared immediately from the window. Being too young to wear a watch, I looked up at the sun and tried to get a sense of the time. Some of the families of my playmates routinely had supper at 5:00 p.m., but for us, it was always at six. Thus, her summons couldn't be right; it was nowhere near suppertime or getting-ready time for supper. I did the only sensible thing: I figured she had made a mistake, and I ignored her. But, in less than ten minutes, she was at the window again: "Paulie, I told you to come in for supper. Get in here!" Then she added, almost as an afterthought, "Your father says we're going for a ride."

My father, who worked the 7:00–3:00 day shift at a local textile mill, often came in the house from work without my noticing, but my mother's reference to him changed my decision calculus a bit. I didn't want to risk his annoyance by dallying in the backyard, but what also stimulated my immediate compliance was the mention of a ride. In the years immediately after the Second World War, factory laborers were transitioning from renters to owners of starter homes. My parents came close to buying a house twice but couldn't quite make it; then my father's untimely death extinguished that dream. Next to a house, the pride and joy of low-income workers of that era was the family car, a huge investment for a wage earner; and a way of celebrating its existence, so to speak, was the ritual of the Sunday drive in the country. Today, when I tell young people about this, many of whom having become somewhat jaded by easy access to or even personal ownership of cars, they struggle to comprehend why I am making such a big thing of it. But a big thing it was. On these rides, my older sister and I would make a game of picking out houses that we would like to live in—in retrospect, an exercise that I think may have caused my parents some pain over their failure to secure one for themselves and us. And my father would sometimes speed up just a bit on the uneven surfaces of the country roads to give us a scaled-back experience of an amusement park ride. But that was all for a Sunday. This was a Wednesday. What was my father up to?

When we sat down for supper, it was *before* five (I had just learned how to read a clock in school), and we were out the door, with no dessert, and on the road before six. Our town, a bedroom community in the Providence metropolitan area, fairly quickly became rural as you traveled away from the city in those days; today, those country areas are densely improved with single-family residences. My sister and I recognized the route we were taking immediately and settled down to a quiet enjoyment. Then, it became joyously clear that my father was also heading for a familiar country ice-cream stand. Having arrived, and later as I devoured my cone, I couldn't help but think that Wednesdays couldn't get much better than this. But it was just the beginning.

As we neared home on the return journey, my father didn't make the left-hand turn onto our street but continued on for about an eighth of a mile and made a right onto an unfamiliar street with houses I had never seen before. It was then that it hit me. Who were the people who lived in these houses, and why didn't I know them? And what did the houses look like inside? What colors were the walls? What was the arrangement of the rooms? I wanted to go inside them right then! As fast as the feeling came, it dissipated when we came to the dead end of the street and a field of scrub grass opened before us. We all got out and advanced into the field. By now, my tonic exhilaration was at such a pitch that I simply ran around in circles, giddy with the delight of a far from normal Wednesday. My sister took me in hand, once I had calmed down, and together we set about the task of searching for any flowers among the wild growth. Once, I looked up at my father and saw that he was checking his watch but then went back to the business at hand. A few minutes after that, my parents started walking farther into the field and motioned for us to come to where they stood at the field's end—a relatively sheer drop to a railroad right-of-way, along which were industrial buildings and warehouses. I knew these railroad tracks well, if only from a distance; our house was a short way south of where we were standing but across the main street and up a hill, so that, from an easterly placed window of our third-floor tenement, I saw many times the switcher engines pulling long sets of box cars back and forth. Indeed, a year later when I received my set of electric trains at Christmas, a rite of passage for boys of that era, it had been a switcher engine that I requested.

We stood at the top of the field for several minutes, waiting ... for what? And then, looking left, I saw it: a diesel, cab-unit locomotive, the kind with a single headlight and the two automobile type windshields, coming from the direction of Providence. I had seen pictures of this type of train before, and my brother's train set was the American Flyer version of the Santa Fe cab unit, but I had never seen the real McCoy. The train was moving at a slow rate of speed, almost groping its way. This gave me time to ramp up my enthusiasm, furiously waving at the engineer (who waved back!) and then to the passengers in the gleaming silver coach cars and the dining car. I continued waving and shouting until the last of the train disappeared southerly, whereupon I collapsed on the ground from exhaustion. I found out later that my father had read in the newspaper that the main line for Boston to New York rail service was under repair in the Providence area and that passenger trains were to be rerouted for a few days onto this industrial spur (hence the slow rate of speed of the train along the unfamiliar track) and then rejoin the main line farther south in Rhode Island. My father turned a transportation inconvenience for some into a kind of holiday celebration for our family.

After the train disappeared, no one moved for a few minutes; it was as if each of us wanted to recapitulate in our minds the several joys of the last two hours and forestall the ending of the day. At last, my parents signaled that it was time to go. We walked oh so slowly back to the car, as the sun was by now into its post–eight o'clock glide path to the western horizon. Then, when we started driving down the street, it hit me again, harder. I wanted to go into the houses, the interiors of which were now illuminated, to see what they looked like and meet and know the people who lived there. It was as if God, who had given me a taste of fullness at the level that I as a child could understand—the ride, the ice cream, the train—now assaulted me with an emptiness without remedy that yearned to be full. These contending sentiments kept me awake a bit after I was put to bed but not for long. I was as spent as an eight-year-old could be and soon fell asleep. The next day would be as typical as this one was atypical. Life went ponderously on.

But I would be changed forever, and because of that, it is worth noting three things about my childhood epiphany. First, the joy of the train and the surrounding activities seemed somehow to be connected with the urgency I felt to know about the houses and the people who lived in them. It was as if fullness and emptiness, as I have described them, were not opposites but coordinating aspects of the same reality. Second, my affective response to the houses and the people in them was not so much perplexity and as much resignation as a child of that age could experience but a deep desire to know that carried with it the implication of fulfillment. And third, and most importantly, in my child's mind, this event and my feelings about it had absolutely nothing to do with religion. I was already going to Sunday school and learning about the Bible and Jesus, but if asked about it, I would not have been able to see how that had anything to do with this wonderment. It would take me years to make the connection.

In a previous book, I named this personal response to reality the "ache of particularity." I consider it a kind of poverty of spirit, to which Jesus, in the Beatitudes, promised as an antidote no less than the kingdom of heaven itself. The idea that human separateness in space and time—for all its existential and functional necessity to the workings of the world—is a kind of wound that needs healing has haunted me at intervals, but in a good way, for all my life. Just a couple of years ago, it assailed me again during a vacation trip Cathy and I took to the Finger Lakes region of Upstate New York. We had dinner reservations at an historic inn on old Route 20. Arriving in plenty of time, we saw that a company had pitched a tent on the grounds and was having some sort of reception catered by the inn. This posed no problem for our dinner inside, but it meant that there was absolutely *no* parking. I dropped Cathy off to secure our table and then went up and down a couple of nearby streets in a fruitless attempt to find a parking space. Finally, a police officer gave me directions down several connecting roads to a commercial area where there was available municipal parking.

By the time I arrived there, the directions back to the inn, though clear to me in the main, were a bit hazy in the details. I struck out walking in the direction of the inn and soon came to the top of a T-shaped intersection. I could go left or right. I had started not so confidently left when I saw a middle-aged couple sitting on the westward-facing front porch of their home, talking, sipping iced tea (or maybe something stronger), and watching the sun go down. I asked them for directions and was told that I had indeed chosen the wrong way. Thanking them kindly, I reversed course and walked on until their home had almost disappeared from view. Then, stopping to look back, I was jolted by that ache to which I have referred. Who were these people; who were their ancestors and their progeny; what music moved them; what name, if any, did they invoke when calling on God; what were the joys that made them laugh or the sorrows that had darkened their lives; about what had they been talking when I interrupted them? The answers to these questions, reason told me, I would never know, but reason, as far as I was concerned, would not have the last word. As I continued walking, my spirit took an imaginary trip across the continental United States, above which the sun was sweeping westward. I reflected that there would be other couples on porches talking together and watching the sun at day's end, people in places like Muncie, Indiana; Lincoln, Nebraska; Laramie, Wyoming; and Sacramento, California—people I would never know or even see. I grieved. By the time I reached the entrance to the inn, I was about as poor in spirit—my own version of this poverty, that is—as it was possible to be, and yet this very emptiness, in the words of Jesus Himself, carried within it the promise of a healing and a fullness to come. Then, before consulting the hostess, I peered into the dining room, and, seeing Cathy waiting for me there with a smile, the longed for yet-to-be was swallowed up by the luminously joyful now.

And now it is time to pose the salient question: what would my muscular atheist friends make of these stories? To interpret my childhood concern about the unknown houses and people, they might summon a pediatric psychologist, who would evaluate my psychosocial development at age eight. It is possible to imagine such a person saying that perhaps I had not reached the level at which children understand that there are families one is not related to who live in separate dwellings and whose acquaintance one is likely never to make. The psychologist could then make a determination as to whether a boy of eight who resisted this reality indicated a slower than normal maturation process. As to such feelings continuing into adulthood, the judgment of an atheist would likely not be as generous. The best I could hope for would be for some sympathetic cultural anthropologist to theorize that I was unaccountably weighted with a kind of herd instinct emotional baggage that, while common and critically useful to my remote hominid ancestors, was rare and decidedly abnormal for a person living in the twenty-first century. My atheist conversation partners, if I had any, would probably be as one in recommending to me a visit to a mental health professional.

It will not surprise anyone to discover that I believe they are wrong. By my lights, what is at work here are tendrils: fragile filaments sent out from the Center of Being that touch us all ever so lightly to remind us that our current quotidian existence is definitely not the whole of human life, tendrils personally crafted for each of our journeys but also sometimes shared with others. In regard to the latter, I read in Ian Ker's massive biography of the aforementioned G. K. Chesterton that Chesterton as a boy wanted to be an artist, though he eventually became a journalist and author. When he looked at landscape paintings in art books, the thing he wanted to know above all was whither the country lanes in the pictures led. When I read this, I almost dropped the heavy volume. I had had a strikingly similar feeling when, viewing *The Wizard of Oz* for the first time, I saw Dorothy and the scarecrow choose a direction at an intersection of the yellow brick road. To where did the other directions lead, I wanted to know—more with my heart than with my mind. I experienced it then and ever after as a yearning, an anticipatory joy, similar to the joy of "The Road Goes Ever On" from Tolkien's *The Fellowship of the Ring*, the joy of pilgrimage, the joy of the quest. A quest in search of what? Save for the most militant of the atheists, the question answers itself.

Yes, it is tendrils such as these that are the poetry of life, what life, in the end, is all about—"billions and billions" of them, to borrow the well-known signature phrase of the late astronomer Carl Sagan, who, I have absolutely no doubt, would highly resent its usage in the current context. And it is tendrils, much more than skyhooks, that are the lifeblood of religion and why it is that religions endure nearly half a millennium after the Scientific Revolution, much to the amazement and annoyance of the Dawkins and Dennetts of this world. That is why I believe that the Dawkensian dichotomy crane/skyhook is so useful; that is, it gives one something of an entree into the muscular atheist mind. In reading the literature of the militant atheist community, it becomes clear that they regard religion, and believe that religion regards itself, primarily as an *explanation* for why things are the way they are, one that is competing with that of science—skyhook versus crane—and one that is entirely fallacious. The idea that religion is much more a medium for experiencing the depth of life or a modality for opening oneself to the delicate witness of tendrils seems to be beyond their ken or never to have occurred to them. The exception is Chet Raymo. This essay has been quite critical of his writing, and I firmly believe that his theory of the real—his ontology, if you will—cannot in the end support what might be termed his *natural spirituality*. In a sense, he wants to be mystical about the impossibility of mysticism. But at least he is alive to the mystery of life and the universe; and while much of his literary effort is in support of the muscular atheist project, other portions of it can be deemed to be a rebuke to it.

So, what in the end is to be done about the current and regrettable deterioration in relations between science and religion? From the domain of science, I believe that we already have something like an answer in the life and career of the abovementioned Stephen J. Gould. In his absolute integrity as a scientist; his detailed, nuanced, and evenhanded studies of the history of science; and the respectful and gentlemanly manner in which he engaged his adversaries in the controversies of recent years, we have, I would argue, a template for the conduct of all future intellectual commerce between science and religion. It makes his untimely passing all the more to be lamented.

A few years ago (2008), there was another hopeful sign, this time from the side of religion: the book *No One Sees God* by Catholic philosopher Michael Novak. Felicitously subtitled "The Dark Night of Atheists and Believers," the book reads like an invitation from the house of religion tendered across the street to the residents of the house of science to come over for dinner and perhaps some wine and good talk. While taking respectful exception to some of the points made by the militant atheists (pp. 30–80), Novak also finds some things to admire about them (p. 58). But, more importantly, by the use of such terms as *The Common Darkness* and his appeal to both atheists and believers to recognize their shared humanity (p. 275), Novak's constant effort is to emphasize how all of us are in this journey together. It is possible that, from this book and the efforts of likeminded persons, we may ultimately achieve what Novak looks to: an atmosphere in which atheists and believers can debate ultimate matters calmly, reasonably, and, above all, with mutual respect (p. 151).

In the meantime, all of us can do our part to advance the cause of amicable relations. We who live in the house of religion should make every effort to dissuade those of our brothers and sisters in faith who are so inclined from disparaging science or failing to acquiesce to what science has shown incontrovertibly to be true. And it might be helpful if some critically situated resident in the house of science would admonish the more militant atheists of that household to the effect that carrying on in the tone and manner to which they have become accustomed is as regrettable in its way as was the trial of Galileo.

CHAPTER 6

MAY

Eschewing the Asphalt Sea

I rejoiced because they said to me, "Let us
go up to the house of the Lord."
—Psalm 122 (NAB)

It is finally the season of superabundant light. Now that the sun is approaching the solstice, our house, with its white-walled interior, is flooded with brightness and will continue to be until the lengthening shadows of mid to late August signal a change. At 6:45 p.m. on May 11, I saw sunlight cast upon the northeast stairway, where it is also hit by the sun in winter through the west-wall octagonal window. But that was the reduced path of the solar journey; in May, its more expansive arc of travel means that the setting sun shines through the window section of the northward-facing front door. I will watch the sun inch across the stairs in the late afternoon until it reaches an omega point in mid-June.

At this time of year, the sun puts in rare appearances in other outlying, mostly northerly areas of the house. At 5:43 p.m. on May 20, I was checking a book in the reading area upstairs when I noted the sun shining through the north window onto the eastern staircase wall and creating perfect shadows of the banisters. On May 31 at 6:45 a.m., the rising sun shining through the northeast skylight, and close to its farthest north, illumined the rocking chair in the TV room.

In May, another convenient phenomenon begins, as I can take lunch in the breakfast unnook at the noon hour, when I am home, since, due to the roof of the box bow window, the unnook enjoys habitable shade at this time, where just an hour or two earlier it was fully illuminated. This of course continues past next month into July on the correlative side of the solstice; but, happily for me, it also extends into late October or early November due to a large maple tree behind the garage in the southwest corner of the yard. When the noonday sun dips below the lip of the box bow window roof—and if I am willing to wait until a little closer to 1:00 p.m.—the tree's leaf complement prevents light from getting through, as it does not in the corresponding late-winter and early-spring weeks when there are no or new leaves. However, the August to November passage is not a complete success. As I note in my log for previous years, on several dates during this period, I was not able to eat lunch comfortably due to gaps in the tree's leaf assemblage. Still, some is better than none, and I will take the days that nature gives me.

In the Northern Hemisphere, March and April see the gradual acceleration of the entire range of earthly activities proper to plants and animals, but in May they reach cruising speed. There is now virtually no fear of snowstorms—April cannot make such a guarantee—or other adverse weather events, at least in this part of the country; in the plain states and elsewhere, it is the beginning of tornado season.

Cathy and I walk year-round, weather permitting, but in May we become more serious pedestrians. Indeed, we have walked (and hiked) thousands of miles together, sometimes, during our younger years, far into the night in the various places in which we have lived. But that is an aggregate of years; for discrete, individual walks, we cannot compete with our ancestors and others who lived before the age of mechanized transport. In his book *The Birth of the Modern*, essentially a history of the world from 1815 to 1830, Paul Johnson tells of a meeting between Thomas de Quincy and Samuel Taylor Coleridge, after which de Quincy walked the distance home of forty miles, apparently thinking nothing of it. Coleridge himself had taken a walking tour of Scotland, accompanied part of the way by Wordsworth, which totaled three hundred miles! When I read these vignettes, I am somewhat saddened that the intimacy with surroundings, engendered by walks of such magnitudes and taken for granted by our forebears, is now largely lost due to the utter domination of motorized conveyance in our time.

A walk that Cathy and I take that becomes more habitual in May is the Sunday stroll to church. I like to think of this walk as the actual beginning of mass and try to hear in my mind the Songs of Ascents recorded in the Psalms, as the grateful pilgrims went *up* to the house of the Lord. The fact that the street from our house to the church is an upgrade aids my imagination in this regard. Our parish church, Our Lady of Mount Carmel, is wonderfully situated in the village portion of Bristol, where we live, and brings me to the principal bête noire of this essay: church parking lots.

The Catholic diocese of Providence, which is coterminus with the state of Rhode Island, includes more than 150 parishes, many of them in suburban locales. During a large portion of my working life, I was employed by the state Department of Transportation, where one of my duties was the inspection of properties (i.e., real estate) that were due to be acquired under eminent domain for highway construction purposes. As a consequence, I viewed many of these parish churches by the by as I traveled around the state in performance of my official function. I used to keep a mental register of the worst ones. Worst? I mean in regard to the church building / parking lot relationship. In some of them, the church building looked like an island surrounded by a sea of asphalt—a parking lot that, if viewed with a jaundiced eye, appeared to approach the dimensions of that of a cinema multiplex.

I realize that on a practical level, there is no help for this; suburban communities are and were planned around the automobile. But that does not atone for the damage done, in my estimation. The pre-experience of the celebration of a sacred rite— unlike the walk to church that is available to Cathy and me—is the arrival at the auto corral with the cacophonous grinding of internal combustion engines turning off in sequence and the staggered bangs of metal against metal as worshipers-to-be close the doors of their cars. And the look! The look is that of strip mall parking and, in my opinion, not in any way invitatory to the approach of the Wholly Other. In the end, the experience of the parking lot does not conduce to a mindset amenable to sacred space but rather to an activity that is another stop in a series of errands—much like picking up a few items at the supermarket, routinely on the to-do list of many churchgoers when the service is concluded.

Fortunately, Our Lady of Mount Carmel provides some surcease from this dreary tableau. The key is the village setting with its nonsuburban and nonplanned characteristics. The church is separated from the parish school by a narrow swath of real estate improved with a small wood-frame building housing the headquarters of the Bristol Train of Artillery. A Rhode Island militia dating from the colonial period, past members fought at such key Civil War battles as Antietam and Gettysburg, while its current membership serves as color guards in patriotic celebrations and parades. I have not researched the particulars, but apparently those who purchased the lots for the church building and school were unable to obtain the militia's headquarters and essentially built around it. From the functional perspective of real estate theory, this is a small disaster: the lots owned by the church are diminished in value, as they would not be if they were in physical assemblage. But that is precisely the point: functional considerations should not have the last word in matters of the spirit, as I fear they do in the case of suburban churches. The presence of this small armory in the midst of the parish buildings is a charming addition to the experience of churchgoing, prompting thoughts of American history to be added to the spiritual enrichment of a worship service.

Of course, not all members of the parish can walk to church; most arrive by auto. Still, it does not cloy. The church parking lot is hidden from view behind the school building, and there is street parking. So, what captures one's attention on exiting from mass is not the few curbside parked cars but the town square with historic vintage buildings—this instead of the suburban church's rank and file of automobiles as far as the eye can see. And then there is the walk home, where Cathy and I can extend and complete the worship experience by discussing the hymns, the readings, or the homily.

It is surely apparent to anyone reading thus far that I am something of a spiritual Luddite—Luddite referring to antimachine sentiments that began in early nineteenth-century England, when the successors of the legendary Ned Ludd, weavers and textile workers, campaigned against machines that they feared would threaten their livelihoods. As a sympathizer of Luddism, of course, I am a complete hypocrite. Living in an era four hundred years after the Scientific Revolution and more than 250 years after the Industrial Revolution, I am utterly dependent on machines and would be lost without them. Still, there is more than a little to be said in favor of neo-Luddism, which takes exception to machines and technology, not so much on the issue of full employment but on the grounds that their pervasiveness is in some way inimical to culture and the human soul.

As a pioneer in this second type of Luddism, I would have to nominate Henry David Thoreau, whose *Walden* is a manifesto of sorts of those who underscore the need to escape the din of machines in order to preserve their humanity. In the same work, he reflected that his contemporaries were in a great hurry to construct a "magnetic telegraph" linking Maine to Texas but wondered whether they would have anything of value to say. In my view, this is the most trenchant criticism that can be contained in one sentence of the perils implicit in the addiction of moderns to machines / technology / mass media. Stated alternatively, machines cannot provide us with reasons, values, and ends, and without these, humankind perishes.

Many have followed the trail blazed by Thoreau, a representative sampling of which can be found in the informative book by Nichols Fox, *Against the Machine: The Hidden Luddite Tradition in Literature, Art, and Individual Lives.* Fox details the efforts of those who have tried to preserve nonmechanized crafts, who have celebrated in verse the wilderness or called for its protection, and others who have deplored the wasteland of modernity. The book is filled with such names as Wendell Berry, John Muir, William Morris, John Keats, T. S. Eliot, and other luminaries. But, perhaps as important, Fox includes the stories of less well-known individuals who have followed the neo-Luddite path, such as that of the married couple who lived for years on an island off the coast of Maine with little or no contact with civilization.

An interesting recent development is the arrival of a kind of neo-Luddite mentality within the precincts of political conservatism. For many decades, a large part of the conservative effort has been focused on the championing of free enterprise, as writings from Adam Smith to Milton Friedman demonstrate. This has given rise to the notion that conservatives are always on the side of any commercial development and are for business, especially big business. Along comes political commentator Rod Dreher with his *Crunchy Cons*, a book that must have the longest subtitle in publishing history (see bibliography). In his book, Dreher delineates a kind of cultural conservatism that includes some interesting examples under the category of "strange bedfellows," such as persons who lean toward traditional moral values *and* are keen to protect the environment. He and likeminded persons believe that true conservatism will value culture over economics and that they (we) must, to the extent possible, shun mass commercialism and the mass media, retreating, like Saint Benedict in the sixth century, to an environment where they (we) may cultivate a life that values the small, the local, the simple, the pious, and the individually crafted.

I first recognized that I had some of these neo-Luddite proclivities when I was a young adult, but it was in regard to a character that I thought I had left behind in childhood: Santa Claus. I realized that I was put out whenever I saw on the news that Santa had arrived at a suburban shopping center by helicopter. The nexus of this guardian angel of the Christmas season with a conveyance powered by fossil fuels seemed discomforting. That is because Santa is a figure from out of time; full of mystery, he is not to be delimited by modern contrivances, and, above all, not to be used sacrilegiously to sell products. If we were polytheists, he would be a god.

I am convinced that children, especially little children, understand the truth about Santa Claus better than adults— another reason Jesus offered the lives and experience of children for our consideration and betterment. My conviction comes from watching them approach Santa Claus actors in malls and department stores. I, of course, understand that malls and stores are every bit as modern a contrivance as a helicopter. But, unlike the case of the helicopter, this is overcome because store/mall management designates an area in which Santa reigns, sometimes going as far as to demark it with a picket fence. Thus, amid all the neon modernity of stores selling wares for Christmas in time, we have a small, mythic space in which a figure from eternity holds sway. As for the children, yes, they are coached by their parents; yes, some are a bit afraid; yes, they know that Santa brings presents; and yes, some of them—the older ones—are greedy for gifts to the point of cynicism, an attitude that is played for laughs in the movie *A Christmas Story*. Still, there are enough who are wide-eyed and receptive to one who is a complete stranger to them and a bit fearful looking too. Why? Because of the beneficence he radiates, regardless of how poorly the individual who plays him acts the part. That, in turn, is due to the fact that Santa Claus is a sacramental—a conduit of God's grace—and children, until they have been corrupted, are drawn to God like iron filings to a magnet.

In his insightful short book *Miracles*, C. S. Lewis makes an interesting observation about the traditional dichotomy between spirit and matter. Typically, persons who believe in spiritual reality tend to think of it as less substantial than the material world: metaphorically, a pale apparition, the wind, or a whisper versus a rock or a tree. But, for Lewis, this is all wrong. Says he, to get our bearings right, we must, if anything, picture spirit as *heavier* than matter. Thus, in the story of the resurrected Christ appearing to His disciples in the upper room, it is *not* the case that He passed through walls like a vapor but that the walls themselves are like a vapor giving way to the hard, dense, blinding actuality of His spiritual body. This is the mentality that I believe a healthy neo-Luddism brings to the Santa Claus of the mall: the activities associated with the mall—the frenetic hithering and thithering between stores, the spending and the getting—are all, in the end, an illusion, the part of the human experience that is crumbling to dust. The mythic space in which Santa Claus receives petitioners is eternal and therefore more real. It is because of this perspective, my experience of watching children interact with St. Nick, and my prior assent to the dogma of the communion of saints, that I can say even in the latter years of my life that, yes, I believe in Santa Claus.

Neo-Luddism and its variants can be found partially hidden almost everywhere in contemporary culture. Another interesting example is what I have come to call the *Star Wars* anomaly. In my view, the Jedi order contained within the *Star Wars* world picture amounts to an inconsistent internal mythology. Here we have a group of individuals dressed like monks—Obi-Wan Kenobi could easily be mistaken for a Franciscan friar—armed with updated swords battling against adversaries in reinforced space suits sporting laser weaponry. And in many cases, the Jedi prevail! But this is akin to a horse cavalry charge against tanks. Why, I have asked myself, couldn't the good guys have weapons and armor similar to those of the evil Empire, just as in shootouts in westerns the heroes and the villains have the same type of guns?

There may be any number of answers to this question, but I have my own theory. It begins with the comments of the aforementioned historian Paul Johnson in another of his books: *Modern Times: The World from the Twenties to the Eighties* (the 1920s to the 1980s, that is; in a revised and updated version, Johnson added the decade of the '90s). Johnson narrates the cultural outflow in the 1920s from the earlier publication of Einstein's theory of relativity, namely the gradual adoption of the idea of relativity of morals, especially in regard to sexual mores. Of course, cultural relativism had been incubating for years previously in Europe and elsewhere, but Einstein's theory seemed to put an end to the discussion with an exclamation point. Everything's relative!

Now there is absolutely no necessary connection between discoveries relating to the physics of the curvature of space, moving bodies at high speeds, and discrepancies in time passage and the acceptability/nonacceptability of an adulterous affair. It didn't matter; cultural elites ran with Einstein's theory into every corner of human affairs, much to his chagrin—another case, as in the Copernican ideology alluded to above, of drawing unwarranted metaphysical (or moral) conclusions from scientific premises. Thus, the connection was irrevocably made, meaning that hereafter when we think of technology, lasers, spacecraft, and the like, we think modernity, and modernity includes relativism in all its pedestrian formulations: "What's true for you is not necessarily true for me"; "I don't believe in victimless crimes"; "Moral codes are culturally conditioned." Every college sophomore knows the drill.

And that was the problem for George Lucas. Lucas, it appears, wanted a story where an absolute goodness, warring with an insidious evil, was unambiguously identifiable. (Has there ever been a clearer cinematic rendering of this than the face-off between Obi-Wan Kenobi and Darth Vader in the first *Star Wars* movie?) But for that, you need knights and swords. Why? Because they were current in an era when men and woman believed that goodness and honor, to which they were morally bound, suffused the universe and originated in a primal reality called *God*. (For the sake of this argument, it matters not that Lucas cannot bring himself to use the word and instead prefers *Force*.) Without such a concept, the screenplay for *Star Wars* might just as well have been written by Woody Allen or Jean-Paul Sartre, where Luke, Han, and Leia, depressed by the Empire's ascendancy, would conduct interminable and angst-ridden conversations in their spacecraft about the ultimate absurdity of existence. *Star Wars?* Call it instead *No Exit from the Millennium Falcon.* On the other hand, the continuing popularity of the *Star Wars* saga, with good guys and evildoers identified with crystal clarity, shows that moderns, perhaps including George Lucas, still have an appetite for neo-Luddite, that is, traditional ideas of moral goodness.

Speaking once again of my own uncomfortableness with modernity, my churchgoing is beset by another spiritual Luddism, this time in regard to the interior of the building. I am speaking of lights. I must start again with a disclaimer: I understand that hard-pressed pastors and other church officials cannot be overly concerned about such matters. When religious denominations and dioceses embark on the design and erection of churches, those in charge are motivated to install the most efficient lighting, available at a reasonable cost, that can aid worship, sometimes opting for the dreaded ceiling insert lights—what I call warehouse lighting. After all, the congregation needs to be able to read the lines in the Bibles, missals, and hymn books. Nevertheless, their choices in this area often diminish the efficacy of candles, which are still in use. In this regard, a question can be asked: With the boon of electrification, why do we still use candles in churches in the twenty-first century? After all, they are as anachronistic as swords would be in futuristic warfare.

A partial and simplistic answer is that they are used in church services because the rubrics still require them. But, in my view, there is much more to this issue. My first stop in this journey of discovery was at the Basilica of Santa Maria Gloriosa in Venice. On leave during military service, I had come to the church to view Titian's oft-copied masterpiece, *The Assumption of the Virgin*, situated prominently above the high altar. It *was* awe striking, but after a short time of gazing at the painting, I became distracted by the interior of the church itself. Except for the flickering sanctuary lamp, it was dark—something new to me, because, not yet a Catholic, I was more used to the brightness of meetinghouse architecture. When I look at photos of the interior of this Venetian church today, it doesn't look so dark, but it seemed so then. What is more, I liked it.

What is it about the semidarkness, illumined by paltry lighting, that attracts us? Why are special dinners often of the candlelit variety? And why do some ecclesial entities still insist on candles as an essential ingredient in the approach to the sacred? There could be many answers to this question, I suppose, but I have my own. Candles and low lighting underscore one half of the human condition. The other half is the triumphant march of human progress: men on the moon, cancer in partial surrender to medical science, sanitation, agricultural productivity, longevity. The candlelit part, if you will, speaks, on the other hand, of the fragility of the human community: we are "dust motes" (as Chet Raymo would have it); we are "wayfarers," a term favored by Walker Percy; and, borrowing from Emma Lazarus, we all belong to the category "huddled masses," in exile, far out in a spiral arm of the Milky Way galaxy.

Besides low-lit churches, nothing brings home to me this hybrid nature of humankind more than looking out the window of an aircraft during a night flight. On one side, we have the engineering marvel of the airplane itself and the skills of the pilot, navigator, and air traffic controller—all attesting to the godlike nature of the human person. On the other, out the window we see Mother Earth wanly illumined by the lights of civilization, set against the greater darkness of the planet—itself in a dark, cold, and nearly empty space, populated by the mostly unreachable other worlds of the solar system and by stars at decidedly unreachable and unimaginable distances.

My faith tells me that this semidarkness of which I speak, and for which candlelight is the most eloquent reminder, is that of a cave. Here human beings are not chained, as in the cave of Plato's *Republic*; nevertheless, they are huddled, forlorn, lonely, yet somehow hopeful. Their hope rests with a man and a woman—a husband and his wife about to give birth. The One born in that cave brings a message to the human community looking on: it is that Someone has taken note of them, though they live in a remote corner of the universe, and that dust to dust is not the end of their story.

CHAPTER 7

JUNE

The Meldung Paradox

> All healthy men, ancient and modern, Eastern and
> Western, know that there is a certain fury in sex that we
> cannot afford to inflame and a certain mystery and awe
> must forever surround it if we are to remain sane.
> —G. K. Chesterton

The sun is now at the culmination of its annual journey for Northern Hemispheric residents of planet Earth, and our house is glorying in the solar reflectivity of its walls, floors, and furniture. At 6:20 a.m. EDT on June 4, the sunlight, at its rising, neared its farthest south in the upstairs TV room, casting light through the northeast skylight well past its northern doorpost and illuminating the hardwood floor south of the rocking chair. At 5:45 p.m. on June 8, I noted that the sun, declining in the northwest and shining through the TV room skylight, lit up the south wall of the staircase, where it will remain for a brief period at this time of day.

In June, Cathy and I have our annual solstice breakfasts at the usual Saturday time frame. We can now sit in the unnook munching our bagels, since the sun by this time has reached the box bow window roof, which, as the sun proceeds westward, blocks nearly all its otherwise unbearable rays. However, the person sitting at the west end of the table facing east (usually me) cannot avoid a slight amount of sunlight on the right forearm, totally manageable. As noted, the season of unnook breakfasts lasts, by my reckoning, from Memorial Day to Independence Day, although at the extremes of this range, such breakfasting is a bit more uncomfortable for the westerly sitting party. But, on the Saturdays immediately surrounding June 20, the sun, being at or near its highest angular distance from the southern horizon, makes sharing a meal here a nearly unalloyed pleasure. Cathy and I never fail to take advantage of this short season.

A different sort of event, at the other end of the house, occurs at this time of year and is made possible by the fact that (a) Cathy has placed some plants on an attractive stand that fits into the corner of the first landing of the staircase to the second floor, and (b) in summer, the late-morning sun transits the skylight near the top of the stairs on the eastern wall of the house. Call me crazy, but what follows I can only compare to a scene from *The Raiders of the Lost Ark*. It will be remembered that, in that movie, Indiana Jones has secured the headpiece to the Staff of Ra, which, when attached to the staff and placed in the subterranean chamber where there is a scale model of the city of Tanis, will reveal the location of the ark of the covenant—but only when the sun is at the appropriate angle to shine through the headpiece. As Indiana and his companion breathlessly await the rotation of the Earth to bring the sun into position, the drama is intensified for moviegoers by John Williams's haunting score. It is that music I hear in my mind as on many a summer morning at home, I stand at the top of the staircase and watch a parallelogram of light on the landing floor or low on the north wall inch ever northeastward until, at the appointed time, it graces me with what I have been longing to see—the burning bush of the northeast staircase.

On this particular Saturday morning, Cathy and I were readying to leave the house when we unaccountably heard the sound of drums and trumpets. I hurried to the north window of the upstairs den and saw a police vehicle slowly advancing down our quiet street, behind which were marchers in colorful garb. Going outside, I asked a couple of bystanders what was up and was told that a neighbor of mine about six houses down had been chosen as the grand marshal of the parade celebrating the annual Portuguese feast of Santo Cristo, sponsored by St. Elizabeth's parish. This was not *that* parade, which would pass along the main street of town later, but the lesser and necessary parade ceremoniously to retrieve the grand marshal. Within twenty minutes, the street was clear. Thus, the unanticipated joys of small-town life.

I had been concerned that we would not be able to exit our property since we were going to the home of my cousin Jan and her husband, Norm, for a day of card playing. Norm is a retired career naval NCO, an aerographer's mate (i.e., weather forecaster), and had served on aircraft carriers and duty stations as widely scattered as Morocco and Alaska. With their growing family, Jan was often able to be with him in the far-flung bases to which he was assigned. She once told me that on a transport ship from Seattle to Kodiak Island, where she and Norm were to be based, they played cards nonstop with other navy personnel. Of course, Norm also had plenty of time for cards on his monthslong cruises.

As a matter of fact, though it is far less so today, card playing used to be a kind of social glue in my family, especially on the French Canadian side. At gatherings, the men would play whist while the women talked and swapped recipes. (In some families, women played as well; ours, however, practiced strict segregation of the sexes.) I remember sitting at my father's elbow, absolutely fascinated by the elements of the game and pining for the chance to be initiated as a partner in the remote future. When the day finally came in my midteens, I soon discovered that being a playing partner was a mixed blessing: I was elated at my new status but intimidated by my dad and uncles, who had absolutely no patience with the inevitable mistakes of card-playing rookies.

As noted, whist was the game of choice of my elders, one of a large number of such games from high-low-jack to bridge, whose rules specify the naming one of the four suits of a standard fifty-two-card deck as trumps—that is, any card of the trump suit beats even the highest card of the three other suits. The games are also similar in that the play phase is preceded by what might be called the contract phase, in which players attempt to outbid each other for the right to name trumps and thereby obligate themselves to take a certain number of tricks. Their opponents do their best to prevent such an outcome.

At Jan and Norm's, we would not be playing whist but their favorite game, pinochle—a word that appears to be of French origin, although the game was most popular among German immigrants to America. It, too, includes the naming of trumps, but in several respects is different from the other trump-like games. For starters, the deck consists of eighty cards, rather than fifty-two, and it features mostly face cards (four sets of ace to ten of each suit; in many versions of pinochle, nines are added). I remember being absolutely dazzled the first time I fanned out a pinochle hand: all those face cards, cards that are at a premium in most other games and therefore highly prized. I quickly learned that face cards can be worse than useless in different game circumstances and strategies and was, in short order, completely jaded.

Another pinochle distinction is that it adds to the contract and the play a third operation, which might be termed the meld phase. After the contract agreement and the naming of trumps, participants lay down those cards that are point bearing—their melds—the points being recorded, and, after the play phase, credited to their score if they take a sufficient number of tricks.

Melds include runs (ace to ten of the trump suit); pinochles (jack of diamonds / queen of spades combinations); and marriages (kings and queens of the same suit). Almost from the very beginning, I was intrigued by the fact that one of the point-bearing combinations was a *marriage*, even more by the fact that this and other combinations were called melds. My fascination took me on a short but, as it turned out, surprising etymological journey.

As a pinochle player, I had always assumed that *meld*, as noted, referred to a kind of joining together or bonding and, in card playing, stipulated cards that somehow go together to make a score—for example, a sufficient number of cards of the same suit (as in a flush in poker), a sufficient number of cards in a numerical series (as in a straight in poker), and pairs. It appears that that is one of the meanings. More than one source I consulted, including the *Oxford English Dictionary*, suggested that the word *meld* was of fairly recent American origin and might have been a conflation of "melt" and "weld." As a further support to this conjecture, another source speculated as to whether the origin of the term could be found in the Middle English *mellen* and Old French *melder* meaning "to mingle, blend."

The preponderance of the evidence points elsewhere, however, when it comes to referring to the word *meld* in the game of pinochle. The origin here is the German words *melden*, to announce, and *meldung*, an announcement. When a pinochle player asks another, "Do you have any meld?" he or she is not only asking what points the player has as a result of cards that go together but what points they have to announce. And the players do so by laying the cards down. Thus, after playing pinochle for a number of years, I was struck by three ideas that are embedded and associated in the game: 1) meld, as in blending together, 2) meld, as in announcement, and ... 3) marriage.

I believe no one would disagree with the proposition that in our time, the institution of marriage is in trouble, undermined in part by new and emerging mores of sexual intimacy. For many years, I kept a file of articles on the changing sexual and marital scene clipped from newspapers and journals. Considering all that has happened in the last half century, they make for interesting reading:

> A report (2006) relating that married couples have slipped into the minority in the United States.

> A review of a movie about the coupling habits of twentysomethings, who, unlike in the past, have no pattern to follow in finding a mate and who discover that, while sex is easier than ever to get, romance is hard to find.

> A newspaper article that counsels parents of teenage children to allow the latter to have romantic sleepovers with their boyfriends/girlfriends.

> An article detailing fashion choices for weddings of expectant brides-to-be.

> A report of a trend that allows wedding vendors to advertise in various ways during the nuptial ceremonies.

> A digest of research indicating that the negatives of marriage outweigh the positives, including statistics demonstrating that middle-age divorce is on the rise.

A report of a new college policy at a local campus: sex with your significant other in the dorm room is fine but not if your roommate is present. That is regarded as inconsiderate.

Several articles in which assorted anthropologists, psychologists, and cognitive scientists attest to the fact that monogamy is unnatural for human beings and that, rather, we are programmed for fornication and/or adultery.

In addition, in the raft of articles I had assembled, I noted a peculiar pairing of opposites in regard to weddings and marriage—opposites because the persons involved were as far apart as the north and south pole in their approaches to the mating process; pairings because, in my estimation, their behaviors originated from a similar sentiment. On the one hand, there was a report of the trend in wedding ceremonies that are thoroughly decoupled from the received rituals of our common civilization and completely personalized. In one case, the bride and groom were, among other things, showcasing their two dogs in the wedding procession. On the other hand, there is the growing practice of cohabitation without benefit of wedding or marriage—not to be compared to such behavior in the past, which was regarded with disdain because of the alleged caliber of people who practiced it, but to a contemporary version that is justified by reasoned argument and the principles of the new morality. In my file is a long, thoughtful article from a regional newspaper detailing the lives of contemporary cohabiters, all professional persons with six-figure incomes and high-powered careers. In the interviews, the couples expressed a perplexity and annoyance with those who urge them to formalize their relationship by what they regard as an outworn, oppressive institution forced on the human race by religion. The article included helpful resources, including websites and the locations of support groups. But one detail spoke the loudest to me: the research finding of a sociology professor who concluded that many young people prefer to cohabit rather than marry because they are unwilling to make a lifelong commitment to anyone. Thus my insistence upon the pairings cited above. Both the wedding personalizers and the cohabiters are afflicted with a common disease that is epidemic in today's advanced societies: narcissistic self-absorption. There appears to be no known cure.

In my estimation, of the two practices described above, cohabiting without benefit of marriage poses the greater danger to civilization because the coming together sexually of human partners has traditionally been seen as linked to the transcendent realities of the universe. What cohabiting proposes is the deritualization of a major life passage, a deliberate withdrawal from participation in the mystery implicit in human living, and, without admitting it, a choice to descend to and join higher animals in their coupling behaviors.

When a lioness comes into heat on the plains of Africa, she and her mate say nothing and may copulate over several days in full view of the pride and any other creature who might look on. With human beings, it has been until recently the complete inverse of this behavior: the persons involved provide the world with a *meldung*, an announcement, that they are going to join together in an exclusive, intimate, lifetime relationship. Traditionally, these announcements have been lavish and redundant, including banns (in some societies), wedding invitations, registries, name changes, dress, public ceremonies, appropriate music, and flowers. But all this is built upon a paradox: the multiform declarations/ announcements refer to a relationship, the consummation and inner dynamism of which is shared in exclusivity, hidden from the world. This is the paradox—announcing/intimacy; this is marriage; this is the irreplaceable arena for human flourishing that is quickly being abandoned by humankind.

Why? The answer is the sexual revolution of the last half century or so, accompanied and rendered irreversible, it seems, by its soundtrack (more about which below). Of course, there has been sexual adventurism in every age, but as noted above with respect to the practice of cohabitation, the sexual revolution also adds something new: a set of ideas that seek to justify or even laud its style of life. Said ideas are a stew that mixes in a bit of Freud, a tad of Rousseau, and generous portions of the emerging science of sociobiology. The ideology that results advances a simple premise, at least in its man-on-the-street version: traditional morality is a repressive and artificial overlay over the natural inclinations of the human person for serial sexual gratification and is, therefore, harmful. In a phrase, "If it feels good, by and large do it."

It is perhaps understandable if adolescent boys, and those who have never advanced beyond this stage, hold to this behavioral paradigm with the fervor of religious converts, but the rest of us are left with a nagging question: is the ideology of the sexual revolution true? That is, is sexual fidelity and exclusivity (i.e., marriage) an artifice foisted upon humankind that, even if it developed over time for pragmatic reasons having to do with the reduction of violence or the stability of society, is, and evermore will be felt to be, unnatural?

I want to attempt an answer to this question in parabolic fashion by looking at cinema and TV series / evening soap operas over the last twenty-five years that were aimed at single twenty-somethings. It goes without saying that the sexual revolution is assumed and approved in these films/shows: countless episodes feature two young persons whose eyes meet at a bar—or in some cases it is coworkers in a firm who have been eyeing each other or making suggestive comments—and the next scene shows them at a doorway of an apartment, making what appears to be vertical sex, unable to endure the merest of preparatory protocols, say, of sipping wine, engaging in conversation, or even undressing as a prelude to intimacy. The implication is clear: human beings are volcanoes of sexual energy, heretofore repressed by Victorianism or Puritanism, but now free to explode; so let's get on with it (or as the phrase has it, "get it on") and to hell with preliminaries or niceties. This is what is *real*, this is what is good.

But then a curious thing happens. The dramatic momentum of many of these stories is fueled precisely by the anger and hurt experienced by a character who discovers that a sexual partner has been intimate with someone else. For heaven's sake, why? Isn't that old hat? Haven't we been freed from the constricting bonds of conjugal fidelity? Multipartner sexual escapades are the most natural behaviors for a human being; the sexual revolution proves it. Right?

Reflecting on this dilemma recalls for me what may have been one of the first blips on the radar screen of the sexual revolution, signaling an uncomfortableness with the emerging paradigm, even as it was being celebrated. I am speaking of 1965 and the film *Dr. Zhivago*. Has there ever been a better date movie than *Zhivago*? It had everything: a love story set against a violent historical upheaval; an unforgettable and award-winning musical score (Maurice Jarre); breathtaking cinematography featuring huge sweeps of the Russian hinterland. It was to this kind of film that a young man might take someone about whom he was getting serious. But there was a problem for the female side of the dating duo (at least in 1965). The young lady likely identified with Lara, because that was the focus of Yuri Zhivago's passion and poetry. On the other hand, as regards her dating partner, she might also be candidating for the role of Tonia—Zhivago's wife—since back then, women were usually hoping to guide a steady relationship in the direction of nuptials. Did she feel the discomfiture of such a contradictory situation? I can only offer a conjecture: the answer is yes, she felt it, if only subliminally. But it was quickly erased, in part due to the fact that the movie provides very little in the way of regret for the adultery on the part of Yuri and Lara. Were the Zhivagos having trouble at home? No, the rationale for the affair, from the point of view of the film, is that Zhivago simply wanted to be intimate with someone other than his wife. And if the female in the dating pair started to have nagging thoughts, they could be quickly lost in the comforting and repeated playing of "Lara's Theme." (For the record, the book from which the film was adapted tells a much more complicated story and includes scenes of Yuri's and Lara's regret over their adultery.)

Now, a half century or more into the sexual revolution, people still feel betrayed if a partner strays. Does that tell us anything? No one denies that the votaries of the sexual revolution have it partly right: sex *is* an irresistible and titanic drive within human persons, prompting all sorts of erratic behavior; hence Chesterton's warning that heads this chapter. But will said votaries also admit that sexual intimacy leading to loyalty and exclusivity is a sentiment felt equally as deeply in the human community and one that cannot be dismissed as a mere socially conditioned behavioral response?

That, anyway, is the view of British philosopher Roger Scruton in his comprehensive study *Sexual Desire: A Moral Philosophy of the Erotic* (hereinafter *Desire*). Scruton ranges over the entirety of the phenomenon of human sexuality, its physiology and psychology, but also its related moral philosophy, poetry, and drama. Like the pedestrian version of the ideology of the sexual revolution, Scruton's central premise can be simply stated: when we unite sexually with another, we are trying to incarnate the first person perspective of the other (*Desire*, p. 121). In other words, sexual desire is the desire for a person, a central truth about humanity that cannot be reduced out. That the progenitors of sexual freedom want such a reduction to the merely physical can be seen in the vulgar terminology and catchphrases of the revolution: "boning," "jumping your bones," "I want your body," as well as in the eradication of the grammar of virtue from the discussion of sex and the overfocusing on skill (deplored by Scruton, *Desire*, p. 91)—a staple of adolescent films and young adult conversations. For Scruton, the concentration on the body to the exclusion of the whole person is the very definition of obscenity (*Desire*, p. 138).

Scruton goes very far with his premise, even insisting that the yearning for another person is present in the basest lust (*Desire*, pp. 89–90). Thus, it is not that Scruton merely differs from the advocates of the new sexual morality; his case is precisely the inverse: the ideological paraphernalia of the sexual revolution is the real overlay and artifice that masks what sex is all about—the desire for a person. That is why, says he, in Dante's *Inferno* (Canto V) fornicators are punished by being forever joined together in body but separated in soul (*Desire*, p. 129). That this would be a punishment is exactly what the sexual revolution challenges. In the end, Scruton's most poignant turn of phrase in giving voice to his understanding is the assertion that when we kiss, we are not kissing a mouth but a smile (*Desire*, p. 128).

So, who is right: Scruton or the acolytes of the new sexual morality? It cannot be proven either way; it is something one senses or not. Believers in sexual freedom are obliged to explain and then dismiss the almost universal experience of humankind over the last three thousand years that has hedged sexual contact about with rituals, safeguards, and waiting periods (i.e., engagements). On the other hand, those who agree with Scruton must confront the reality of the sexual drive to gratification that all human beings experience at one time or another and that does seem to struggle against societal and religious restraints. It is probably not a surprise to the reader that I believe that Scruton is right. However, it is not just that my mind is persuaded by his arguments; my heart affirms the truth emerging from a lifetime partnership with my beloved Cathy.

For those who see themselves more or less as Scrutonites, there is an additional problem. If the desire for a person and conjugal fidelity is natural to the human community, as we would affirm, how is it that the sexual revolution has been pretty much able to demolish millennia of its structures in less than a half century?

There are likely many responses to this question. Those on our side of the issue often point to human weakness or even sin. That is, even though for centuries official or semiofficial sexual morality stipulated some kind of conjugal fidelity, many persons were not able to abide by it. This does not prove that it is invalid, only that it is difficult to live. But this would only be a Scrutonite account of human behavior prior to the sexual revolution. The question before the house, as noted, is why the sexual revolution as a *philosophy* has permeated so completely our public discourse and entertainment and sent conjugal fidelity packing. In my judgment, there may be a partial explanation in regard to what I have termed the *soundtrack* of the sexual revolution, alluded to above.

I hesitate to put to paper my thoughts on this issue, believing that it very well might lose me whatever meager readership this book still has. But there is no help for it, so let me state plainly my contention: rock and roll music is primarily about sex, has significantly contributed to the goal of making the sexual revolution permanent, and is, on balance, a disaster for world civilization. I advance this thesis with several reservations. First, I like some rock, though it is mostly a matter of nostalgia, associating in my mind events of my past with what was then playing on the radio. And, doing a mental inventory, I realize that it is the least rocklike rock for which I have an affinity. Is "Bridge over Troubled Water" by Simon and Garfunkel rock? Is "Norwegian Wood" by the Beatles rock?—to name two pieces that I enjoy and were performed by rock artists. Second, I am fully aware that many rockers are or were highly accomplished musicians and composers: George Harrison, I am told, was a virtuoso guitarist, and Frank Zappa may have been a genius. Third, I understand that rock is not the only kind of music that has been labeled as sexually suggestive; there are certainly others (e.g., the tango, prerock bawdy drinking songs, jazzlike music formerly used in striptease performances). However, in regard to this assertion, I would argue that none of these other musical styles has achieved anything like the global dissemination of rock. Finally, there is the argument that rock, especially in its infancy, was not about sex. What is sexually suggestive, for example, about "Yakety Yak" by the Coasters? This is a point worth discussing and was the basis of the campaign of Tipper Gore, wife of Vice President Al Gore, to put warning labels on some of the racier rock music—an effort that earned her the opprobrium of the rock community. She felt constrained to say how much she loved rock and that her concern was that certain lyrics should not be part of the hearing of youngsters of an early age. The point here is that her argument—which, in my mind, was totally valid—was about lyrics. But rock *music* by itself, especially in regard to its egregious use of electric guitar and what I would term its bloated percussion, is (admittedly with the help of deplorable lyrics) the perfect musical setting for the sexual revolution.

Keeping all these caveats in mind, what I am talking about is something—including words *and* music—that unites Bill Haley's 1950s classic "Rock around the Clock" with the raunchiest contemporary rock video, namely the desire to throw off constraints to any spontaneous behavior, especially sexual, and to thumb one's nose in the face of a moral matrix that urges the postponing of gratification in the cause of the formation of character ("I wanna rock 'n' roll all night and party every day!"). A perfect metaphor for this thesis and for what I believe constitutes the demolition project of rock could be seen in the early 1980s. Back then, cable TV was just taking off, and MTV, the rock and roll station, was campaigning to be included in basic subscription services. Their ad spot in support of this outcome featured the plaint of a spoiled child—"I want my MTV!"—followed by a guitar neck being smashed through a television screen. In view of such provocations and the general tenor of rock music, it is amusing to listen to Bob Seger's song about "Old Time Rock & Roll" and how it "soothes the soul." That has to be the most misbegotten lyric in the history of song writing. Rock cares nothing for soothing the soul; for that, you listen to Samuel Barber's Adagio for Strings. The mission of rock and roll, rather, was and is to excite the body and release it from the soul's suzerainty.

I suspect that critically situated persons knew this even at rock's beginnings in the 1950s, at least as early as the portentous arrival of Elvis Presley on the scene. One of these individuals was early rock impresario Dick Clark of *American Bandstand*, who, with his well-coiffed looks and engaging style, served as something of a rock ambassador to concerned parents and teachers. He once penned an article in a teen magazine that, while pledging fealty to the rock genre, at the same time urged youngsters to be well groomed, respectful of elders, and attentive to homework. I believe that Clark knew well that the emerging rock ethos encouraged none of these things, and thus he perpetrated a scam on parents and older Americans that anticipated by a decade a similar charade in the Eugene McCarthy presidential campaign of 1968, in which young adult and student volunteers, who had nothing but contempt for the values of the older generation, nevertheless promised in their canvassing for votes to be "clean for Gene."

Very few of my contemporaries agree with me on the subject of rock and roll. After they chide me for my priggishness, they often take the quasi–Tipper Gore tack, insisting that much of rock and roll is harmless, innocuous, and just plain fun; claim that I take lyrics too seriously; and point out that most people who love rock have lived productive and upstanding lives. My answer is simple: if people live productive lives these days, it is because there are other components to their character than their affinity to rock. By my lights, the promptings of rock, if taken to heart, lead to a life of dissolution.

This I feel is an important point. My contemporaries and I can remember a time before there was rock, when one might hear on the radio a song as innocent as "How Much Is That Doggie in the Window?" by Patti Page. By the early sixties, such music was being forced off the airways by the rock juggernaut, and baby boomers were there to welcome its ascendency. Now boomers are classified under the category of rock grandparents. Next to the pathos of an aging rock performer—pitiable because of the unseemliness inherent in a person over sixty, who should have by now achieved some wisdom, nevertheless indulging in sexually explicit lyrics and dance moves—nothing is more regrettable than the sight of aging boomers at a Rolling Stones nostalgia concert, grooving behind the innuendo-laden "I can't get no satisfaction" and, at the same time, hoping, in another compartment of their brain, that their grandchildren will not fully incarnate the sentiments implicit in the songs and in the lifestyle of the musicians. But, as noted, these older boomers can remember something else; their grandchildren, by contrast, have been born *inside* rock and roll and know little else musically. What, therefore, can be expected of them absent strong countervailing influences?

As to this question, I sometimes suggest to my pro-rock interlocutors that they take a look at what is happening on the dance floor, then and now. My wife, Cathy, is a devotee of the writing of Jane Austen, having read all her novels. We also have video adaptations of some of them, including *Pride and Prejudice.* In them, there are scenes of early-nineteenth-century dancing, the elements of which were elaborately choreographed and chaste, as was required back then. Almost every successive move in the dance as it unfolded found the partners signaling mutual respect through bows and other symbolic gestures. The music—and this is also true of the dance suites of the Baroque era—is often very grave, a fact that puzzled me for some time. After reflection, I have concluded that our forebears of these eras regarded life in all its aspects—conversation, dance, interpersonal relations—much more seriously than we do today. Of this traditional dancing, Scruton says that it was an enterprise of shared skills, a supreme expression of our rationality, and an integral part of moral education (*Desire*, pp. 271–272).

Rock dancing? In many cases, it is little more than vertical sexual foreplay. I should know: I chaperoned a few high school dances during my brief teaching career and witnessed such behavior already taking hold in youngsters of secondary school age. When they achieve the age of majority and later—now beyond parental control—it gets worse. An enterprising videographer in our area roams the nightclubs of downtown Providence, filming the dance floors filled with persons in their twenties, and posts the videos on public access TV. When I cross that channel by accident, I sometimes watch the video for a moment: young adults, in some cases scantily clad, at times pasted against each other, beer bottles in hand, moving in what Scruton calls "formless vibrations"

(*Desire*, p. 272), and listening to lyrics that have far transcended the merely suggestive. I find myself wondering what kind of husbands, wives, parents, what kind of citizens they will become. Many, I am sure, will fulfill these roles admirably, but, I would insist again, not if they adopt the philosophy embedded in rock dancing.

As noted, for many years I felt that I was absolutely alone in my views, the only person of my age group, with the possible exception of Dan Quayle, to have missed the sixties. Then I read *The Closing of the American Mind* (hereinafter *Closing*) by Allan Bloom. Writing in the 1980s, Bloom, the late professor of philosophy at Cornell, Yale, and the University of Chicago, addressed what he saw as a decline in standards, academic and otherwise, along the way taking note of what motivated students with whom he interacted, including rock music.

Of rock, Bloom states flatly that it has one appeal only— to sexual desire, untutored and undeveloped—and that it induces an attitude that sex should be served on a silver platter (*Closing*, p. 73), not approached as a serious matter with serious consequences. Bloom is bemused by the way rock midwifes a sentiment of exaltation in its devotees, one that seems misplaced and is more fittingly attached to great endeavors (*Closing*, p. 80). I must confess the same thought has crossed my mind when watching the behavior at a rock concert, both of the performers and the concertgoers. What are they celebrating while shouting and swaying with arms raised, eyes closed? Not passing the bar or getting an acceptance letter from Harvard. No, what merits such triumphant approval is the victory of libido over decorum, of hormones over rationality.

A final point that I take from Bloom is that young people "live for music" (*Closing*, p. 68). For me, this rather simple assertion is weighted with meaning and explains why the sexual revolution and its musical accompaniment have achieved hegemony over our civilization. Simply put, I believe that rock and roll is a religion. Other than Bloom's commentary, the event that suggested this idea to my mind was a news report about a rock awards show in the 1990s. Rocker Billy Idol was a winner, and, after thanking a number of people, he raised his trophy and bellowed, "Rock and roll forever!" Whatever did he mean? I tried to imagine a similar music awards show about forty years earlier with someone like Perry Como shouting, "Popular music forever!" It wouldn't come. That is because for the greater part of humanity, musical styles of the past—whether the Charleston craze of the 1920s, ragtime, swing—were enjoyable diversions. Rock and roll, by contrast, is a way of life—hence the term *rock on*. When Billy Idol proclaimed, "Rock and roll forever," he meant self-indulgence, sexual libertinism, nonstop partying, and adolescent rebellion in perpetuity.

If rock is a religion, as I claim, it would have its sacred places. This, I suspect, is what you would find at the Rock and Roll Hall of Fame in Cleveland, Ohio (I have never been; *not* going there is engraved on my bucket list). A religion also has sacred events, one of which for rock has to be the Woodstock happening of August 1969. My guess is that, at the Rock and Roll Hall of Fame, this bit of rock history is treated with the circumspection other religions accord to the Red Sea crossing, the resurrection of Jesus, or the Buddha's enlightenment under the bo tree.

It is sobering to reflect that almost exactly a quarter of a century before Woodstock (note: one does not even have to say the "Woodstock concert" or "Woodstock event"; "Woodstock" alone is sufficiently indicative, such is the sway of rock over our culture), twenty-something American males were storming the beaches of northern France in an attempt to break the grip of Nazism over Europe. Twenty-five years later, the next generation of twenty-somethings invaded a small town in Upstate New York and did what? While listening to their sacred music, got high on drugs, laid waste the landscape, and had sex with persons whose names they had just learned or didn't even know. With this in mind, it occurs to me that one surefire way to divide Americans into camps is to discover whether they regard the road from Normandy to Woodstock as one of progress or decline.

In any case and to repeat, by my lights, rock and roll is a religion. It is pervasive in our culture, a sea in which we swim. A dubious choice for elevator music, it attends and makes difficult selecting greeting cards in a pharmacy. It is an addicting drug that must be had even in some cases as background to news reporting or narrated sports highlight reels. Its legendary performers are treated with the deference once accorded to moral heroes or unquestioned benefactors of civilization. It is everywhere present and everywhere honored. Those who would criticize it risk excommunication from what now passes for civilization. I have called rock the musical accompaniment to the sexual revolution. But that is too tepid. Rock *is* the sexual revolution; the sexual revolution is incarnated in rock. Whatever rock once was, it is now identified with licentious sexual expression. Anyone who doubts this need only watch any random rock video, concert, or music awards show.

Thus the sexual revolution—the mythology and the never-ending music video—stands alone in the arena, having defeated all rivals in its program of revolutionizing mores and social customs. One of those rivals was the morality of mating that specified an announcement, a *meldung*, prior to sexual intimacy and cohabitation. What has been our response to this almost complete dismantling of the institutions of weddings and marriage in a few short decades?

At the risk of testing the patience of my readers, I wish to answer the question by relating a story—actually a story within a story. When I was a seminarian, I participated in field education placements as part of the professional education for priesthood. One of them was at a state hospital for mentally disabled persons in the Boston area. I and several interdenominational divinity students performed ministry among the patient population and then met as a group to evaluate our experience under a format known as clinical pastoral education. Each of us would prepare a verbatim of our visitation and ministry with the patient or patients—that is, a complete record of what we and the patient said and did—and then, by turns, present it before the group, the others already having copies in hand before the session. The group dynamics that followed—discussion and commentary—had as its goal seeing oneself through the eyes of others and thereby discovering aspects of personality or ministry style that facilitated or impeded one's effectiveness as a clergyman-to-be. The process was always illuminating for the presenter, if sometimes sobering or even brutal. The group was led by two psychologists, one of whom was a priest and with whom each member of the group also had private supervisory meetings.

Once, during a lively group session, one of the psychologists related an incident at the hospital to illustrate a point. The point is now lost to my memory, but her story I will never forget. In the ward for severely mentally disabled persons, a resident died. The psychologist went to the ward in the aftermath to be of service to the other residents in their grief. Though she suspected what the outcome would be, she was still struck by what she encountered. There was no grief; incapable of the responses, rituals, and protocols appropriate to marking significant life passages, the patients didn't know how to grieve. Rather, the psychologist experienced their singular resolve to maintain their usual daily routine, almost as if the death had not occurred, as a disquieting void and discomforting emptiness. It anticipated Dustin Hoffman as the autistic savant "Rain Man," for whom nothing, not even the Second Coming, could bar him from watching the daily broadcast of *The People's Court.*

This, in my judgment, is where we are headed in regard to our individual and collective responses to the phenomenon of cohabiting—to a mental ward. Everyone reading these words has by now been told by someone that a distant, or not so distant, relative, or a friend of a friend has moved in with another person. It is then that the perplexity assaults us: what to say or do. Deprived of the rituals that mark important passages in human life—rituals that we still preserve in, for instance, graduation ceremonies—we, after a few stumbling inquires or remarks, sense the void and, like the mentally disabled patients alluded to above, quickly move on. With regard to our collective responses to the epidemic of cohabitation and recohabitation, we are all rain men now.

From at least the time of the Lascaux cave paintings, it has been the human vocation to narrate life as well as live it. Perhaps as far back is the ritualization of the joining together of partners in the marriage bond. Marriage has not always been well lived, but up to very recently, there had always been the sense, even in failures, that human beings created something in joining together: there was you and I—and now you and I together. That third person, most times but not always, symbolized by children was regarded in some sense as alive and therefore never to be treated with anything less than respect. It has been the work of the sexual revolution to obliterate that third person and to midwife the phenomenon of cohabiting—a joining together for gratification and convenience, for as long as the partners, as they said in the sixties, "dig it."

Those who have misgivings about this new social artifact are doing their best to get used to it. That is a mistake. For cohabitation without benefit of melding and *meldung*, whatever else it is, is a terrible foreshadowing of barbarities to come.

CHAPTER 8
JULY

A Death in the Morning

Only the dead have seen the end of war.
—Statement attributed to Plato

It is still the season of solar mastery in the Northern Hemisphere; sunlight seems as bright as in June, but the air is heavier. On a Saturday morning early in the month, Cathy and I pushed the envelope in the matter of solstice breakfasts in the unnook at the 9:00–10:00 a.m. hour. The sun, now a bit lower than in June, uncomfortably lit up the right side of my body in the eastward-facing chair. This will definitely be the end of such breakfasts—barring cloudy days—until next year. On the eleventh, I noted the rising sun shining flat against the west wall of the computer room, illuminating the star map I have suspended there. It surprised me because, not having kept up with solar events in this room, I had remembered only the late-winter sun feebly casting light on the north wall and moving left, that is westerly, in the smallest of increments. On the twenty-fourth of July, I was in one of my favorite spots—the top of the staircase in the northeast corner of the house—watching a parallelogram of light on the first-floor landing of the stairs moving slowly toward the north wall, where it became a Nevada-shaped projection.

Another phenomenon confined to this season concerns our northward-facing porch, which is illumined twice a day, morning and evening, due to the generous sweep of the sun in its diurnal journey. I had already noted the sunsets bathing the porch in light at this time of year, because I was often sitting there in the late afternoon; but on the second of July at 7:00 a.m., I saw at the other end of the porch a reciprocal glow that had eluded my notice up till then.

It got me to thinking about how folks in other locales on the globe experience the sun's journeyings. I had read once in an astronomical magazine that north of certain latitudes but well south of the arctic circle, say, fifty-five to fifty-eight degrees, the sky never really darkens to pitch-black at the time of the summer solstice but remains a lingering twilight all night long. On the other hand, I have been told that near the equator, where the sun descends to the horizon at less of an acute angle than in temperate latitudes, the onset of darkness occurs with a duskless suddenness.

On the morning of the fourth, I awoke in relative darkness at 3:45 a.m. for a solitary breakfast while watching the *Twilight Zone* marathon on the Sci-Fi channel. After showering and dressing, I was out the door at 4:55 a.m. when the eastern sky was brightening but the sun was not yet at porch level. Why was I up so early? For a Bristolite, the answer is easy: to ensure a place on the sidewalk for a viewing of the annual Independence Day parade. The parade route is one street over from our house, and at the five o'clock hour—the earliest that local police will allow for the staking out of spots—I was found to be walking down a connecting street, encumbered with two folding chairs, a blanket and sheet, and a crossword puzzle book. I would choose a spot under a leafy tree on High Street near the end of the parade route, the chairs at the limits of the space I had commandeered and the blankets and sheet in between. (An informal code of parade-viewing etiquette stipulates taking no more room than is necessary for a contingent of family and friends.) I will have to wait for hours for the parade; in the interim, Cathy will bring me a cup of coffee, and our relatives will gradually arrive with their own chairs to fill up the space I have secured. I say *gradually* only in the sense that they will arrive serially. They also will have to be early, because by midmorning the downtown area of Bristol is inaccessible by auto, and there is absolutely no parking surrounding the parade route. Our driveway, as a consequence, will be packed with vehicles.

The Bristol Fourth of July parade is the biggest annual event in these parts, planned meticulously by a municipal committee beginning on the week after the previous celebration and complemented by other events—fireworks, concerts, lectures—in the days surrounding. The oldest continually held Independence Day parade in the country (since 1785), it features the usual assortment of military units, floats, bands, and notables. Though people from around the state, and the country for that matter, come to watch or participate, the parade throughout places a heavy emphasis on the local, which, in the end, is perhaps the most compelling kind of patriotism.

Later in the day, after our cookout, I was sitting on our porch festooned with flags and, while sipping wine, turned my thoughts again to love of country. My mind was prompted in this direction even more than was usual for a Fourth of July, because Cathy and I had planned a short vacation for the end of the month to another place with many patriotic resonances—Gettysburg, Pennsylvania.

I came late in my adult life to an appreciation of the American Civil War and the Battle of Gettysburg in particular. When I was a high school student, an English teacher, preparing our class to write a term paper, recalled a student of years past who took as his topic an aspect of the Civil War. She seemed almost awestruck as she recalled the boy's absolute devotion to that episode in American history. At the time, I was already considering whether to make history my major in college; but I only marveled at the teacher's story, for I could not summon feelings about the Civil War as that boy had. Years later, in 1986, Cathy and I traveled to West Virginia to visit an old friend. On the way back, we stopped at Gettysburg, but all that interested me was the search for the possible location of Lincoln's address in November 1863. The drama of the battle itself, the principal personalities who contended there during charges and countercharges, the courage and sacrifice of the combatants—none of this registered in my consciousness at the time.

Things changed in the 1990s. I viewed the PBS documentary *The Civil War* and discovered emotions that I never knew I had about the horror of the conflict and yet its redemptive character. Individuals all over the country, it appears, had similar experiences. About the same time, I read Michael Shaara's compelling novel of the Battle of Gettysburg, *The Killer Angels* (Cathy read it too) and saw the movie *Gettysburg*, based on the book. As I did more reading about the war and the battle, I began to see what entranced that boy my high school teacher had described; I could understand why men and women became Civil War buffs and people with careers and families nevertheless spent large amounts of their time in Civil War encampments and battlefield reenactments. I didn't know whether I would ever qualify as a buff, but one thing I did know: I had to get back to Gettysburg. With Cathy's cordial assent, we made plans for the vacation trip.

I could hardly contain my enthusiasm almost from the first moment of arriving at the battlefield but initially could not tell why. After an hour or two, it hit me. I had developed quasi-religious sentiments about the Civil War and this battle in particular, and here the land characteristics looked familiar—rolling hills, deciduous trees; in short, it reminded me of home. Why was this worthy of note? Because, being a Christian, the landscape of my religious history is somewhat alien, the biblical story being largely told against the geographical backdrop of Middle Eastern deserts and wadis. This poses no problems for the elements of faith, but it means that, for Christians from more temperate climates, topographical references are grasped only with the mind and not inhabited, as it were. On the other hand, for individuals from the same areas who also have religious sentiments about the battle, Gettysburg provides a spiritually supporting landscape—maple trees, not fig trees; moderate climate, not excessive heat; grassy, rolling hills, not a water-starved wasteland. What more could one want? The battlefield was, in essence, familiar and much-loved topography covered with a rich layer of history.

Our accommodations were conveniently near the site of General Lee's headquarters on the Chambersburg Pike. From there, Cathy and I spent two days touring the battlefield— walking part of it and driving the rest with a self-guiding CD. We were at Seminary Ridge, Cemetery Ridge, the "Angle," where Confederate troops temporarily broke through the Union lines during Pickett's Charge, Devil's Den, and, of course, Little Round Top. I had most urgently wanted to see the last named location, the hill where Joshua Lawrence Chamberlain and the Twentieth Maine repelled assaulting Confederates with a bayonet charge on the second day of the battle. Also there on the hilltop, I had my picture taken at the monument to Chamberlain's commander, Colonel Strong Vincent (no relation, as far as I can tell).

I was in a celebratory high for much of this tour, especially when striking up conversations with other visitors who were similarly enthused. But two things happened that brought me back to earth and stayed with me as a kind of balancing consideration. The first occurred at the outset of our excursion at the northwest sector of the battlefield near McPherson's Ridge. There on the first day of the battle (July 1, 1863) Union General John Buford and his dismounted cavalry were attempting to hold off advance units of the Confederate Army near the Lutheran Theological Seminary. He was awaiting infantry support under General John Reynolds, which arrived before he was overwhelmed. Reynolds, a young (age forty), handsome major general, believed in leading his soldiers from the front and was so doing when, around 10:30 a.m., he was shot off his horse, dying instantly. As we were viewing his monument at the edge of a wooded area where he fell, his death began to haunt me and continued to do so for the rest of our time there. The evidence is not conclusive, but there is the possibility that Reynolds was taken down by a Rebel sharpshooter, perhaps lodged in a tree. It may seem disproportionate amid all the carnage of a battle like this, where indiscriminate musket fire mowed down nameless enemies in bunches and artillery barrages dismembered fighting units wholesale, but there is something about having an individual person's life in your sights and therefore in your power over the space of several seconds and then ending it at your discretion that absolutely terrifies me.

The second incident occurred later in the afternoon of the same day. Cathy and I were exploring monuments in the famed wheat field west of Little Round Top when an afternoon thundershower threatened, much needed in this locale due to a rainless summer. We made it to the car just before the storm broke. Since we had the whole next day to complete our battlefield survey and museum visit, we decided to drive down to Maryland on the Emmitsburg Road. We ended up at St. Mary's College and Seminary and drove to the top of the hill immediately behind it to the shrine where St. Elizabeth Ann Seton attended mass. By the time we parked the car, the downpour was over, and Cathy and I were able to walk the grounds. Along with my continuing discomfiture about John Reynolds's death, it began to dawn on me that in all my exulting about Civil War battles, I was perhaps forgetting that I was a Catholic. Maybe my enthusiasm should be tempered a bit. What indeed would the Founder of my religion have to say about my unabashed celebration of the clashing of armies and the slaughter of men by the thousands? In fact, should a Catholic or Christian come anywhere near war or war making?

As I understand it, the Christian faith has a complicated history in regard to the use of force. There is much in the teaching of Jesus and his lived responses that suggest that a kind of pacifism is integral to Christianity. Some Christian denominations—the Quakers come to mind—have accordingly made it an absolutely core value to their faith community. Others, like Roman Catholicism, while forbidding the perpetration of violence to *some* within the church—usually those who are in holy orders or who have taken religious vows—have reserved the prerogative to laypersons to participate in wars under certain defined conditions. It must be added here that in recent times, some Catholic thinkers have urged that the church move closer to a Quaker-like posture and emphasized that the evils inherent in weapons of mass destruction in the modern era render the prospect of war making under any circumstances as immoral.

In regard to the conditions alluded to above that might justify the use of force by Christians, theologians such as St. Augustine, St. Thomas Aquinas, and others have addressed the topic, their findings often being summarized in the term the *just war theory*. A comprehensive treatment of the theory can be found in *In Defence of War* (hereinafter *Defence*) by Nigel Biggar, Regius Professor of Moral and Pastoral Theology at Oxford University. Biggar has addressed two issues in his volume, one theoretical and one practical. First, he has defended the just war theory against the competing claims of Christian pacifism and absolute nonviolence, including an assertion that one cannot with certitude deduce the imperative of pacifism from the teaching of Jesus (*Defence*, p. 47). Second, he has evaluated several recent and historical conflicts using the just war criteria: the Battle of the Somme in World War I, the Kosovo intervention of the 1990s, and the Iraq War of the first decade of the twenty-first century.

Biggar discusses the elements of the just war theory throughout the book but gives a particularly helpful summary on pages 251–253. He divides the components under two headings: 1) ad bellum (i.e., the decision to go to war—five criteria) and 2) in bello (i.e., the conduct of a war once undertaken—two criteria). The five ad bellum stipulations are as follows: 1) the war must seek to rectify a grave injustice; 2) it must be prosecuted by legitimate authority with right intention (i.e., rectifying the injustice, not acquiring territory or other collateral reasons); 3) the war must be undertaken as a last resort, presumably after the exhaustion of negotiations or other remedies; 4) there must be an element of proportionality, in that those who prosecute the war must not perpetrate greater evils than they seek to remove or fail to account for problems related to postwar restoration; and 5) there must be a reasonable prospect of success. The in bello criteria are: 1) there must be no intentional attacks upon noncombatants; and 2) there must be proportionality in tactical and small-unit operations as there is in the overall prosecution of the war.

Biggar, while a proponent of the just war theory, is not uncritical of it, noting that some criteria carry more weight than others (*Defence,* p. 319) and averring that sometimes the criteria could lead us astray. For instance, if British authorities had applied the stipulation of "reasonable prospect of success" to the situation after Dunkirk in June 1940, they might not have carried on the war (*Defence,* p. 319). Still, as noted, he is convinced of the general validity and applicability of the theory as against the position of Christian pacifism.

After reflection, my own inclinations have been to support the just war theory in principle while admiring pacifists and nonviolent activists for their courage and fidelity to a difficult and utterly counterintuitive way of life. But this admiration is in a sense for their hearts rather than their heads; that is, the way of pacifism, while hard and even dangerous to live, seems to me to be easy to conceptualize, there being no distinction making or shades of gray. On our walk to mass, Cathy and I pass a home with a sign in the window that reads, "War is not the Answer." The statement has always puzzled me. For starters, I assume that *answer* in this sentence means "answer to a problem" or "solution." If war is never the solution, then what is? Negotiations, diplomacy? How would negotiations have stopped the extension of the hated institution of slavery into the territories in 1850s America, keeping in mind that for thirty years prior to this era, there had been a series of painstaking compromises forged to prevent such an outcome? Or how would diplomacy have stopped Adolf Hitler in 1940, it having so measurably failed to prevent his enslavement of whole populations in 1938 and 1939? It is as if pacifists believe we live in a perfect world. In a perfect world, negotiations would not only be sufficient, they would be superfluous; in an imperfect world—that is, the world in which we live—negotiations when not backed by the threat of force are not only insufficient but impotent.

To the extent then that the pacifist position remains with the principle of the pricelessness of human beings—that is, emphasizes its heart—I commend it; when it offers itself as a viable alternative solution to all conflict resolution—its head, if you will—I cannot in the end take it seriously. But I am primarily critical of it for its above-noted lack of distinction making or—let me call it what it is—fault finding. I can illustrate with an allusion to a movie and an existential situation.

In the motion picture *Witness*, Harrison Ford plays a police detective on the run from dirty cops and hiding among the Amish of Lancaster County, Pennsylvania. In one scene, the Amish grandfather shows his grandson Ford's police revolver as the prelude to a lesson in their faith community's ethics. He begins by saying, "Many times wars have come ..." in which the Amish refused to fight, that being one of the reasons, he goes on to say, that they have separated themselves from the larger societies they inhabit. It is a poignant scene to watch as he lays out the hard path of the Amish way of life, so it is easy to let slip from notice the bit of base stealing usage in his discourse. "Many times wars have come" is a semipassive construction that really does not do justice, in many cases, to the reality of the occurrences he is citing, a phrase that is more fitting for something commonplace like "Many times weeds will grow on your lawn." What if he had said, "Many times men have unjustly invaded the territory of other nations, burned their homes, stolen their property, raped women, and killed children"? I would have been much more interested to find out how he defended the Amish response to events like this with which history is replete.

The real-life situation that prompts a similar analysis is that of road rage. Police spokespersons rightly urge motorists not to get out of their cars after an incident where, say, the individual is cut off or suffers aggressive tailgating. Point well taken, but the impression often left is that, like the pacifist view of war, there is an undifferentiated entity called road rage that we should avoid. The truth is that in many of these instances, *someone is at fault*, and while the injured party is well advised not to act on his or her rage, that doesn't mean there isn't a case of a wrong that in some way should be righted. (My solution: draconian punishments for egregious violations, such as excessive speeding or road racing, which put others' lives at risk.)

It is this seeming reluctance to give weight to culpability in situations leading to violence that bothers me about the pacifist position. Pacifists sometimes reply that that consideration is nugatory when weighed against the horror that war, any war, wrecks upon humanity. However, as Biggar points out (*Defence*, p. 33), not going to war or not going to war in a timely fashion can also have as its result particularly horrendous evil. The now silent crematoria at Auschwitz and Dachau are eloquent testimony to that truth. It seems therefore to me that the just war position is the only rational and consistent course to follow in certain situations for an imperfect humanity. Without it, how will the world be made safe for pacifists?

And yet ... I cannot leave it there. I am haunted by the fact that, despite all the arguments of the just war philosophers, pacifists and advocates of nonviolence are on to something that is much deeper than can be expressed in the point/counterpoint of a theoretical debate. I have become dimly aware of it in my own marital relationship, which is why I believe marriage is such an irreplaceable school of life. Sometimes, when Cathy is not noticing, I look at her meditatively in profile. I think I know her, but there is so much more in there, hidden even from a husband's view—yearnings, sufferings, wonderings, a whole unfathomable universe of being that, sanctified by the divine indwelling, is hers and hers alone. And this is God's way with every human being who was ever conceived—even the thousands and the millions whose lives were and are cut short by malnutrition, disease, and warfare. Somehow all of them are indispensable to something God is doing, something He is building, that is partially veiled from us in the here and now. With such a prospect in view, the very thought of justifying the deliberate and intentional taking of a human life reaches a level of repugnance that cannot, it seems to me, be overborne.

My favorite author, C. S. Lewis, dwells on this notion of the pricelessness of the individual human person in two locales in his writing. One is the too little heralded religious fantasy *The Great Divorce*, the plot of which involves the trip of some residents of Hell who are bused to the outskirts of heaven and are given a chance to go in. Lewis is there as an observer (actually, the whole book is a dream), with George MacDonald, the Scottish pastor and writer, as his guide—that is, the Vergil to Lewis's Dante. In one episode, a wife who is already dead and living in paradise comes down to appeal to her husband to enter. As she approaches from Deep Heaven, she is attended by a grand processional with music and flowers and accompanied by birds and beasts of all kinds. Lewis at first thinks it is the Virgin Mary, such is the woman's splendor and beatitude. It turns out that she was an ordinary housewife from England who was, nevertheless, extraordinarily kind to children and animals. Her death and entrance into paradise demonstrate the inversion of values that prevails there; to wit, it is persons like this kindly woman, and not necessarily kings, presidents, movie stars, and sports figures, who are to be honored and celebrated.

I wrote that the lady was an ordinary housewife, but this is a misstatement. At least that is the view of Lewis in his essay, originally a sermon, *The Weight of Glory*—the nonfiction companion piece to the above cited episode in *The Great Divorce*. Says Lewis, there are *no* ordinary people. Such is the glory hidden in every human being that, he says, we would be strongly tempted to fall at the feet of one another in worship if we could see in the here and now what Heaven will, by our cooperation with God's grace, ultimately reveal. Lewis concludes by urging his listeners to conduct all their interpersonal relationships with these awe-striking possibilities in view.

The hidden glory of the human person—this was the idea, unarticulated, that was a weight on my spirit as I viewed the monument to John Reynolds on the Gettysburg battlefield and that put a restraint on my tonic exhilaration during our visit there. Thus am I divided, mind versus heart, but also within my heart, on the issue of war and peace. In the end, I must cast my lot with the defenders of the just war theory, believing, as I do, that the perpetration of justified violence is in certain cases the only rational course to follow to prevent unspeakable evils that exceed even the horror of warfare itself. But I do so reluctantly, even grudgingly; for what I have learned of the human person through the teaching of Jesus, through a lifetime relationship with Cathy, and through the imagination of C. S. Lewis suggests to me that, in a way I wish I could call my own, my pacifist sisters and brothers have not only chosen the better path but the truer one as well.

CHAPTER 9
AUGUST

The Angel from the Tomb

The stone *is*, it always remains itself, it does not change—
and it *strikes* man by what it possesses of irreducibility
and absoluteness and, in so doing, reveals to him by
analogy the irreducibility and absoluteness of being.
—Mircea Eliade

As I intimated earlier in the book, August is a melancholy month for me because within its borders we reach the two-month mark past the summer solstice, the Northern Hemisphere's projection forward toward the sun now significantly receding as we approach ineluctably another equinox and shorter spans of sunlight.

The signs are everywhere to see in our house. On August 3, I checked the large square of afternoon sunlight projected onto the floor of the den through the northwest skylight and onto the southern extremity of the bed in the bedroom through the southwest skylight. Soon these reflections will move more northerly—in the bedroom, the light projection will fall onto the floor north of the bed—as the sun moves south. On the twentieth, in the 6:00 to 7:00 a.m. hour, I noted that the rising sun—the appreciably later rising sun—is now hitting the bookcase north of the doorway to the upstairs den, where through late spring and early summer it cast light *through* the doorway. On the twenty-fifth in the morning, I sat in the upstairs reading area, unvexed (as Mr. Lincoln might say) by the sun for the first time in a while.

On the same day, I noted the midday sun had slipped noticeably below the roof lip of the box bow window, though it will take a few more days for it to fall behind the leaves of the maple tree in our yard, enabling me to take lunch in the unnook. Finally, and sadly, I realized at month's end that the rising sun, blocked by my neighbor's house, now illumines but a small sliver of our northwest-facing front porch.

August is not so somber in its entirety or for everyone. Many young people, a bit jaded at this point by the long summer, are, unbelievably, beginning to get excited by the prospect of school opening at month's end or after Labor Day. And for Cathy and me, there are a few bright spots. One is Cathy's birthday, August 21 (saint of the day—Pope Pius X, the beloved but controversial pontiff, my favorite anecdote about whom is that, as patriarch [i.e., cardinal archbishop] of Venice and attending the 1903 conclave that would elect him pope, he had purchased a round-trip train ticket). Another is the annual Perseid meteor shower (August 11), also known as St. Lawrence's tears. And finally there is the East Coast Rock, Gem, and Mineral Show held every year on the second weekend of the month.

To understand why the latter is a highlight of our year, I must go back in history a bit. As narrated in the prologue, before Cathy and I moved to Bristol, we lived for a number of years in the semirural town of Smithfield, northwest of Providence. As is most likely true across the United States, towns are routinely composites of previously founded villages, in New England quite often mill (i.e., textile mill) villages. Thus, when a Rhode Islander says he or she is from a part of the state, they are at least as likely to refer to one of these villages as to one of the state's thirty-nine cities and towns. When Cathy and I lived in Smithfield, we were situated right next to the village of Georgiaville, where we would often take walks. It is uncommonly small, featuring mill houses, a textile mill converted into residential condominiums, other single-family residences, two churches, and a firehouse. There was almost nothing in the way of commerce or retail establishments, except for one signless storefront with shuttered windows by which we would regularly pass. One day we decided to go in, and that was the beginning of a lifetime adventure, especially for Cathy,

The store was in fact a mineral shop. When you entered its precincts, you were immediately dazzled by what the inanimate Earth could bring forth: violet amethyst, green malachite, alternative green dioptase, red rhodochrosite, yellowish wulfenite, cobalt-blue azurite, various types of quartz, and fossilized life-forms. Best of all was the proprietor, an older gentleman named Sal, now sadly passed, a warm and engaging porter at the gates of the avocation known as rock/mineral collection. Because of Sal, Cathy, who was always attracted to stones, began her journey of serious collecting, but she was far from the only one Sal enticed into the hobby. It was always edifying to watch him lure others, especially children, to start collecting. He would spend a protracted amount of time with the tots, helping them to assemble the best collection their allowances would accommodate and, no doubt, taking many a monetary loss in service to the greater good of inculcating in children an appreciation of what lay hidden in Mother Earth.

Sal then was a facilitator, which in my mind is another name for angel. After meeting him, I have tried to recognize others whom I would term angels in our midst—that is, persons we encounter who, in one or way or another, guide us into the deeper realms of life. In Sal's case, the moniker "angel" was doubly appropriate because his first name was actually Seraphino—Italian for angel, or at least one class of them. He once told me that he liked to compare himself to the angel from the tomb—that is, the angel or angels who were situated at the tomb of Jesus to announce the good news of the resurrection. In Matthew 28:2, the angel actually sits upon the stone he has rolled back from the tomb entrance—a somewhat modified image for me of Sal, sitting not upon a stone but among them, beckoning anyone and everyone to see the grandeur of rocks and minerals.

Largely due to Sal's influence, Cathy became a serious collector, continuing to shop at his store and visiting mineral shows that sometimes made appearances locally. After several years of this routine, she took a measured leap into a venue of greater choices—the East Coast Rock, Gem, and Mineral Show. Held on the fairgrounds of the Eastern States Exposition in Springfield, Massachusetts, on the second week of August each year, it takes over one of the fair's display buildings with thousands of square feet of floor space. To these premises come mineral and fossil dealers from all over the country and beyond, with wares in all price ranges, even to six figures.

It is fun for me to watch Cathy in her foray at the gem show. Flush with her own savings over the course of a year, plus an advance birthday monetary donation from me, Cathy walks the whole arena to get a sense of the items for sale, all the while taking notes and recording vendor numbers. She gradually narrows her search to a few dealers until, by show's end, she has made one or two purchases to augment the array of minerals and gems situated in various places around our house. I usually accompany her for part of the time, but she is, as they say, on a mission, and I have as a goal a more relaxed enjoyment. Separating from her after a while, I stroll through the various displays—especially the high-end specimens—as if I were in a museum, except in this case the credit goes to one Artist alone. In addition to the constant exhaling at the awe-striking beauty of many of these objects, a mantra, as it were, keeps repeating itself in my mind—*under the radar*—a phrase that, in this context, requires a rather longish explanation.

I made reference in the prologue that my mind and spirit were of a traditionalist bent. Statements I have made subsequently in the book, as well as the chosen sources in the bibliography, I would venture to say have reinforced that assessment in the minds of readers. Simply stated, I regard myself as a conservative. But it is not in relation to politics that I own this self-designation; I never feel more like a conservative than when I am walking the arena of the mineral show or doing night sky observing with my mounted binoculars. To explain why, it is best to begin with a more conventional look at the term.

It is a bit hard to arrive at a definition of conservatism since there are as many takes on it as theorists who have attempted to distill its essence. Moreover, there is some fluidity in its components over time. Some contemporary conservatives actually call themselves liberals, referring to the nineteenth-century, John Stuart Mill sense of the latter term. In his book, *The Conservative Mind*, Russell Kirk, the foremost taxonomist of Anglo-American conservatism, identified the following components (in slight paraphrase) of the conservative mindset: belief that a divine intent pervades society, linking the living and the dead; affection for the proliferating variety and mystery of traditional life; conviction that true equality is moral equality and that the enforcement of all other types leads to despair; belief that property and freedom are inextricably combined; faith in prescription and tradition; and belief that society must alter slowly, incrementally, organically. Kirk goes on to explore these ideas and their variants in thinkers and political actors such as Edmund Burke, John Adams, Walter Scott, Benjamin Disraeli, John Henry Newman, and Henry Adams.

Out of the aforementioned ideas come the multiplicity of contemporary conservative persuasions: paleoconservatism, neoconservatism, libertarianism, fiscal conservatism, national defense conservatism, social conservatism, to select a few. Usually, if one adopts a self-designation of conservative, he or she will choose one or another of these descriptions as their primary focus, which makes a comment of William F. Buckley Jr. of interest as regards my own thinking. Buckley, it will be remembered, was the impresario of the post–World War II conservative revival with his founding of the journal of opinion *National Review*— the beginning point of the growth over the last half century of a conservative intellectual infrastructure to include other journals, think tanks, publishing houses, and even colleges. Buckley once averred that, while he regarded himself philosophically as a conservative, temperamentally he was not of the breed. The "isms" mentioned above are all such philosophies or policy emphases that Buckley would recognize and, to varying degrees, endorse, but I find my conservative juices running at the mineral show precisely because I, unlike Buckley, am temperamentally— at least at first—rather than philosophically of the breed. That is, my desire to conserve and reverence, say, the beauty of minerals flows from me instinctively rather than as an adopted position.

To illustrate further, an axiom of conservatism is a selective opposition to the modern administrative state, which, as the historian John Lukacs once noted in a public lecture, is the product of a one-way vector toward centralization as the history of the last four hundred years has unfolded. He went on to say, by way of further elucidation, that, although on many points, the government and society of, say, France in the revolutionary period (1789–1799) was markedly different from that of France under the Old Regime (drawing such contrasts has traditionally been a standard of lectures and testing in courses in modern European history), this was not the case with regard to centralization of governmental functions, which continued to expand in a gradual, serenely uninterrupted fashion, even as monarchies toppled and the month of August was now called Thermidor. To this trend, conservatism, as noted, has been in large part opposed, stressing the need to cultivate those private institutions—families, churches, voluntary societies—where, so the argument ran, virtues are taught and character formed.

Two things have happened in recent and contemporary conservatism that have altered this stance a bit. First, such is the addiction of modern societies to centralized government that conservatives, while still in theory opposed to its growth, have nevertheless jumped on the bandwagon, proposing and implementing huge expansions of federal activity. In this regard, it is interesting to hear presidents at the State of the Union speech, when addressing the American people, say something like "Four years ago (or five or six), when we began this journey together ..." (I have heard lines or something very close to them from several presidents)—as if the whole American populace were on a public policy / programmatic adventure with him, daily noting additions to the Federal Register and slavishly following the march of government into every nook and cranny of society. When I heard Ronald Reagan utter these words, I was dumbfounded; he, of all persons, should have known better. Yes, citizens of a republic have a duty to keep themselves informed of what their government is doing, and, yes, in certain crisis situations, they will be asked to do much more; but for conservatives, it is the highest duty of government to preserve the arena of private life, to the imperatives and enrichment of which, citizens ought to devote themselves.

The second issue for me is highlighted by Roger Scruton in his book *The Meaning of Conservatism*. Scruton notes that *conservatism* is a term of political discourse, and for most practicing politicians, that means a preoccupation with economics. Elected conservatives, therefore, have a tendency to define the private sector as preeminently the business sector and spend most of their time thinking of, talking about, and advocating for lowering taxes, extinguishing undue regulations, promoting free trade, and celebrating entrepreneurship. Thus, when Steve Forbes, running for the Republican nomination for president in 2000, was asked what his campaign was all about, without missing a beat, he answered, "Hope, growth, and opportunity." And if asked about his conservatism, the late Jack Kemp, a most creative and engaging congressman, would almost certainly have responded with something about what the Laffer Curve implied relative to tax policy or the promise of urban enterprise zones.

There is nothing wrong with these emphases, and perhaps a lot right. And, to be fair, there are some conservative writers who focus on elements of the position other than an obsession with economics. I referenced in an earlier chapter Rod Dreher's *Crunchy Cons*, with its emphasis on a simple and local way of life. Roger Scruton, in *The Meaning of Conservatism*, has stressed the importance of clubs and societies that relate individuals, in his words, to the transcendent. And that great icon of conservatism, Alexis de Tocqueville, keen observer of 1830s America, was insistent on the critical contribution of voluntary (i.e., nongovernmental) societies to the moral and intellectual life of the nation.

But these are not the loudest voices under the conservative tent, and, for me, that is too bad. As I see it, I qualify as a conservative because I believe that the important business of life is transacted in the private sector, but I am not in its mainstream because I further hold that the important business of life is not about business. What it is—what life is really for—is the development of the faculty of informed appreciation. That is why I find such a balm for my soul at the Rock, Gem, and Mineral

Show and why I keep repeating, "Under the radar." There is nothing about the government here: no reports from the 24/7 cable news channels about the Congress, the president, or the judiciary; no Democrats or Republicans; no handwringing about campaign-finance reform, defense readiness, taxes, deregulated markets, or income redistribution. Instead, the human person is simply invited to see and respond with gratitude. And no one is left out. For once, it is true that race, ethnicity, or religion do not count. All that is required is the ability to be aesthetically transported. In this enterprise, there is true equality—not before the law but before the beautiful.

It seems to me that the protection of the space and time where this most essential human vocation—appreciation prompting gratitude—can survive is an absolute imperative. But is it not presumptuous to designate conservatives as the ones who follow this path, as if liberals, socialists, and those of other political attachments do not qualify? The answer is, of course, yes, it is presumptuous; conservatives are not alone in and may not even be the best at this calling. But, based on my studies and life experience, the aggrandizing, centralized state is a threat to the private areas where contemplation, religious ecstasy, wonderment, and aesthetic rapture take place. As one moves away from the conservative position, the percentage of space within human society occupied by the government increases, putting the pursuit of such activities at risk. Though it is certainly a debatable proposition, insisting on the freedom to discover the "proliferating variety and mystery of life" seems to me like a conservative thing to do.

Thus the cultivation of informed appreciation rather than devotion to reducing marginal tax rates characterizes my brand of conservatism. But there is another personal departure or, better, emphasis that makes me a bit different from my conservative brethren. It seems to me that there has arisen over the last half century a new behemoth-like entity that, in its way, is similar in power and menace to the modern centralized administrative state, a phenomenon I like to call the public discourse / mass entertainment complex. It is a pastiche of distasteful offerings: news mixed with comedy that breeds terminal cynicism about elected public service and those who engage in it and threatens the health of the republic; the cult of celebrity, expanded beyond anything that could have been extrapolated from the movie magazines of the 1950s, to the point where celebrity itself is an object of worship rather than notoriety based on accomplishment; entertainment that is more and more marked by vulgarity, the allure of voyeurism, and utter mediocrity; and what I like to call the *din* of news, provided by twenty-four-hour cable TV news networks, where events are repeated and analyzed ad nauseam, ultimately numbing rather than informing the populace.

It seems to me that a conservatism critical and fearful of the modern centralized state should be equally opposed to the malign, many-sided colossus just described. I frankly do not understand why our intellectual, cultural, and moral leaders do not inveigh more strenuously against these and other clear and present spiritual threats to the survival of our civilization. Their failure to do so means that these dangers have become routine and commonplace or what I like to call *cultural wallpaper*; that is, gross indecency or extreme vulgarity barely register on our moral radar, prompting little more than a collective shrug of the shoulders. That is why to the definitional list of the components of conservatism, I believe a new item should be added: the maintenance of the capacity to be appalled, without which the well-being of the world is imperiled.

All this is, as noted, subject to debate. But there is one thing I do know: when a television listing invites me to keep up with people whose activities, in saner eras, would not merit a moment's notice, or another apprises me that housewives in a certain city are to be interviewed in regard to slights one of them believed she received from another at a recent luncheon, and afterward I go downstairs to look at the sun glinting off Cathy's mineral collection in the china cabinet, well, it is then that I know why I am a conservative.

CHAPTER 10
SEPTEMBER

One and a Half Cheers for an Elder Brother

Everything I have is yours.
—Luke 15:31b (NAB)

"Back to school" is the watchword for this time of year as academic life resumes after the long summer hiatus. Actually, that is the wrong way to describe it. It isn't as if June represented a suspension of studies, to be resumed in September; June was an end, the end of the academic year. And September is widely felt not as a resuming but as something more akin to a fresh start. Hence, to many, September is the true beginning of the year, though to the flora and fauna of our surroundings, it is more like the beginning of the end.

Around our household, Cathy is still harvesting tomatoes, green beans, and broccoli from our small garden, and I am looking forward to some spectacular astronomical observing now that September brings earlier sunsets, crisper nights, and skies of superior transparency. Speaking of earlier sundowns, the sun is seemingly in retreat everywhere in the interior of our home. At 5:40 p.m. on the eighteenth, I noticed it blazing through the northwest window in the downstairs parlor but was frustrated that the full power of its luminosity was blocked by the air conditioner, which will not be removed until next month. Well, at least I have the vernal equinox to look forward to, with the sun in a similar position and the entire window free of any obstruction. The import of this preoccupation with the downstairs northwest window is that the sun, at its more southerly declination, is almost entirely disabled from casting light through the north face of the house—the windows and the front door, which were bathed in early-evening sunshine in June and July.

I noted what I have referred to as the sacred parallelogram of the northeast staircase in a previous chapter. It is now leaving for the season in its morning apparition: on the third, it had lost its shape and was only grazing the top of the plant; on the eighth, it cleared the plant altogether. From here on in, whatever light is left, as the sun plummets toward the winter solstice, will be a new quadrilateral illuminating, however briefly in the morning, the north wall of the stairwell. Another sign of things to come: on the thirtieth, at breakfast at the south end of the dining room table, I feel the first warmth on my right arm as I face east. The September/October passage of the sun between the unnook and the dining room table is in progress; soon Cathy and I will be exiled to the north end of the table as the sun establishes hegemony over its southerly half.

The liturgical year of Catholicism in Year C is winding down as well this fall, as the priest at Sunday mass proclaims the Gospel from St. Luke. For those unfamiliar with this framework, a number of churches of Christendom rotate the Gospels on a three-year cycle wherein they read through one for an entire year in installments at Sunday services as the basis for sermons and homilies, Cycle A being devoted to Matthew; Cycle B, Mark; Cycle C, Luke. The Gospel of John is inserted partially in Cycle B—Mark being a very short narrative—and is used at some of the highest holy days, such as Good Friday. The final weeks of the liturgical year, which ends most often on the last Sunday of November, usually contains passages related to the last incidents and stories of Jesus before His passion. In Cycle C, these include some of His most memorable parables, especially the one many regard as the greatest of them all—the Prodigal Son—almost always read in September.

Years ago when I was studying theology, I came across an article that urged students of scripture not to overanalyze parables but instead submit to "being parabled." What the author meant I can illustrate with reference to the incident in Jesus's ministry known as the "woman caught in adultery," recorded in the Gospel of John and on which my seminary faculty advisor, a venerable Jesuit priest, once delivered a memorable homily. In his meditation, my advisor appealed to his listeners to enter this story, to become part of it: were they like Jesus, inclined to forgive; were they like the woman, in need of forgiveness; or were they like the scribes and Pharisees, anxious to condemn? This is exactly what being parabled means, and one can see the possibilities for ourselves across the whole gamut of Jesus's stories. Are we wise or foolish virgins, sheep or goats, Lazarus or the rich man?

The story of the prodigal son fits well into this framework and has a correlative, threefold focus to the incident of the adulterous woman for our consideration: there is the beneficent, forgiving father; the erring, dissolute son; and the dutiful but resentful older brother. Which one are we? But there is something more about this story with which to grapple. For some exegetes who have tried to grasp Jesus's intentions in this narrative, there is some sentiment that the older brother, who apparently never gave his father a moment's trouble, is, due to his implacable disdain for, and unforgiving attitude toward, his younger brother, more blameworthy than the latter, who was guilty of manifold sins of moral turpitude and wasteful living. Even C. S. Lewis gets into act, having his more experienced devil in *The Screwtape Letters* advise the apprentice devil always to remember the elder brother in Jesus's story.

Why is the older brother cast in the role of the villain? Perhaps it is because the younger brother has come to his senses and seeks forgiveness, while the older brother appears to remain frozen in anger. There is almost an exact parallel here to another Lucan parable—the Pharisee and the Publican—where the former lives a seemingly upright life but is proud of it, and the latter is a sinner but knows it and begs forgiveness. The publican rather than the Pharisee receives Jesus's approval. In both cases, the apparently righteous one is ignorant of the fact that, no matter what our moral record in life, we all fall short and have no business looking down on anyone.

With this as a basis, I have decided to be parabled with the story of the prodigal son, though I suspect the author of the above-noted article would be taken aback by the results. My version of this process is not to identify with the characters in turn but to ask a series of questions of the story. The result, as described below, is to offer an encomium to the older brother consisting of one and a half cheers, a numerical assessment that recalls the 1978 book by Irving Kristol titled *Two Cheers for Capitalism*. At the time of the writing of the book, Kristol was a prominent neoconservative—that is, a former leftist who had become disillusioned with bloated government and top-down solutions to economic and political problems and was giving free markets and limited government a second look. The title of his book—two cheers rather than the customary three—equated to an approval with reservations and quickly elicited a public debate and written responses with analogous titles such as "Three Cheers ..." or even "Four Cheers ...". The phrase *two cheers* thus entered the public domain as shorthand for a qualified endorsement of anything.

My praise for the older brother in the parable is an even more qualified endorsement because it goes against the grain of the story offered to us by none other than the Founder of my own religion. If Jesus is telling me in the parables titled the Prodigal Son and the Pharisee and the Publican that refusal to forgive, condescension, disdain, and resentment are more deadly sins than riotous living or collecting onerous taxes for a foreign authority, which nevertheless give rise to repentance, then perhaps I'd better listen. And asking the questions I am about to pose amounts, according to experienced exegetes and biblical theologians, to a misunderstanding of this kind of storytelling that typically does not probe characters but uses them one-dimensionally to make a single salient point. But, hey, when you are parabled, anything can happen.

My summation questions for the parable of the prodigal son are these: Is the older brother really so bad? Who would you like better as a neighbor—a person who could not control his appetites and had wild parties every weekend or a tight-lipped prig who, at the same time, kept his lawn mowed, paid his taxes, and went to work on time every day? Who is to be emulated—the hardworking, rule-obeying citizen who finds it difficult to forgive or the wastrel and debauchee who tardily comes to his senses? Can the world in fact function without older brothers, even if their condescension is hard to take?

As noted, Irving Kristol offered two cheers for capitalism; sometimes I reflect on whether, in rendering one and a half cheers to the older brother, an uncomplaining, nose-to-the-grindstone type, I am actually endorsing a capitalist or, at least, a middle-class striver. Since in everything from poetry to social science analysis, the distinction is often made between rich and poor, haves and have-nots, first world and third, that would cast the younger brother in the role of or as a symbol of the poor—which does not exactly fit, since the younger brother's troubles are the result of his own unwisdom and imprudence, while many of the poor of this world have little choice about the contours of their lives and are trapped in poverty by systemic social and political forces. Put in a more generalized form, the older brother is the one who is self-sufficient and successful in life; the younger brother is the one who needs help. How does Christianity, especially its Roman Catholic version, look upon the two?

The present occupant of the see of Peter, Pope Francis, has made several statements that appear to be less than enthusiastic, to put it mildly, about capitalism and free markets—the pathway that so many have used to achieve success. On the other hand, one of his recent predecessors, Pope John Paul II, in his encyclical *Centissimus Annus*, appeared to give a restrained approval to the capitalist system while being careful to condemn its excesses. Rolling these views into one might yield something slightly less than one cheer for capitalism. As for the poor of the world, the other pole of our comparison, the Christian religion seems to have its arms wide open: Pope Francis has in fact called for the church to be a church for the poor; and there are many theological constructions in the last fifty years that have approved of liberation for the oppressed or a so-called preferential option for the poor. None of this bodes well for the older brother.

It gets even worse for the capitalist / middle-class striver / older brother when one turns from the teachings of popes and theologians down through the ages to the attitudes and statements of the Founder of the religion Himself. There can be no doubt that in His historical existence, Jesus loved and cared for the poor, the unfortunate, and the outcast and indicated that they were objects of God's special favor. The episodes are too numerous to mention. Likewise in his teaching, there are redundant warnings about the perils of riches and the necessity to relieve the poor. This seems to me to be God speaking to us in no uncertain terms—to us, that is, who have resources and are called upon, no, compelled in conscience, to share sacrificially with those who have less and much less.

The means, manner, and timing of this sacrificial sharing is another question altogether: I simply mean by this that, when we account for the distinctive features of Jesus's teaching—His habitual use of surprise, hyperbole, and the reversal of conventional wisdom—it is difficult indeed to infer His specific instructions, in many cases, about how to implement our service to the poor. Another layer of difficulty confronts us when we consider the limitations on His human consciousness as a consequence of the self-emptying implicit in the mystery of the Incarnation—if, that is, one is willing to consider that He experienced such a radical kenosis as is suggested previously in chapter 1. To illustrate the dilemmas hinted at, I offer for consideration another moral imperative that Jesus enjoins upon His followers: care and concern for the incarcerated. Many prison ministers of various denominations, clergy and lay, have appealed to Matthew 25:36 ("I was in prison and you visited me") to justify inmate advocacy, sentence reduction. and, as one such minister had it, the "recycling of human beings." My question is, Could the Jesus of His cultural horizon imagine a modern legal and penal system such as ours with constitutional guarantees, endless appeal processes, plea bargains, and work-release programs—this instead of what prevailed in a remote province of the Roman Empire in the first century where unfortunates could be thrown into airless dungeons at the whim of petty tyrants, never to be heard from again? Again, that it is God speaking to us in the moral injunction of Matthew 25:36, I have no doubt, but a belief in a kenotic Jesus means that no single format can be stipulated with finality for ministerial praxis.

The same dilemma, I submit, attends Jesus's many commands to care for the poor. In Galilee and Judaea of the first century AD, poverty was not just a lack of the material goods of human life; it was a caste, a status in life in perpetuity, a prison with no way out. Truly, in this historical milieu, the poor, as Jesus said, were always with us. But what would the human Jesus say if He knew of societies where socioeconomic classes were fluid; where the impoverished at least had the chance to rise through hard work, available education, and (I am almost afraid to say it) a kind of worldly ambition; and where government was more responsive to the popular will, and advocates for the poor could succeed in enacting programs of income redistribution and the weaving of social safety nets? I am not qualified to answer; it is a question for professional biblical theologians but, to my mind, one well worth asking.

I have strayed off topic. To get back to what I am struggling with, I refer to the aforementioned Catholic philosopher Michael Novak, who, in his book *The Spirit of Democratic Capitalism*, entered the discussion alluded to above about the compatibility/noncompatibility of capitalism with the Christian religion. The book is an extended argument that a market economy, a polity guaranteeing rights and liberty, and a system of cultural institutions that promotes justice and the dignity of the human person affords the best chance for human flourishing and is hence much more than minimally in harmony with Christian values. But that is not what concerns me; it is rather Novak's incisive argument that the middle class has no literature lauding its essential character as there is for kings, warriors, aristocrats, and even the poor. Rather, it is the object of ridicule and mockery. This gets me back to the older brother, to the extent he is seen as a middle-class striver, and to the issue that Novak has broached, with perhaps a slightly different twist. How does God regard the middle-class person—an individual with means, blessings, and sufficient worldly goods? I fear saying it, but the cumulative effect of reading the Gospel parables, papal encyclicals and other statements, and the writings of some modern theologians is almost to wish that one were poor, if only to change the face of God from a frown to a smile.

And that is why I love the parable of the prodigal son, especially under its allegorical modality in which the father represents God. On this reading, we are all younger sons, in need of forgiveness and happily astonished at the depths of God's forgiving love. But under this framework, we also learn, I suggest, something new about the older brother, the patron saint of the middle class—that is, the middle class consisting of persons with worldly goods and opportunities, homeowners who sacrifice to give their children a better life, not perfect and subject to failure, at the same time not being unmindful of the poor but seeing to their care through the volunteering of time and the giving of treasure. The father as a symbol of God is right to appeal to the older son—as he appeals to us—to be more gracious and forgiving, the aspect of their relationship that has received the most ink from commentators down through the ages. What is sometimes lost is that he prefaces his entreaty with a remark that is not associated with similar characters in other parables—the rich man in the parable of the rich man and Lazarus or the Pharisee in the Pharisee and the Publican. He says to the older son, "You are always with me and all that I have is yours." By my lights, the development of a theology of middle-class self-esteem could begin right there.

CHAPTER 11

OCTOBER

The Fall of "Man"

What is man that thou art mindful of him?
—Psalm 8:4a (KJV)

October is the apotheosis of New England, the time of year when New England realizes its true self. Leaf peepers come from far and wide to take in the glory of the maples and other trees as their foliage flames out in blazes of color. Locals such as Cathy and I also make sure not to miss out; together with my sister Barbara and her husband, Norm, we have for years taken October weekend excursions to northern or western New England, primarily to Vermont, where we have sampled bed-and-breakfast establishments from Bennington to Montgomery Center. One year, as an exception, we stayed in Lenox, Massachusetts, and enjoyed what may have been our greatest foliage ride on the way to Hyde Park, New York. There we visited the Franklin D. Roosevelt home and museum and discovered, much to our joy, that the attached research library had a copy of Norman's doctoral dissertation on diplomatic relations between the US and Argentina during World War II.

The science fiction writer Ray Bradbury once compared October to a country where the hills are fog and the rivers mist; where noons go quickly and twilights linger; where it is always turning late in the year. The sense that it is late in the year afflicts me now, despite the vivid colors of the leaves. On the eighth, I noticed that the rising sun through the northeast skylight now casts light onto the north wall and entirely misses the bookcases in the reading area. There is a corresponding bookcase on the other side of the wall—that is, the east wall of the upstairs den—where at 5:15 p.m. on October 11, I noted that the light of the setting sun through the northwest skylight also completely cleared the bookcase northerly. When the sun is hitting north, that means it has traveled south and is ebbing in its power to banish melancholia from residents of the Northern Hemisphere.

On the other hand, I was utterly astonished on the twenty-eighth to notice the return of the burning bush of the northeast staircase, albeit in its late-season, reduced-intensity version. The facilitator here was the west-wall octagonal window, through which at 3:25 p.m. the sun shot a beam across the living room onto Cathy's house plant. Speaking of octagonal windows, I have written little in these pages of the other larger one in the south wall immediately west of the box bow window. At this time of year, due to the juxtaposition of the two windows, the dining room is bathed in low-declination sunlight from midmorning till well past noon.

As October is still good walking weather—maybe the best— Cathy and I continue our strolls to church. But on a walk back from mass of a recent October Sabbath, I was in something of a foul mood due to a hymn we had sung, the substitution of words in it and the reason for the substitution ... which brings me to the subject of this chapter—the movement for gender-neutral usage for nouns and pronouns and its consequences for human communication. But first, full disclosure: with regard to the concept of a plurality of genders and their so-called social construction, I am both fearfully ignorant and perhaps a little skeptical; for the purposes of this essay, I assume that there are two genders—male and female—and wish to explore the issue of whether the human community should continue to use male-denominated nouns such as *man* and *mankind*, along with the pronoun correlative *he*, as a synecdoche for the whole human race.

The answer is a qualified no; that is, I am all for using *humanity, human person,* or *person* rather than *man* in speaking and writing. To me, such a policy symbolizes a positive change in recent decades involving the emergence of women into a fuller partnership with men in the life of the world—one that was heretofore unavailable to the them—where now they may pursue, alongside their male counterparts, all the nongender-based callings of the human community: law, medicine, plumbing, carpentry. Moreover, I believe all males should cultivate an empathy with women for the loss, which may be incalculable, of appearing to be excluded linguistically from meaning networks using masculine-accented terminology. As men, we simply cannot know what that feels like. On the other hand, the recent and current regime of plenary exclusion of male-denominated language has a *1984* (i.e., Orwellian) resonance. When I see such substitutions effected wholesale, I think of Winston Smith rewriting all those past newspaper articles to conform to present policies. The insistence on such changes, heedless of their artificiality and awkwardness, suggests to me a diktat from a Ministry of Political Correctness or, in the argot of Oceania, MiniPoliCor. By my lights, the world community should pursue the goal of a gender-neutral language, as stated, but marked by reasonable qualifications.

And that is the nub of the issue with regard to the hymn we had sung recently in church, "I Am the Bread of Life." The lyrics are drawn from the Bread of Life discourse in John, chapter 6, especially of verse 44, which in most translations has Jesus saying, "No one can come to me unless the Father who sent me draw him; and I will raise him up at the last day." The lyrics of the gender-sanitized hymn, based on the biblical passage, is sung thusly: "No one can come to me unless the Father beckons; and I will raise you up on the last day."

As can be seen, from the priority of gender neutrality, we have the problem of the two hims in the biblical text. The lyricist deals with the second of these by an unforgivably awkward, grammatically inconsistent sudden shift to the second person *you* from the third person *him* based on the antecedent *no one*. That is bad enough. But the hymn writer deals with the first *him* by substituting *beckons* for *draw him* and thereby elicits my first qualification to the program of gender-neutralizing language: ungendered terminology must not render the original thought or term as something significantly different or less than that of the original; that is, it must not mislead or fail to convey the fullness of the text as received.

I consulted six English translations of the Bible, admittedly published before the age of concern with gender-neutral language. All translate the verse with "draw him." The Greek word in question is a derivative of *elko* ("draw"), which has a variety of meanings (e.g., to draw a sword) but in the context of the verse means "to attract," one of the synonyms given. My Greek dictionary adds a further refinement: It reads "to attract, especially as of a magnet." The question before the house then is as follows: is *beckon* a nonmisleading, equivalent-meaning holder to *draw*? In my view, the answer is most emphatically no.

Consider the following two uses of *beckon*:

> After the student threw the paper airplane across the room, the teacher, with a wagging finger, beckoned him to the front of the class and, after scolding him, sent him to the principal's office.

and

He had always loved sailing but had only dabbled in it due to the time limits imposed by a demanding career; but now that he had taken an early retirement, this most beloved avocation beckoned again.

Let us stipulate that *beckon* and *draw* are not utterly dissimilar; both have the sense of *attract*. The problem is that *draw* is a much richer verb than *beckon*. In almost all uses of the word *beckon*, the beckonee is fully aware of the entity summoning him in a certain direction; with *draw*, that is not always the case. In the more esoteric sense of draw, the person is pulled in a direction that may not be completely clear to him or her. This is the arena of God as a still, small voice; of the God who prompts rather than demands; of the Divine One whom the drawee sees only fleetingly, out of the corner of his eye; of the implicit rather than the explicit; of the beguiling, half-heard music rather than the fortissimo anthem. (A good example of a person being drawn to God in this sense, of being slowly reeled in rather than summoned, can be found in C. S. Lewis's autobiography, *Surprised by Joy.*)

My contention is that all these possibilities, in play with the use of *draw*, are emptied out with the substitution of *beckon*. If the literature in question were a training manual, it might not make a difference, but since we are dealing with a sacred text and matters of the spirit, the decision for *beckon* is disastrous. My conversation partners on the other side of the issue might say that it is justified by the higher imperatives of gender neutrality. Though I recognize the legitimacy of their goals, in cases like this, I cannot agree.

The second qualification stems from my belief that human life at its highest—and when we are in the arena of spirituality and holy writ, we are in these higher realms—is a prose story constantly endeavoring to become a poem. Poetry extracts out of human activity precisely what is eternal, what we are ultimately in search of. Hence, in matters of literature, especially of this kind, protecting the poetic must win out over all other considerations.

An illustration: In Acts, chapter 16, Paul and Silas are in Philippi, where they are thrown into prison by magistrates who charge the jailer to guard them most carefully. The jailer accordingly commits them to what almost all translations render as an *inner prison*. Much to my surprise, a Bible I was once using translates the same as *maximum security*. I was immediately put off by the use of such an anachronistic, insipid, utterly prosaic term from modern penology. It simply doesn't belong there; what is wanted is *inner prison*, with its poetic and metaphorical power, addressing not just the situation of Paul and Silas but that of the jailer himself.

As another example, I ask the reader to turn his or her attention to the English word *ghost*. When I was young, the term *Holy Ghost*, used to designate the third person of the Trinity, was a commonplace. Then, over my lifetime, a replacement term *Holy Spirit* seemed to be preferred. It may have been that the word *spirit* was a more faithful translation of the Greek *pneuma* from the New Testament or that *ghost* in English was less than useful as a divine denominator because of its terrifying, Halloween-related meaning or even its comic overtones (think *Caspar, the Friendly Ghost*). For the sake of this argument, the historical background does not matter; let us stipulate that the word *spirit* is the preferred and correct term to use when referring to the third person of the Trinity. What are we to do then with the musical setting of the Old Hundredth psalm, using the alternative lyrics that are sung in many churches of Christendom as a doxology, as follows: Praise God from whom all blessings flow/Praise Him all creatures here below/Praise Him above ye heavenly host/Praise Father, Son, and Holy … Spirit? Of course not. We use *ghost* because, though outmoded, it has a recognizable historical usage pedigree and, most importantly, *the poetry demands it!*

Similarly, sometimes the words *man* and *mankind*, as opposed to, say, *humanity*, feel better, fit better poetically, like a key to a lock that opens the door to meaning in all its resonances. An example is found in the biblical verse that heads this chapter, the terse, monosyllabic *man* and *him* posing the question starkly to the reader, where "What is/are humanity / human persons that Thou art mindful of it/them?" is, in either case, both more awkward and less poetic. However, just as valid is the fact that *humanity* on other occasions is to be preferred. President Franklin Roosevelt took to radio during the D-Day operation in 1944 to offer a prayer for its success, stipulating as the last of several purposes for the operation "to set free a suffering humanity." (A necessary excursus here: can you imagine a president today leading the nation in a nondenominational prayer? We are now light-years away from what in historical terms is essentially the day before yesterday.) The multisyllabic *humanity* seems to fit the bill here better than *mankind*, as it does in this musically rhythmic line from Longfellow's poem on the American republic: "Humanity with all its fears, with all the hopes of future years …"

Of course the argument will rage on, and persons can agree or disagree with the qualifications set forth above, but for me, and to repeat, the good to be accomplished by the use of gender-neutral language must not be at the expense of accuracy in the delivery of meaning or in the sacrifice of the poetic.

Before ending the discussion, mention must be made of a related and perhaps more profound issue for people of religious faith: the gender of God. The good news for all combatants on this issue is that God transcends gender; the bad news is that transcending gender is not the same thing as lacking one altogether. That is because gender is a perfection, a characteristic of higher forms of life, and when deploying metaphorical language for God, we must always aim higher. Sometimes a particular religion wishes to aim so high that it attempts to match the above-noted transcendence of gender in its tenets by refusing to use metaphorical language. It is well known that some religions of the East, particularly Hinduism, favor the concept of God without attributes, believing that any descriptive language constitutes a diminishment of the deity. A noteworthy example of this can be found in the Hindu scripture the Brihadaranyaka Upanishad, where the writer states that, when approaching the divine, there is no higher teaching than "no, no." This idea that no words are better than any when thinking about God is not entirely absent from the West, which in general has put a stronger emphasis on the idea of God as a person. Frederick Copleston, in his magisterial and comprehensive history of philosophy, notes that the Neoplatonic philosopher Plotinus (AD 205–270) was unwilling to ascribe to God any positive attributes, no duality of substance and accident, insisting on the mantra "neither 'this' nor 'not this.'" A similar trend in the West is the theology associated with the so-called *via negativa.*

On the other hand, as philosopher of religion John Hick has noted in his book *Death and Eternal Life,* even some strains of Hinduism conceive of God as a person, a Bhagavan, as the perennial adoration of the divine incarnation Krishna demonstrates. Such observations prompt the aforementioned Roger Scruton to aver that even the most abstract religion attributes a gender to God (*Desire,* p. 274). It might be better to say that the idea of God as a person, and hence regarded as having a gender for conceptualization purposes, is not entirely absent from any major religion, even the most abstract. In most cases, and especially in the West, the choice of a divine gender has been male. Is there anything that can be done about this from the point of view of achieving some kind of gender neutrality in thinking and writing?

From one point of view, there seems to be little room for change. For some, perhaps not all, of those who are strong advocates of gender neutrality, gender itself is a mere functional placeholder, there being no difference in the sexes for nearly the entire range of human enterprise. But there is another view, which holds in matters of the spirit and other areas as well: gender is a mysterious esoteric reality of which individual males and females are pale reflections. On this view, gender matters in ways that cannot be fully understood in the here and now, as we see in a number of languages that attribute gender to animate and inanimate nouns. Scruton goes so far as to say that the inability to see that masculine and feminine reaches through all nature amounts to an impoverishment of perception (*Desire*, p. 273). In this way of thinking, the choice of a gender for God is largely nonarbitrary.

A second obstacle to the project of degenderizing a religion is the importance of tradition in most faiths. A religion does not belong to some but all of its adherents, *all* referring not only to the worldwide community of the faithful at any given time but to the dead of millennia who worshiped in the same way. For this way of thinking, it is repugnant to affront those for whom in ages past words and concepts translated to devotion, moral heroism, and even martyrdom by ransacking holy writ to sanitize passages that were not just read but lived out.

But I believe there is hope for those in the gender neutrality community who are disappointed by such strictures where they are held. If it is true that gender refers to something deep within the divine comedy that is human history, it is also true that at some time and in some way, it is also set aside. St. Paul's assertion that in Christ there is no male or female is not a bromide but an article of faith. And, it bears repeating, God *transcends* gender. Second, as referenced in chapter 1, my view is that dogmas are less like prisons than they are like homes with rooms to explore. For instance, sometimes I reflect on the Trinity in the following terms: First Person, Unattributable Oneness; Second Person, male expression; Third Person, female expression. I like this framework because it preserves the idea of a God without attributes and, at the same time, gives due regard to maleness and femaleness as coordinating aspects of a fundamental reality with no subordination. Is this a heresy? I do not know, but, in a sense, it does not matter, since it is a personal departure that I hold only as a fleeting image under correction and would never seek to impose on anyone. When I am worshiping with my faith community, I respond as my brothers and sisters, using the nomenclature of the received tradition.

Then there is the novel *The Shack* (later made into a movie) written by Canadian author William P. Young, the son of Christian missionaries. What follows is in no way an endorsement of the book; it has received both praise and criticism, and I am severely equivocal about it. Without giving too much away of the story, a father, the protagonist, suffers the loss of his daughter on a camping trip, where she is abducted, raped, and killed. In the aftermath, he struggles with his faith over a period of time, when one day he receives a mysterious letter inviting him to a small shack in the same woods where some of his daughter's clothes were found during the investigation of her kidnapping. When he arrives there, the shack is transformed into a dwelling, and he meets all three persons of the Trinity! Much of the rest of the book is devoted to his conversations with said personages.

Who are the persons he meets? The first person of the Trinity appears as an African American housekeeper and cook; the second person is a Middle Eastern–looking man wearing a tool belt (get it?); the third person appears as an Oriental women who has charge of the garden outside, over which she flits and hovers (get it, part 2?). (I hope the reader will pardon this digression. There is one scene where the protagonist and the Middle Eastern man are lying on a dock at night, looking up at the sky, when the latter remarks about how much he enjoys gazing at the stars— that is, the incarnate Son of God, with respect to His human nature, expressing a preference for certain things as contrasted with all things, which, with respect to His divine nature, He has created. To me, there is a wealth of Christological meditation and speculation embedded in this incident, along the lines suggested in chapter 1.) The point? The author has let his imagination run wild with regard to the dogma of the Trinity. Good for him! But this is not a worship service; it is not a rewriting of the Bible.

In this matter, I cannot speak for other faith traditions, nor can I speak with authority for my own (Christianity), but I believe that the above analysis yields reasonable parameters for the contemplation of the deity: exploring alternative terminologies and understandings of the mystery of the divine precisely because it transcends any and all methods of human communication and, at the same time, and at all times, honoring those received terminologies and understandings that have incarnated a sacred tradition, belonging not to some but to all the faithful across the ages.

CHAPTER 12
NOVEMBER

The Joy of Sacred Doublethink

He that is not against us is for us.
—Luke 9:50 (KJV)

Needless to say, now that the sun has moved more than halfway south from the autumnal equinox to the winter solstice, some of our perceptions of solar reflectivity within the house that were oncoming as fall progressed are now firmly settled and will be for some months to come. For instance, I now have no fear of using the chair in the upstairs reading area at any time—the sun being confined to the north wall of the staircase and a mere needle of light, rather than the usual parallelogram, as I noted at 9:55 a.m. on November 6. And, of course, Cathy and I are exiled to the north end of the dining room table for Saturday-morning breakfasts, our customary late-fall and winter station.

The sun is now so far south that—as I noted at 1:00 p.m., also on November 6—it projects light through the west-wall octagonal window onto the couch downstairs at the northern extremity of the house, where it will remain in early afternoon all through December. On the eleventh at 3:00 p.m., I noticed that in the upstairs master bedroom (southwest corner of the house), the sun was back again on the east wall north of the bed. On the twenty-eighth, just after noon, I observed the sun bathing the kitchen floor in light through the box bow window, courtesy of a low arc of travel and the now bare yellow maple in the backyard.

Two thoughts occur to me about this season of the sun's journey. One is the fact that, paradoxically, the sun invades the house more insistently at the very time that it is at its weakest with respect to the Northern Hemisphere. That is because its low declination allows it to shine through windows during most of the day, whereas, in spring and summer, its midday transit takes it over the roof. Indeed, a cursory glance through my solar log shows a relative dearth of entries for midday from about the middle of April to the end of August, while there are many for the other months. Still, if there is more house sun quantitatively in November, it is the very definition of *muted*, with a melancholy-inducing wanness.

The other reflection relates to what I call *Golden November*. To me, afternoon sunlight is golden in hue and aura when a combination of favorable circumstances obtain: the sun is at a lower declination, and the air is cooler and less encumbered by water vapor. In New England, we have a name for this phenomenon: October. But while October in New England receives all the attention when discussing such matters, I would claim that what I refer to as *goldenness* reaches its apotheosis in the first two weeks of November. That is because yellow maples tend to hold on to their leaves longer than other trees, and in November, with no rival colors remaining, sunlight and maple make for an aesthetically transforming experience of the purest of gold.

In the ritual of the Catholic faith, November is primarily about endings: the end of the liturgical year and the end of life as underscored by the celebration of All Saints' Day and All Souls' Day. When glancing over the calendar of what is known as the sanctoral cycle—that is, the list of saints' and feast days celebrated by Catholics throughout the year—another one in November caught my eye, the Feast of the Dedication of the Vatican Basilica in AD 324 (celebrated on November 9). With all the personages and events in the history of Christianity, the church still saw fit to mark off a day to celebrate the beginnings of *one* church—albeit the pope's own, St. John's Lateran—among the tens of thousands that exist in the world.

It got me to thinking of a phenomenon that I call Catholic "subdividability." I once gave a talk called "Catholicism by the Numbers" (fourteen stations of the cross; seven sacraments, seven deadly sins, five wounds of Christ—that sort of thing). The Catholic religion is replete with highways and byways down which a believer can travel and separate devotions in which he or she can become consumed—the Sacred Heart, Padre Pio, the Shroud of Turin, to name but a few. To incipient Protestants of the sixteenth century, the sheer weight of these subdividables, this religious paraphernalia, if you will, was crushing; and they affirmed, not without some justification, that it got in the way of the basic message that Christians were called to propose to the world. On the other hand, there were and are many, among whom I number myself, who, within limits, kind of enjoy it.

In any case, a religion with so many facets that direct one's attention inward, paradoxically, raises for me the question of the world's other religions with their own packages of subdividables—an issue to which I now direct the reader's attention, as promised in chapter 2. The question I wish to consider at some length is how one holds to a received faith tradition—that is, one's own denomination—which in some sense has pretensions to definitiveness over the identity of the One who lies behind/within the universe, therefore animating it, and with regard to the ultimate destiny of the human community and at the same time account for religious systems other than one's own that make competing claims in these very same matters.

Before proceeding, I must make my readers aware of the tools that I will use in attempting to find some personal clarity in this issue. They include two limiting conditions, a paradigm, a metaphor, a dichotomy, a "baptized" Orwellian construct, and a cautionary note.

As noted in chapter 2, I converted from Protestantism to Catholicism at a young age. With respect to the religions of the world, I consider that transition as akin to a puddle jump. Though I write as a Catholic Christian, I regard Protestantism, Catholicism, Anglicanism, and Eastern Orthodoxy as part of one revelation system to be compared as a whole to the other religions of the world. Thus the first limiting condition. The second concerns the concept *religions of the world*. The world, in its long history, has produced thousands of religions; I am an expert on none of them. To allow the discussion to be at all doable, I have concentrated on only the major religions of the globe— that is, those that were founded centuries ago, are still practiced, and have adherents numbering in the millions. For the sake of further practicality, I consider these major religions to be Judaism, Christianity, Islam, Hinduism, Taoism, and Buddhism. (I am aware of the incompleteness of this list—it can't be helped—and that some experts do not consider Buddhism to be a religion per se, or at least an utterly unique one, a taxonomical conundrum discussed by, among others, Huston Smith in his *The Religions of Man*, later renamed *The World's Religions*).

The paradigm I offer is expressed in the rather crude diagram immediately below, with an explanation to follow:

CREED	CULTUS	CODE
I believe in God	I	I
I	I	I
I	I ⟵——————— I ⟶
I	I	I ⟵
I	I	I
v	v	v

The above schema, which I used for years in parish adult education programs, attempts to break down the morphology or component parts of any major religion. I regret to say that I do not know to whom to attribute it, realize that it can be considered more or less applicable depending on the religion in question, and am aware that there are variations on the three Cs noted above (some versions add a fourth C for *Community*). In any case, I have found it useful in the past and relevant to the subject of this essay.

The contention implicit in the diagram is that each of the major religions of the world features a set of assertions about the nature of reality and, most especially, *ultimate* reality, such as are, for example, contained in the Christian Nicene Creed or the Buddhist Four Noble Truths (Creed); have a set of ritual/ceremonies for worship (e.g., Passover meal in Judaism, Catholic mass) that celebrate these truths and/or the primordial events of the founding of the religion in question (Cultus); and enjoin on faithful followers a set of moral precepts as standards for membership in the religious community (Code). The diagram invites three further comments, two short and one somewhat longer. First, the vertical dashes and downward arrows simply signify the content under the category that would be filled in relative to the respective religion under consideration and, of course, would vary from faith community to faith community. However, under Creed, I have entered one statement ("I believe in God") for reasons that will become clear at the end of the essay. Second, I have named the second category Cultus when I really meant to use *cult*, referring again to the array of ceremonies and rituals that pertain to a given religious tradition. I found over the years in adult education venues that the word *cult* was so associated with the concept of a small secretive religious sect that used various forms of coercion on its members that it was stripped of any usefulness to denote its more fundamental meaning referring generically to religious ceremonies and have therefore, to avoid confusion, latinized it.

The longer explanation has to do with the section under Code and the horizontal arrows—one pointing toward the Cultus section, one pointing *outward* from the diagram, and one pointing *toward* the diagram from outside. This refinement in the diagram is my own, so far as I know, and I referred to it tangentially in chapter 2; however, I'm sure others have thought of it long before me. It refers to the inward-facing moral precepts of a religion—that is, those that are enjoined upon followers in support of the rituals of the faith community (arrow pointing from Code section to Cultus section), and the outward, those that transcend the boundaries of the religion itself (arrows pointing beyond the boundaries of a religion and those pointing inward from outside). An example of the former: On Ash Wednesday, Catholics have ashes smeared on their foreheads to symbolize both their mortality and their renunciation of sin (Cultus); on the same day, they are mandated to fast and abstain from meat (Code in support of the Cultus). To understand the other wing of a religion's ethics, I think it is best to offer a hypothetical situation, this time involving the Jewish faith.

In Exodus, chapter 12, there are listed the specifications for the celebration of Passover, including the imperative of eating unleavened bread. Now, imagine a public high school principal who got it in his head to require all students, of whatever religion or no religion, to eat only unleavened bread for lunch during the Passover season, with anyone found with leavened bread subject to detention. Would this be a violation of the establishment clause of the First Amendment to the Constitution? Would he have to field a spate of phone calls from irate parents? Would this incident make the evening news? Place all the answers to these questions under the *yes, definitely* column. Now imagine the same principal confronted by a rash of locker break-ins, with the concomitant loss of students' property and belongings. He instructs the teachers to announce in homeroom that they have several leads as to the identity of the perpetrators and that they will shortly install security cameras on every floor. As a final point, he says, "And I want you to tell the students that stealing is wrong." In Exodus, chapter 20, we read, "Thou shalt not steal." Would anyone accuse the principal of trying to impose biblical Judaism on the student population? Of course not.

This was the point that I tried to forward in chapter 2. Using a similar analytical standpoint, one can say that the Catholic position on, say, abortion is not Catholic in the way that the Rosary is Catholic. It, like the proscription against stealing, is based on legitimate, if disputed, inferences from the principle of the dignity of the human person—in this case of preborn infants—that transcend the teaching of any one religion. Thus, a given religion offers these moral precepts to the world at large and is edified by receiving similar precepts from other faiths; its moral standards for participation in the Cultus, by contrast, are kept *within* the borders of the individual religious community. The failure to honor the distinction between inward- and outward-facing moral norms of a faith community has greatly hampered the discussion of the legitimate role of religion in the public square under our constitutional order; and, as I hope to show, understanding this distinction is necessary to arrive at a balance between faithfulness to one's own religious tradition and respect for religions that are not one's own. (For a useful list of outward-facing moral norms, see the appendix to C. S. Lewis's *The Abolition of Man*.)

To recapitulate the list of analytical tools thus far, I have offered two limiting conditions and a paradigm. Now, in quick succession, I advance for consideration the metaphor, the dichotomy, and the borrowed Orwellian concept. In my graduate studies, I for a time was researching sources related to the borderland between theology and political theory and came across the title of a doctoral dissertation deploying an intriguing metaphor—"A dance along a precipice." For some reason, I didn't note it down and hence lost track of it. Later, I saw it used in other contexts and even discovered a book on international debt by William N. Eskridge that had the term as its title. Thus, if Mr. Eskridge is the originator of the concept, I offer him my thanks and admiration; I, however, wish to deploy it in a setting far from the field of global finance.

In my opinion, true faith in God according to a specific religious tradition, a sensible and sensitive religious belief and practice, involves one inevitably in a dance along a precipice (thus, the metaphor). The religious believers who will not even approach the precipice are those who regard other faith systems with scorn, condescension, or animosity or simply believe that all religions other than their own are inefficacious. There are others who gladly come to the precipice but to jump off, believing that all major religions are basically the same and showing at least a minimal aversion to the custodianship of their own tradition. In my judgment, the faithful who will not approach the precipice are afflicted with an over regard for their own "fromness"; those who jump off, with an over concern for otherness (thus, the dichotomy). In an attempt to baptize Orwellian language for a good purpose, to turn a negative into a positive, I have dubbed the process of holding these two aspects in a creative tension, of actually dancing at the precipice without falling off, *sacred doublethink*.

And finally, the cautionary note. The remainder of this essay will sketch out proposals for the correct proportions of the two wings of sacred doublethink. Along the way, I will likely use or, better, fall into the use of words like *proper* or *sufficient*; I ask readers to give the weight to these adjectives that a book of essays, as opposed to a learned treatise, merits. In addition to those who eschew an approach to the precipice and those who readily jump off, there are believers who wish to dance without falling off, who, nevertheless, have a different calculus of sacred doublethink from my own. What follows is, as they say, what works for me.

Otherness

In my hometown, I used to frequent an interfaith religious bookstore—now out of business—that featured on one of its interior walls a large photograph of Pope John Paul II embracing the Dalai Lama. In the photo, John Paul appeared to whispering in the Dalai Lama's ear. Whatever was he saying?

It should have been something like, "You must believe in Jesus to be saved"—"should have," that is, if you keep in mind the foundational documents of the Christian religion, especially the Pauline corpus of writings; the copious writings of saints and divines down through the centuries; the missionary impulse of Christianity right from the beginning, in which the faithful, clergy and lay, have felt the obligation to bring the Christian story to the four corners of the world; and the peculiarly Christian phenomena of altar calls, deathbed conversions, and emergency baptisms.

Members of Protestant churches, especially in that wing known as evangelical, have been at this for years in churches, under tents, in arenas, and on street corners. For Catholics, it has historically been more a question of bringing the sacraments, especially baptism, to those who had never heard of Jesus, and keeping them within the ambit of grace by administering the sacraments that are repeatable: penance and communion.

However, since the Second Vatican Council and with such recent renewal events as the Charismatic movement, the Protestant emphasis on the message as opposed to the rituals has seeped into Catholic faith and practice in a number of quarters. (A short excursus here: For those unfamiliar with the term, the Second Vatican Council [often called Vatican II] was a meeting of all the world's Catholic bishops with the pope, lasting from 1962 to 1965, and treating of the entire range of Catholic faith and practice, to which it made important changes [e.g., mandating vernacular liturgies] explained in a number of documents that it issued. For Catholics, outside of sacred scripture itself, there is no higher authority than directives emerging from a convocation of the pope with the entire global episcopacy.)

A good example of a Catholic contemporary evangelical effort that is a product of the above-noted trend can be found in *The Urgency of the New Evangelization* (hereinafter *Urgency*), a short book, more accurately described as a tract, by Ralph Martin. Martin, a professor of theology at Sacred Heart Major Seminary in Detroit, has been active in Catholic evangelization efforts related to an entity known as Renewal Ministries for several decades. Except for the passages that are pointedly Roman Catholic, to the bulk of the narrative, its main message, there is almost nothing that a Protestant evangelical would object.

One can encapsulate the thrust of the volume in several points: Martin states that many Catholics believe that wide is the way that leads to eternal life, but scripture teaches just the opposite (*Urgency*, p. 23–24); he notes that the Second Vatican Council teaches that some who haven't heard the Gospel might be saved, but he thinks that this is a narrow eventuality (*Urgency*, p. 26); and Martin asserts that the clear implication of John 3:16 ("For God so loved the world that He gave His only begotten Son that whosoever believes in Him should not perish but have everlasting life") is that *not* believing means perishing (*Urgency*, p. 57). He goes on to state in a manner that would have brought a smile to the face of Jonathan Edwards that we deserve God's wrath (*Urgency*, p. 58). And for good measure, he invokes the writings of the Polish mystic Sister Faustina, to the effect that wrath is coming, and the souls of sinners will be tortured in hell for all eternity (*Urgency*, pp. 62–64).

It is reasonable to assume therefore that, from the point of view of Ralph Martin, John Paul II would have been derelict if he said anything to the Dalai Lama other than "You must believe in Jesus to be saved." And it would appear that, for Martin and others of his ilk, John Paul had something approximating a pontifical senior moment when in 1986 he invited representatives of the major religions of the world to Assisi to pray *with* him for peace—this, instead of warning them of the peril of eternal damnation if they did not convert to Christianity.

Martin says that all who reject Christ's sacrifice will be condemned by God's just decree (*Urgency*, p. 85). In the light of this assertion, I ask the reader to consider the following hypothetical situation, which, in my view, does not greatly tax the imagination. Christianity—including Catholic Christianity— has had a presence in India for centuries. Now consider two contemporary young men from that country—one Catholic, one Hindu—who have been friends for years, who are both studying to be engineers at a local polytechnic institute, and who are more serious than the average person about their respective religions. The Catholic invites the Hindu to his parish church for a series of talks explaining the Christian religion and inviting, at its end, all inquirers who are so motivated to receive the sacraments of initiation. At the conclusion, the Hindu tells the Catholic that, while he is attracted, even, at times, moved, by the Christian story, he is more comfortable with his native Hinduism and will not convert.

For Martin, such a person, whose decision cannot be otherwise characterized than a "rejection of Christ's sacrifice," is to be condemned. But is this in any way fair? If Christ's sacrifice must be accepted by anyone who wants to be saved and gain eternal life, then people in the West have an enormous advantage over those in the rest of the world whose cultural and religious patrimonies take them in a different direction. This is not a problem for Calvinist Christians who believe that all humankind is totally depraved and unspeakably evil, and the fact that God saves any at all, even if their salvation is a result of unconditional election, is a sign of His infinite mercy. Ralph Martin is a Catholic, not a Calvinist, but he sounds like the latter, and an enthusiastic one at that, when he avers that God's wrath is deserved and is coming (*Urgency*, pp. 59, 62–63).

I fully confess that all this makes me depressed, but an argument can be made that there is no way out. As noted above, supporting the case of Ralph Martin and my evangelical Protestant brothers and sisters are dozens, if not hundreds, of scripture verses attesting to the necessity of believing in Jesus to be saved. How all these passages are to be explained away in the service of a wider amplitude of God's saving action, I do not know. But it must be done. As has been my practice previously in this volume, I, perhaps unfairly, leave the task to the professional theologians.

Why do I say it must be done? In the first place, there is my intuition that the God we meet in Jesus the Christ does not operate thusly. Evangelists like Martin might comment that to be a Christian believer is not to be a judge of holy things, including scripture, but to subject oneself, intuition and all, to them. However, it has taken me a lifetime to learn to trust my spiritual instincts and to regard my intuition not as an obstacle to faith but as an integral component of it. I will not surrender on this point. Second, there is the behavior of John Paul II cited above, which appears to be totally out of compliance with the Martin program. And third, there is the Declaration on Non-Christian Religions of the Second Vatican Council. In that document, the council fathers exhorted Catholics to engage in dialogue and collaboration (I ask the reader to remember these two nouns) with followers of other religions and to preserve and promote their spiritual and moral goods and stipulated that the Catholic Church rejects nothing that is true in these other religions but looks upon them with sincere respect. Can any of these directives to the faithful be mined for the urgency that Ralph Martin declares should characterize a Catholic's dealings with persons of other faith traditions? To put it bluntly, if the council fathers are right in this matter, then Ralph Martin is wrong.

So what is the truth here? Who in the end is right about such weighty matters? For my response—one of a Catholic layman with no authority but his own opinion—I offer for consideration a question I used to pose to expectant parents at baptismal preparation classes: what does Al Pacino as Michael Corleone in *The Godfather, Part I* have in common with Catholic grandmothers? Answer: each of them represents an extreme with regard to the respect that should be paid to the sacrament of baptism.

In an absolutely arresting extended scene in *The Godfather*— one reason, I would claim, that *The Godfather, Part I* is one of the greatest movies ever made—Michael Corleone is participating in the baptismal ceremony as godfather to the son of his brother-in-law, Carlo. While the priest asks him a series of questions as to his fidelity to God and the Christian faith, his henchmen are fanning out over the city of New York and simultaneously murdering his rivals in the mob. The scene conveys a level of depravity and hypocrisy perhaps unrivalled in the history of cinema and leaves me numb and exhausted every time I view it. Conclusion? To vastly understate the case, Michael Corleone does not render to the sacrament of baptism the respect that it merits, at, it must be added, the extreme of disrespect.

To probe the other extreme, I used to ask the attendees at baptismal preparation classes if anyone in their extended families had cautioned them not to take the baby out until it was baptized. Invariably, hands would go up, as participants shared the comments of their grandparents or great-aunts to that effect. Why did older members of their families offer such advice? Because many of these folks received their religious instruction under a paradigm similar to that of Ralph Martin: to wit, the world is perishing the beyond the borders of God's grace, a necessary gateway to the salvific efficacy of which is the sacrament of baptism. Accordingly, taking the baby out unnecessarily risks his/her salvation should the unthinkable (i.e., a fatal accident) befall.

My response to such believers on this point was that God is far greater than the means that any religious system affirms He has explicitly bestowed on humankind to find Him and is not handcuffed by a specific soteriology, however elaborate. (Scene at the gates of heaven, Peter speaks: "Lord, John here just passed away and was never baptized but spent large amounts of his time volunteering in hospitals and working to relieve the sufferings of the poor." "Peter," says the Lord, "you know there is nothing I can do; send him to the other destination.") This is not to diminish baptism; those of us who are Catholic, as well as others, believe that all the sacraments are definitively endowed arenas to encounter God and to which He with love and compassion invites us. But it is a form of spiritual pride, in my judgment, to believe that God is prevented from operating outside the path to redemption a faith community stipulates He has revealed. (And speaking of spiritual pride, I have detected in persons with views similar to those of Ralph Martin—I do not say so of him since I have never met him—a certain delight in their own inclusion among the "saved" and an incipient sentiment of disappointment were they to discover that God is more generous with others not of their creed than they expect Him to be.)

This then, for me, represents the correct building materials for the otherness pole of doublethink and one half of the appropriate choreography for precipice dancing: whatever our beliefs, whatever our evangelical practices, they should not be held or forwarded, respectively, with the notion that a person, simply because he/she believes and wishes to continue in another faith system, is irretrievably lost and beyond God's reach. The Ralph Martins of this world will not approach the precipice; as Jesus is pictured as lamenting in the hymn "Lord of the Dance" (sung to the same tune as the Shaker hymn "Simple Gifts"), they simply will not dance. As I hope to show, there are others who love the precipice but only to jump off—that is, their understanding of the otherness pole of sacred doublethink requires of them more, much more than simply positing that God's grace can be effective outside of a given faith community.

But before proceeding to them and a consideration of the aspect of "fromness," there is one more issue that remains to be addressed. When I was in the seminary, I had a long discussion with a religious brother of a missionary order who had arrived in his thinking at the same point of this essay thus far; that is, it appears that those outside of the Christian faith are not lost after all, the many scripture passages to the contrary notwithstanding. But if that is true, he mused, what is the point of missions, of evangelization, of carrying the story of Christ to the four corners of the world?

A salient question and one that has captured the attention of George Weigel in his book *Evangelical Catholicism,* a kind of manifesto for Catholic self-confidence and a catalog of proposals for top-to-bottom reform of the church. Weigel is a well-known Catholic writer and theologian and the definitive biographer of Pope John Paul II, and his writing in some ways shares the triumphalist tone of Martin but, in my judgment, is far more nuanced. Says Weigel in the matter at hand: For believers, the truth of Christianity is not to be forwarded as one option in a supermarket of religious possibilities but as *the* truth that demands to be shared with everyone.

I agree with Weigel … up to a point. As I suggested in chapter 1 of this book, there is no reason why Christians cannot propose the story of Christ to the world, provided they do it with sufficient sensitivity and discretion. Humankind is pining, afflicted with galactic loneliness, and prone to evil. In the view of Christians, Christ is the medicine for these ills and also the giver of eternal life; believers will naturally want to proclaim His story with love, enthusiasm, and even urgency. But to be at the precipice—the only location for commonsense faith—means to regard such urgency differently from the manner of Ralph Martin and his ilk, for a proper urgency does not admit of those who are not persuaded by the Gospel that they are therefore automatically destined for the infernal regions.

Fromness

It is time now to investigate the other pole of doublethink using the invented word *fromness.* As noted in the previous section, it has been the contention of this essay that, with respect to religion, it is possible to have too much fromness coupled with too little respect for otherness. In this part of the essay, I wish to investigate the dangers of too *little* fromness. But before proceeding, there are two preliminary points for consideration.

The love of fromness in general can be a dangerous inclination, as can be seen from just a cursory glance at the human story: Cosa Nostra, tribalism, racism, ethnocentrism, nationalism, and that peculiarly malevolent species of fromness on steroids—*ein Volk, ein Reich, ein Fuehrer*. It would be understandable if human beings, anxious to avoid the cataclysms of the past hundred years, which gave us global wars, mass crematoria. and concentration camps, sought to ban fromness as a legitimate sentiment forever. That, in my opinion, would be a mistake; for love of the familiar and the close, what I would call the patriotism of small spaces, is both natural and enriching for the human person. Roger Scruton calls this characteristic of our species "oikophilia"—love of place, home, community, country, and tradition. In his book *The Four Loves,* C. S. Lewis notes that, while love of country becomes a demon when it becomes a god (the best short, cautionary note on fromness I have ever seen), he nevertheless avers that differences in national character are to be relished and declares that if the French like café *complet* and the English bacon and eggs, well, more power to both of them. And, as I noted in the prologue, if the play *Our Town* is about the universal village—that is, the universal experience of being human—it is also about a particular village described by the stage manager in a detailed list of etceteras. That is why I must now partially amend comments I made in chapter 5 regarding the ache of particularity, for that is only one hemisphere of our experience of the particular and the singular. The other is the joy of particularity: this field, this woodland, this pond (Thoreau), my home, my family, and finally, my faith.

When the particularity in question is a person's religious faith, we are again faced with the precipice: whether to approach or whether to jump off. As outlined in the previous section, the nonapproachers make the mistake of crafting a grim-faced, unyielding triumphalism of their own religious tradition. Those who readily jump off are, in my view, motivated by a belief in or an attraction to various modalities of syncretism—that is, the notion that all religions are at bottom the same and/or the attempt to blend them, an effort that draws pointed criticism from the aforementioned theologian John McQuarrie. Says McQuarrie: Though all religions teach in some way the impinging of Holy Being upon the being of man, syncretism is impossible (!) for finite historical persons. I would add that this is true because a religion is so much more than a set of assertions about what lies behind/above/within the universe; it is rather a constellation of lived experiences that variously include aromas, music, food, bodily postures, sounds, clothing, vessels, visual art, architecture, relics, writings, and, of course, rituals. In spite of these impediments, the syncretistic preoccupation is alive and well. I have in my files an article from our local metropolitan newspaper's "News of Religion" page (When it had a "News of Religion" page!) showing a pastor of a church in a denomination within the Christian family of churches presiding over a liturgy in celebration of Christmas, Hanukkah, and the winter solstice, featuring sacred objects from all three traditions. By my lights (pardon the pun), this is not a jumping but a diving from the precipice.

What follows is my own evaluative critique of this jumping/diving, but nothing I write in the ensuing pages—and this is my second preliminary point—should be construed as a diminishment or disrespect of religious traditions other than my own or should serve to mask the real appreciation of these communities of faith that I have been mandated to foster by the council fathers of Vatican II. But said appreciation is more than a response to an injunction; I love the other major faith systems of the world: I love their architecture, sacred art, and their history, and I am grateful for the wisdom I have gained from their foundational writings. This love, this affection is, nevertheless, that of an onlooker who delights in another family's celebration; my home is elsewhere.

As noted above, the jumping from the precipice is almost always into a kind of syncretism or what has been described by the aforementioned John Hick approvingly (and in another gratuitous use of a scientific principle in a religious setting) as the Copernican versus the Ptolemaic view of the world's religions. The Copernican view sees the sun as the basic truth common to all religions, while the planets (the different faith traditions) both receive sustenance from it and revolve around it in their separateness. (The Ptolemaic posture, it appears, would apply to persons like Ralph Martin.) Two religious writers who subscribe to the Copernican view more or less are Frithjof Schuon in his *The Transcendent Unity of Religions* (hereinafter *Unity*) and Bede Griffiths in his *The Marriage of East and West* (hereinafter *Marriage*). Schuon (1907–1998) was born in Basel, Switzerland, and spent a good deal of his life traveling and investigating the world's religions, small and large, their singularities and their commonalities. The result was *The Transcendent Unity of Religions* and other books. Bede Griffths, OSB, (1906–1993) was a Benedictine monk and Oxfordian (where he was a student of C. S. Lewis) who later left his monastery in England to travel to India. There he lived in an ashram, immersed himself in Eastern thought, and wrote books on the relationships of the world's religions. The respective books of these two gentlemen, cited above, are fascinating—full of useful information, brilliant comparative analysis, and, most importantly, sufficient nuance. On the other hand, if Schuon and Griffiths are nonsimplistic Copernicans, they are also ardent precipice jumpers.

Schuon's version of Copernicanism is summed up in his theory of religious esoterism and exoterism: esoterism is the depth of religious truth, shared by all faith communities, in which one escapes the particularities of an individual religion; exoterism is keyed to those particularities and adherence to them. It need hardly be said that esoterism is superior and the approved destination of all religious striving. Says Schuon: Esoterism is the truth beyond individual expressions, religions are those expressions (*Unity*, p. 20); the primordial tradition lives in every orthodox form (*Unity*, p. 84); dogmas atrophy when separated from esoterism (*Unity*, p. 9); while it is true that certain religions are adapted to certain collectivities, the contradictions among religions are just appearance (*Unity*, p. 97); and, with reference to Christianity, if one can say the Jesus is God, it is also true that God is not Jesus (*Unity*, p. 28). To be fair, Schuon is, as stated above, nuanced. He admits the possibility of exoterism being of the divine will (*Unity*, p. 17) and declares that the outward dogmatization of religious truth is the foundation of a faith community (*Unity*, p. 3). One gets the impression that, for Schuon, the exoteric experience is an absolutely necessary way station on the journey to the esoteric and is therefore not to be despised; on the other hand, it most definitely exists to be transcended.

And how is this to be accomplished for the millions of adherents of the many faith communities of the Earth? Answer: it is not. That is because esoterism is reserved for an intellectual elite (*Unity*, p. 33). It is in this statement that one perceives the dark underbelly (to adapt the Churchillian metaphor) of Schuon's thinking and that of many other like-minded individuals who labor in the vineyard of comparative religion: spiritual pride and condescension. It is especially unpersuasive to me since throughout my life, and especially during my years in lay ministry, I have made the acquaintance of many persons who, under the Schuonian paradigm, would be adjudged to be operating at the exoteric level and who, nevertheless, practiced and exhibited a spirituality the depth of which could in no wise be doubted.

Another of Schuon's organizing principles, one he shares with Griffiths, is the superiority of the religious East over the West (*Unity*, pp. 82, 104fn). In the case of Griffiths, it appears, East and West are not so much to be married, as the title of his book would imply, as that the former is to take the latter on as a disciple. I confess I find this generalization annoying, and for the same reason, I am put off by Schuon's concept of an intellectual elite. As noted above, I have great respect for the spirituality of the East; on the other hand, I have seen a number of people in my life who dabbled in it or practiced it faddishly in response to the reported doings of movie stars and rock musicians. In this regard, no one should indulge in characterizations of the sort that Schuon and Griffths specialize in; spiritual depth (and for that matter, spiritual superficiality) is not confined to any compass point. In any case, we now turn to the writing of Bede Griffiths on the relationship of the world's religions.

In my first reading of *The Marriage of East and West*, I was all agog as I discovered in its pages a treasure trove of spiritual concepts from the Vedic tradition, the Upanishads, and Buddhism. But that was in part because Griffiths was all agog about India and its religious patrimony (see chapter 1, "The Discovery of India"). Griffiths appears to wave aside the poverty of the Indian people and the difficult conditions of life for many of them, since they live from the unconscious or intuitive (*Marriage*, p. 8)—an orientation he prefers to that of the West's with its Industrial Revolution, which he was led to reject (*Marriage*, p. 39). As noted, he, like Schuon, believes that the West must learn from the East and does not fail to remind his readers of this imperative again and again (*Marriage*, pp. 27, 46, 47, 152, 199). He is passionate about the necessity of the West to reject mind/

matter schizophrenia (*Marriage*, p. 57) and notes that the West is beset by intolerance, which, he claims, does not plague the East (*Marriage*, p. 22). For good measure, he adds that he fears nuclear energy and that a shortage of natural resources by the end of the twentieth century will bring about fundamental changes in living standards (*Marriage*, p. 40). If at times Griffiths scales spiritual heights, at others he descends into a kind of sophomoric analysis of issues outside his expertise.

To be fair, Griffiths lets it be known that both the West and the East have strengths and weaknesses and can be complementary, one to the other. For this reason, his book is replete with dichotomies: rational/intuitive; conscious/unconscious; male/female; mind/matter; active/passive; communicative/receptive. Griffiths sounds like Schuon when he avers that each religion is a face of the truth (*Marriage*, p. 25); but instead of a vertical analysis—esoteric/exoteric—he opts for a horizontal effort across religious lines, looking for commonalities. One to his liking is the concept *Saccidananda* originating in the Upanishads (as David Bentley Hart notes, there are variations in the spelling of this term, another being *Satcitananda*)—an approach to describing ultimate reality that translates into "Being-Consciousness-Bliss" and one that has, for Griffiths, striking similarities to the Christian dogma of the Trinity. In the end, Griffiths would favor a melding of the world's religions—an idea that it appears would be anathema to Schuon. On the other hand, both Schuon and Griffiths, in differing ways, are undoubted Copernicans in their perspectives on the truth of religion.

And, it may be asked, is there anything wrong with religious Copernicanism? After all, it is a kind of doublethink: my religion *and* other faiths, perhaps in a grand synthesis. For me, the answer is yes. I come back to John McQuarrie's comment that such syncretism is impossible for a finite historical being. Religion, whatever else it is, is a way of life, one that, by my lights, cannot be lived encumbered by the bicameral religious consciousness proposed by either Schuon or Griffiths. To illustrate my point, I offer two hypothetical situations, attended, I fully admit, by more than a dash of hyperbole:

Scene 1

A Seder supper. The youngest child asks his father, "Why is this night different from all other nights?" His father, well schooled in comparative religion, replies, "Well, in all honesty, it isn't that different. We have a symbol system by which we celebrate the divinely assisted escape from slavery to freedom, which is in fact another way of conceptualizing the movement from ignorance to enlightenment or death to life—passages that have their correlatives in all the major religions of the world."

Scene 2

A man, a Roman Catholic, is on his deathbed and is prompted to cry out, "Jesus, be with me!" Instead, having read Schuon and Griffiths, he says, "Jesus—although if I were of another faith tradition, I would call upon another avatar of mercy—be with me!"

Over the top? Perhaps. But the point, I believe, survives the exaggeration. What these two examples illustrate is the manner in which I believe Schuon and Griffiths, with differing emphases, go wrong: their failure to cultivate adequate religious fromness.

How can such fromness be properly understood? A good starting point, in my judgment, can be found in the 2010 motion picture *The Way*, starring Martin Sheen. Sheen plays a California doctor whose son (played by his actual son, Emilio Estevez, who also wrote the screenplay and directed the movie) is accidently killed while making a foot journey along the Camino de Santiago in Spain—the ancient pilgrimage trail that extends across the northern coast of Spain from the Pyrenees to the Compostela de Santiago, burial place, tradition dictates, of the apostle James. Sheen travels to Europe to identify and claim the body, has his son's remains cremated, and then decides to make the pilgrimage himself with his son's ashes, along the way meeting and befriending three other pilgrims with whom he has conversations about the beauties and tragedies of human life, among other things.

Neither Sheen's character nor that of his companions could be described as a conventional Catholic. So why are they going to Compestela? In a sense, because it is there; and it is there because there are others, conventional and more than conventional Catholics, who believe in the mystery that surrounds the destination shrine. It is possible to imagine persons who walk the Camino de Santiago for the exercise, and it is also possible to imagine others who, arriving by motorized transport, wish to view Compestela for reasons of tourism that would motivate them to travel, say, to the ruins of Pompeii. But, in my judgment, no one would do the walk as pilgrimage—and this includes nonbelievers and skeptics—if they were not convinced that at its end there was a place deemed holy by others and in whose cultus they wanted to participate, if only from a distance.

Another example. Over about a nine-year period, my brother-in-law Norman and I went on retreat every May to Benedictine and Cistercian monasteries, Catholic and Episcopal, in the New York / New England area, there to observe and participate, as far as possible, in the monks' daily regimen of work and prayer. During free time (other than the Grand Silence), Norm and I would often discuss the world's religions and their connectivities. Also, during periods of silence, I often did readings concerned with the religions of the world. But at the prescribed times for the liturgy of the hours—matins, lauds, vespers, and compline—we would assemble with the monks for prayer using the scriptures from this *one* faith community, in the regulated order laid down by this *one* monastic tradition, and in the sacred space of this *one* religion.

Such an attitude, such a posture is required for the survival of this or any religion and reveals to us, I believe, the irreducible minimum for a fromness pole of sacred doublethink. A religion, to exist, must look inward to its own sacred truths, must regard them as somehow definitive; for Christians, this means believing that Jesus the Christ is the Word of God in singularity. To believe in this manner does *not* represent religious condescension or bigotry; as noted, it is the way of all religious faith communities (and I would include here Hinduism, which is often regarded as highly latitudinarian). A refusal to subscribe to what I would call, with positive, not negative connotations, a prejudice in favor of one's own faith tradition is to fall off the precipice into a syncretism that, despite its manifest attractions, cannot realistically be lived.

Conclusion

By way of (an extended) conclusion and in order to summarize my sense of an acceptable content for doublethink, of a commodious balance between fromness and otherness in religion, I turn the reader's attention again to the diagram included at the beginning of this chapter—Creed-Cultus-Code. There we saw that there was an outward thrust and a receiving capacity of any religion with regard to its Code component, where a multiplicity of religious traditions could agree on an affirmation, with perhaps differing accents, of the dignity of the human person and at times foster cooperation in the furtherance of this moral good. In my opinion, there is another part of this diagram where such conceptual convergence with certain practical implications can be found.

For that, I turn to the aforementioned David Bentley Hart in another of his books, *The Experience of God: Being, Consciousness, Bliss* (hereinafter *Experience*). When I first opened the book, I expected something a la Griffiths, especially in view of the fact that a Christian theologian chose to title his effort using terms from the Hindu tradition. And, yes, Hart does make passing reference to the similarity of the Hindu concept of *Satcitananda* to that of the Christian Trinity (*Experience*, p. 42). But a passing reference is all that is included; the rest of the book could not, in my judgment, be more dissimilar to *The Marriage of East and West*. It reads instead like a tour de force response to the claims of modern muscular atheism discussed in chapter 5 of this book.

Hart is deadly on the oversimplifications of the modern militant atheists, especially in their view that Western theism, whatever specific revelatory content a respective faith tradition adds, ultimately depends upon the notion of God as something on the order of a Watchmaker or Demiurge (*Experience*, p. 36). Arthur Koestler in *The Sleepwalkers* has noted this too, relating that in the early phases of the Scientific Revolution, some thinkers acquiesced only in a God who was in essence a constitutional monarch, brought in for the sake of decorum. It is God as this kind of monarch—a bland placeholder for some in the early scientific community, a deistic nonentity to the later philosophes of the Enlightenment—that atheists with grim satisfaction easily depose; and, with this God gone, much more so, in the mind of the atheists, is the God of revealed religion, the dispenser of additional skyhooks to the invincibly ignorant of Christianity and other faith systems.

The problem is that, with regard to the great religious traditions, this is but a reductionist caricature of their theologies, as Hart shows with his discussion of the "Divine Mind" (*Experience*, pp. 228–229). In the middle section of the book (pp. 153–235), Hart demonstrates how inadequate reductive evolutionary theory is to an account of consciousness and intentionality, echoing in some respects the argumentation of Thomas Nagel discussed previously in this book. Indeed, readers of this book might wonder why I didn't deploy the analysis of Hart in *Experience* in chapter 5, where scientific atheism was the primary topic.

I believe, however, that Hart's book is more important for the issues of this chapter. Hart mentions the terminologies of a variety of religious traditions to get at the basic "whatness" of God and human interactions with Him. On the surface, this looks similar to the analysis of Bede Griffiths, but, as noted, it is not. For Griffiths, there are several divine revelations emanating from several faith traditions, all of which must be melded—a necessary step to which is the obliteration of the separate creeds. Hart's analysis, by contrast, is nothing about creeds; rather, he mines the conceptual terminology of the world's major religions to enhance a description of divine transcendence, pure and simple. The best way to understand this is to recall the distinction between foundational theology (the term goes by several names: philosophical theology, fundamental theology, natural theology), and dogmatic theology, touched on in chapter 5: dogmatic theology is concerned with explicating the content of the revelation of a specific faith community; foundational theology is the effort to distill what, if anything, can be predicated about God from the use of language, the application of reason, and the observation of nature, apart from the consideration of any specific revelation or faith tradition. Unlike the books of Schuon and Griffiths, Hart's entire effort is at the level of foundational theology; it is there that he wishes to "dialogue and collaborate"—using the words of the council fathers of Vatican II—with his opposite numbers in other traditions and to do so for a variety of purposes, not least among which is to counter the challenge to all religion of modern militant atheism. The result is the closest thing I have seen to an interfaith foundational theology.

It is for these reasons that I included the statement "I believe in God" from the shorter Christian Apostles' Creed under the Creed section in the diagram Creed-Cultus-Code. In my view, the statement (or if you prefer to recast it as "I believe in Holy Being") is a summarizing affirmation of that part of a religion governed by foundational theology; identifies the vineyard in which David Bentley Hart (as opposed to Schuon and Griffiths) and likeminded scholars toil; and marks out an appropriate locus for cooperation across denominational lines. In the case of the Apostles' Creed, the very next term after "I believe in God" is "the Father," and, with that, we have begun to step across the threshold into dogmatic theology. The crossing is complete just a few words later with the utterance "and in Jesus Christ."

To recapitulate then and with the Creed-Cultus-Code diagram in view, my understanding of the balance between fromness and otherness in religious faith is as follows. The very initial part of the Creed section—the affirmation of the existence of God / Holy Being—and the outward-facing/moral-receiving capacity of the Code section—the affirmation of the dignity of the human person—represent any religion's duty to honor otherness and constitute legitimate arenas for productive intercourse among the adherents of the different faith traditions. The rest of the diagram's elements—the details of the Creed; all the Cultus, that is, all the rites and ceremonies; and that part of the Code section that supports the way of life believed in the creed and celebrated in the designated rituals—is inward looking, cultivating the tradition's fromness, and about the business of the specific faith community and no other.

I leave it to others to judge whether I have gotten the balance right between the two wings of doublethink or whether doublethink and associated ideas are even valid concepts at all. For me, there is only one more question to answer: why do I believe that the values I give to each hemisphere of doublethink occasion joy? Answer: because, on the one hand, I do not worry about the salvation of others who follow a different path to the divine from mine but seek dialogue and collaboration with them where possible even as I propose, in a sensitive manner, my own faith tradition—not as an urgent summons to someone who is in danger of falling into a pit of unquenchable fire but simply as genuinely good news; but, on the other (I write now as a Christian), I regard myself as part of a story that I celebrate with my sisters and brothers in faith, as we take a yearly journey through the life, death, and resurrection of the One who has spoken a definitive word of healing to human beings and, to their everlasting gladness, restored them to fullness of life.

AFTERWORD

The Great Appreciation

In everything give thanks.
—1 Thessalonians 5:18a (KJV)

At the end of the movie *Batman Begins*, Lieutenant Gordon (much later to be Commissioner Gordon) is on the roof of police headquarters discussing the status of, and prospects for, Gotham City with the Caped Crusader, after the latter almost singlehandedly saved it from destruction. At the end of the conversation and as Batman turns to leave, Gordon blurts out, "I never said thank you." To which Batman replies, "And you'll never have to."

I find myself unaccountably moved by this exchange, as I have viewed this scene again and again and have tried to discover why. I made some progress in this quest when recalling from the misty past another legendary figure: the Lone Ranger. Like Batman, the Lone Ranger was a masked man about whom we had only fragmentary knowledge but whose mission appeared to be to set things right. As he and Tonto rode out of town at the end of the half hour program, one townsman would typically ask another, "Who was that masked man? I wanted to thank him."

And that brings me to a third figure from fiction or near fiction—one who is masked but not wearing a mask—Boo Radley from *To Kill a Mockingbird*. The conventional wisdom about this book/movie (both splendid) is that it is about racial injustice in the South in the 1930s and one man's bravery in standing up to it. A variation on this assessment is that it is concerned with the same topic but as viewed through the eyes of two children. A third possibility is that the whole story is about children and the voyage of discovery that is growing up (a view taken by Elmer Bernstein, who composed the musical soundtrack for the movie). Of course, it is all these things. But I would add a fourth perspective: in *To Kill a Mockingbird*, we have an account of the discovery of God in the person of Boo Radley—a mysterious, shrouded, and fear-inducing figure who nevertheless turns out to be a benefactor, leaving gifts for Jeb in a knothole in a tree and saving Scout's life at the end of the book.

And what is the fitting response of those who have received such gifts or help in perilous situations from the likes of Batman, the Lone Ranger, and Boo Radley? There is only one possible answer: to say, "Thank you."

I have always marveled at the assertion of some philosophers, often of the atheist/existentialist/nihilist breed, that reality is absurd. It is *not* absurd; on their premises, it simply *is* and can be described in detail using the methodologies of natural science and mathematics. What should be regarded as absurd on their presuppositions is the human search for meaning in a landscape putatively empty of purpose, goodness, and spirituality. But it appears that human beings can do no other than to search for such meaning, which is why even some existentialists propose that one should strive for authenticity amid the barrenness of reality.

Most human beings are not existentialists. They simply believe that reality is meaningful beyond their wish that it be so and find that they are, sometimes even unintentionally, filled with gratefulness. As suggested in this book, that is one reason that militant atheism has made only modest headway in the wider culture.

The philosopher Blaise Pascal said that man was like a reed, feeble and easily crushed by the universe, but that, in reality, he is greater than the universe because he is a *thinking* reed! I would suggest that human beings are not only searchers for meaning, thinking reeds, but that they are also foundationally *thanking* reeds; that is, expressing gratitude for them is not just a pragmatic response to a situation—say, someone holding the door open for you—but is an existential, primordial orientation attendant on the joy of simply being called into existence. With this in mind, it is my view that appreciation prompting gratitude is the highest vocation of the human community—in the end, its only vocation.

As the solar journey of the analemma approaches completion at the end of November, these are the summation ideas that I take away from a year of reflection: that human beings are called to be a race of appreciators; that all human intercourse should be suffused with reciprocal gestures of gratitude, rather than rude manifestations of entitlement; and that the world community should strive in various ways to give thanks to that One who mercifully rescued it from nothingness.

I began this book/journey in the Christian season of Advent; it was not originally part of the plan but, for me, a most accommodating piece of temporal fittingness that it ends with the American feast of Thanksgiving. It also ends on my part with a gesture of gratitude to all who, having read thus far, have done me the honor of traveling with me.

BIBLIOGRAPHY

Abbott, Walter, S. J. *The Documents of Vatican II.* Baltimore: American Press, 1966. pp. 662–663.

Aguirre, Edwin. "What Is an Analemma?" *Sky and Telescope* (March 2003). p 78.

Alighieri, Dante. *The Divine Comedy.* Translated by Henry F. Carey. New York: P. F. Collier and Son, 1909. pp. 23–25.

Bachelard, Gaston. *The Poetics of Space.* Boston: Beacon Press, 1958.

Barzun, Jacques. *From Dawn to Decadence: 1500 to the Present; 500 Years of Western Cultural Life.* New York: HarperCollins, 2000. p. 75.

Becker, Carl. *The Heavenly City of the Eighteenth Century Philosophers.* New York: Yale University Press, 1932. pp. 79–80.

Berry, Wendell. *Life Is a Miracle: An Essay against Modern Superstition.* Washington, DC: Counterpoint, 2000. p. 98.

Beston, Henry. *The Outermost House: A Year of Life on the Great Beach of Cape Cod.* New York: Henry Holt, 1928.

Biggar, Nigel. *In Defence of War.* Oxford: Oxford University Press, 2013.

Bloom, Allan. *The Closing of the American Mind.* New York: Simon and Schuster, 1987.

Brinton, Crane. *The Anatomy of Revolution.* New York: Random House, 1938. pp. 7, 13–20.

Brown, Raymond. *Jesus: God and Man.* New York: Macmillan, 1967. pp. 41–45, 93–105.

Buckley, William. *American Conservative Thought in the Twentieth Century.* Indianapolis: Bobbs-Merrill, 1970. p. xviii.

Burckhardt, Jacob. *The Civilization of the Renaissance in Italy*, 2 Vols. New York: Macmillan, 1946. (See Vol. 1, introduction, p. 14, for yet another discussion of how the paradigm for inquiry emerging from the Scientific Revolution could be deemed to have more in common with medieval scholasticism than it did with Renaissance humanism.)

Carter, Stephen L. *Civility: Manners, Morals, and the Etiquette of Democracy*. New York: HarperPerennial, 1998. pp. 108, 213–219.

Churchill, Winston. *The Grand Alliance*. Boston: Houghton-Mifflin, 1950. p. 200.

Copleston, F., S. J. *A History of Philosophy*, Vol. I (Greece and Rome, Part II). Garden City, NY: Doubleday, 1946. pp. 209–210.

Cross, F. L., ed. *The Oxford Dictionary of the Christian Church*. Oxford: Oxford University Press, 1974. p. 777 ("Kenotic Theories"), p. 1479 ("William Wilberforce").

Daniels, Anthony. "Differently the Same," *National Review*, Vol. LXIV, No. 9, May 14, 2012, p. 28.

Dawkins, Richard. *The God Delusion*. Boston: Houghton-Mifflin, 2006.

Dawson, Christopher. *Progress and Religion*. Washington, DC: Catholic University of America Press, 2001. pp. 191–192.

——————————. *Religion and the Rise of Western Culture*. New York: Image Books, 1957. pp. 189–191.

Dennett, Daniel. *Breaking the Spell: Religion as a Natural Phenomenon*. New York: Viking, 2006.

DiCicco, Dennis. "Photographing the Analemma," *Sky and Telescope*, March 2000. pp. 135–139.

Dreher, Rod. *Crunchy Cons: How Birkenstocked Burkeans, Gun-Loving Organic Gardeners, Evangelical Free-Range Farmers, Hip Homeschooling Mamas, Right-Wing Nature Lovers, and*

Their Diverse Tribe of Counter-Cultural Conservatives Plan to Save America (or at Least the Republican Party). New York: Crown Forum, 2006. p. 243 (also the manifesto preceding chapter 1).

Eliade, Mircea. *The Sacred and the Profane.* New York: Harcourt, Brace & World, 1959. p. 155.

Fellman, Michael. *The Making of Robert E. Lee.* New York: Random House, 2000.

Fitzmyer, Joseph. "The Letter to the Philippians," *Jerome Biblical Commentary.* Englewood Cliffs, NJ: Prentice-Hall, 1968. p. 251, Section No. 19.

Foote, Shelby. *The Civil War: A Narrative,* Three Vols. New York: Random House, 1958. See Vol. II, p. 469.

Fox, Nichols. *Against the Machine: The Hidden Luddite Tradition in Literature, Art and Individual Lives.* Washington, DC: Island Press/Shear-Water Books, 2002. See especially pp. 3–23.

Gaines, James R. *Evening in the Palace of Reason: Bach Meets Frederick the Great in 'The Age of the Enlightenment.'* New York: Harper Collins, 2005. p. 81.

Gingerich, Owen. *God's Universe.* Cambridge, MA: Belknap Press, 2006. p. 13ff.

Gould, Stephen J. *Rocks of Ages: Science and Religion in the Fullness of Life.* New York: Ballantine Books, 1999. pp. 3–10, 49–89, 150–163.

Griffiths, Bede. *The Marriage of East and West.* Springfield, IL: Templegate Publishers, 1982.

Guelzo, Alan. *Abraham Lincoln, Redeemer President.* Grand Rapids, MI: William B. Eerdmans, 1999.

Hamilton, Edith. *Mythology.* Boston: Little, Brown, 1942. pp. 39–40.

Harris, Sam. *Letter to a Christian Nation*. New York: Alfred A. Knopf, 2006. pp. 65–66.

Hart, David Bentley. *Atheist Delusions: The Christian Revolution and Its Fashionable Enemies*. New Haven: Yale University Press, 2009. p. 72.

——————————. *The Experience of God: Being, Consciousness, Bliss*. New Haven: Yale University Press, 2013.

Herman, Arthur. *The Cave and the Light: Plato versus Aristotle and the Struggle for the Soul of Western Civilization*. New York: Random House, 2013. p. 424.

Hick, John. *Death and Eternal Life*. New York: Harper and Row, 1976. pp. 30–32, 453.

Hitchens, C. *God Is Not Great: How Religion Poisons Everything*. New York: Hachette Book Group, 2007. pp. 37–41.

Hughes, H. S. *Consciousness and Society: The Reorientation of European Social Thought 1890–1930*. New York: Alfred A. Knopf, 1961. p. 359.

Johnson, Paul. *The Birth of the Modern: World Society, 1815–1830*. New York: Harper-Collins, 1991. pp. 702–703.

——————————. *Modern Times: The World from the Twenties to the Eighties*. New York: Harper and Row, 1983. p. 4ff.

Kagan, Jerome. *An Argument for Mind*. New Haven: Yale University Press, 2006. pp. 211, 213.

Ker, Ian. *G. K. Chesterton: A Biography*. Oxford: Oxford University Press, 2011. pp. 9, 648–649.

Kerferd, G. B. "Aristotle," *Encyclopedia of Philosophy*, Vol. I, Paul Edwards, Editor-in-Chief. New York: Macmillan, 1967. p. 161.

Kimball, Roger. *The Fortunes of Permanence: Culture and Anarchy in Age of Amnesia*. South Bend, IN: St. Augustine's Press, 2012. pp. 201–204.

Kirk, Russell. *The Conservative Mind: From Burke to Santayana.* Chicago: Henry Regnery, 1953. pp. 7–8.

Knille, Robert, ed. *As I was Saying: A Chesterton Reader.* Grand Rapids, MI: William B. Eerdmans, 1985. p. 30.

Koestler, A. *The Sleepwalkers: A History of Man's Changing Vision of the Universe.* New York: Grosset and Dunlap, 1959. pp. 51, 207, 509.

Kohauk, E. *The Embers and the Stars: An Inquiry into the Moral Sense of Nature.* Chicago: University of Chicago Press, 1984. pp. 32–34.

Lewis, C. S. *The Abolition of Man.* New York: Macmillan, 1947. p. 90 and appendix.

_____. "De Descriptione Temporum," *Selected Literary Essays.* Cambridge: Cambridge University Press, 1969. p. 7.

————. *English Literature in the Sixteenth Century excluding Drama.* Oxford: Clarendon Press, pp. 1–14.

————. *The Four Loves.* New York: Harcourt Brace Jovanovich, 1960. p. 42.

————. *The Great Divorce.* New York: Macmillan, 1946. pp. 108–117.

————. *Miracles: A Preliminary Study.* New York: Macmillan, 1947. pp. 75, 94–95.

————. *The Screwtape Letters.* New York: Macmillan, 1961. p. 18 (Letter No. III).

————. *Surprised by Joy: The Shape of My Early Life.* Harcourt, Brace & World, 1955.

_____. "The Weight of Glory," *The Weight of Glory and Other Addresses.* Grand Rapids, MI: William B. Eerdmans, 1949. p. 15.

Lukacs, John. *Five Days in London: May, 1940.* New Haven: Yale University Press, 1999. p. 189.

Martin, Ralph. *The Urgency of the New Evangelization: Answering the Call.* Huntington, IN: Our Sunday Visitor, 2013.

McLaughlin, Dean. *Introduction to Astronomy.* Boston: Houghton-Mifflin, 1961. pp. 91–93.

McQuarrie, John. *Principles of Christian Theology.* New York: Charles Scribner's Sons, 1966. pp. 156, 244, 261.

Morehead, A., ed. *The Official Rules of Card Games.* Racine, WI: Whitman Publishing, 1963. p. 156.

Nagel, Thomas. *Mind and Cosmos: Why the Materialist Neo-Darwinian Conception of Nature Is Almost Certainly False.* Oxford: Oxford University Press, 2012.

Novak, Michael. *No One Sees God: The Dark Night of Atheists and Believers.* New York: Doubleday, 2008.

————. *The Spirit of Democratic Capitalism.* New York: Simon & Schuster, 1982. p. 154.

O'Grady, J. *Models of Jesus.* Garden City, NY: Doubleday, 1981. pp. 97–102.

Pascal, Blaise *Pensees.* New York: E. P. Dutton, 1958. p. 97 (Thought No. 347).

Pasternak, Boris. *Doctor Zhivago.* New York: Modern Library, 1958. (See for example pp. 302–303.)

Pegis, Anton., ed. *Introduction to Saint Thomas Aquinas.* New York: Modern Library, 1948. p. 606.

Percy, Walker. *Lost in the Cosmos: The Last Self-Help Book.* New York: Farrar, Straus, & Giroux, 1983. pp. 85–126.

Plait, Philip. *Bad Astronomy.* New York: John Wiley & Sons, 2002. pp. 11–20.

Rahner, K. *Foundations of Christian Faith.* New York: Seabury Press, 1978. pp. 236, 249.

Raymo, Chet. *Natural Prayers.* St. Paul, MN: Ruminator Books, 1999.

——————. *Skeptics and True Believers: The Exhilarating Connection between Science and Religion.* New York: Walker and Co., 1998.

——————. *The Soul of the Night: An Astronomical Pilgrimage:* Englewood Cliffs, NJ: Prentice-Hall, 1985.

——————. *Walking Zero: Discovering Cosmic Space and Time along the Prime Meridian.* New York: Walker and Co., 2006.

Ruhemann, H. *Artist and Craftsman.* New York: Chanticleer Press, 1948. pp. 9, 14, 68–69.

Schuon, Frithjof. *The Transcendent Unity of Religions.* Wheaton, IL: Theosophical Publishing House, 1984.

Scruton, Roger. *How to Think Seriously about the Planet: The Case for an Environmental Conservatism.* Oxford: Oxford University Press, 2012. pp. 262, 369.

——————— *The Meaning of Conservatism.* Houndmills (UK): Palgrave/Macmillan, 2001. pp. 31, 87–88.

——————— *Sexual Desire: A Moral Philosophy of the Erotic.* New York, Free Press, 1986.

Smith, Huston. *The Religions of Man.* New York: Harper and Row, 1958. pp. 101–109.

Swafford, Jan. *Johannes Brahms.* New York: Alfred A. Knopf, 1997. pp. 348–351.

Tarnas, Richard. *The Passion of the Western Mind.* New York: Ballantine Books, 1991. p. 210.

Thoreau, H.D. "Cape Cod," *Thoreau.* New York: Library of America, 1985. p. 971.

——————. *Walden.* Gorden S. Haight, ed. Roslyn, NY: Walter J. Black, 1942. pp. 76, 206–207, 310–314.

Throckmorton, B. ed. *Gospel Parallels: A Synopsis of the First Three Gospels.* Nashville: Thomas Nelson, 1949. p. 130 (displays the story of the rich young man in Matthew, Mark, and Luke).

Tocqueville, Alexis. *Democracy in America,* Vol. II, Henry Reeve, trans. New York: Alfred A. Knopf, 1945. pp. 102–110 (especially p. 110).

Toynbee, Arnold. *A Study of History,* Vol. I, Abridged Edition, D.C. Somerville, ed. New York: Oxford University Press, 1946. p. 258.

Vawter, Bruce, C. M. "The Gospel According to John," *Jerome Biblical Commentary.* Englewood Cliffs, NJ: Prentice-Hall, 1968. pp. 446–447 (Section Nos. 124–126).

Walsh, John E. *Moonlight: Abraham Lincoln and the Almanac Trial.* New York: St. Martin's Press, 2000.

Warren, James P. *John Burroughs and the Place of Nature.* Athens: University of Georgia Press, 2006. p. 53.

Weigel, George. *Evangelical Catholicism.* New York: Basic Books, 2013. p. 58.

Wheelwright, P. ed. "The Nichomachean Ethics," *Aristotle.* New York: Odyssey Press, 1951. pp. 189–192.

Whitman, Walt. *Collected Poetry and Collected Prose.* New York: Library of America, 1982. p. 409.

Wilder, Thornton. "Our Town," *Collected Plays and Writing on Theater.* New York: Library Classics of the United States, 2007. pp. 149–151, 159–160, 173.

Williams, Frank J. *Judging Lincoln.* Carbondale: Southern Illinois Press, 2002.

Winik, Jay. *April 1865: The Month that Saved America.* New York: HarperCollins, 2001. pp. 362–363.

Wolff, Christoph. *Johann Sebastian Bach: The Learned Musician.* New York: W.W. Norton, 2000.

Young, William P. *The Shack.* Newberry Park, CA: Windblown Media, 2007. pp. 60, 82–84, 112, 136.

Zaehner, R., trans. *Hindu Scriptures.* New York: Everyman's Library, 1966. p. 44.

Printed in the United States
by Bookmasters

Printed in the United States
By Bookmasters